Cultural Pluralism in Education

Cultural Pluralism in Education

Theoretical Foundations

Nicholas Appleton
Arizona State University

Longman
New York & London

Cultural Pluralism in Education
Theoretical Foundations

Longman Inc., 1560 Broadway, New York, N.Y. 10036
Associated companies, branches, and representatives
throughout the world.

*The material reported herein was partially funded and
prepared pursuant to Grant No. 300-78-0560 with Teacher
Corps, Department of Education. Grantees undertaking such
government-sponsored projects are encouraged to freely
express their professional judgment in the conduct of the
project. Points of view or opinions stated do not, therefore,
represent official Department of Education position on policy.*

Developmental Editor: Nicole Benevento
Editorial and Design Supervisor: Diane Perlmuth
Production Supervisor: Marion Hess
Manufacturing Supervisor: Ferne Y. Kawahara

Library of Congress Cataloging in Publication Data
Appleton, Nicholas.
   Cultural pluralism in education.
   Includes bibliographical references and index.
   1. Minorities—Education—United States.
2. Educational equalization—United States.
3. Ethnicity. I. Title.
LC3731.A78   1983   371.97   82-12741
ISBN 0-582-29009-0

Manufactured in the United States of America

Acknowledgments

The author would like to thank these publishers and individuals for their kind permission to reprint the following:

Three charts from *Ethnicity in the United States* by Andrew Greeley, © 1974 by John Wiley and Sons. Reprinted by permission of the publisher.

"The Power of Medicine Men" by Jeannine Dunnell. Reprinted by permission of Jeannine Dunnell Dahl.

"An Asian American Perspective on Multicultural Education: Implications for Practice and Research" by Robert H. Suzuki, ERIC ED 205 633, November 1980, © by Robert H. Suzuki. Reprinted by permission of Robert H. Suzuki.

Thirteen simulation descriptions from *Handbook of Simulation Gaming in Social Education, Part 2: Directory* by Ron Stadsklev, © 1975 by the Institute of Higher Education Research and Services. Reprinted with permission of the Institute of Higher Education Research and Services, The University of Alabama, and Ron Stadsklev.

"The City," a simulation game, originated by Wilford A. Weber. Reproduced by permission of Wilford Weber.

"Freeway Planning Game" was created by Michael Chester. Reproduced by permission of Michael Chester.

Appreciation is extended to Dr. Carl Grant and Teacher Corps Associates whose partial funding and support made the preparation of these materials possible. I also wish to thank Dr. Lou Carey for her help and encouragement in pursuing the project initially. I am especially indebted to Dr. Bob Suzuki, who read earlier drafts of this manuscript and provided very helpful suggestions for improvement. In addition to constructive feedback, Bob Suzuki, with the exception of minor editing, contributed the sections "Historical Background" in Chapter 1 and "Goals and Principles of Multicultural Education" in Chapter 7. Of course, I remain totally responsible for any shortcomings or limitation of the book. Finally, I would like to thank the office of Secretarial Services at Arizona State University, which spent many hours in the typing and technical preparation of the manuscript.

Contents

1

The Problem

CULTURAL PLURALISM AS A GUIDE TO POLICY DECISIONS

Some theorists suggest that Anglo-Protestant domination and the ideals on which it was based have begun to decline in the United States,[1] and the time seems right to consider an ideal such as cultural pluralism. This is important because our society is extremely dependent on having social ideals that project the future for the development and evaluation of social policy. "[T]he society's mass culture, its major institutions, its social structure, and its rationale for being all lean toward the future. . . ."[2] Ideals function to guide and evaluate our social development. They play a prominent role in the construction of our cultural identity and provide the criteria to define the past, present, and future. Moreover, they function to link beliefs to action.[3] That is, they tend to prescribe how we ought to behave under particular circumstances.

The United States appears to be on the verge of embracing cultural pluralism as a social ideal. The evidence is broad and varied: It can be seen in legislation on federal and state levels responding to minority demands; in the availability of funding from federal, state, and private sources to support ethnically focused projects; and in the increasing willingness of schools, colleges, and universities to acknowledge the presence of culturally different clientele in curriculum construction, courses, programs, teacher training, and affirmative action. The acceptance of pluralism might also be inferred from the fact that ethnicity has emerged to rival the prominence of social class as a social force in contemporary society and from the increasingly serious and scholarly treatment of the subject in the literature of the social sciences and education.

Yet if we are to adopt cultural pluralism and if it is to guide and provide a sense of purpose and identity for the American society, it must be understood clearly, for when an ideal is expressed as a broad and ambiguous concept or principle, its effectiveness as an aid in deciding social policy is severely reduced. It is not useful for discriminating among alternative positions and for establishing a clear direction for society. Unfortunately, at present the ideal of cultural pluralism appears to be in this state. The concept is plagued with ambiguity, generality, and confusion, particularly in educational circles. As James Banks notes, "concepts such as multicultural education, multiculturalism, multi-ethnic education, ethnic education, ethnic studies, cultural pluralism, and ethnic pluralism are often used interchangeably or to convey different but highly ambiguous meanings."[4]

The purpose of this book, then, is to develop a clear understanding of cultural pluralism as a theory, as an ideal, and as a way of life. More precisely, the purpose is to aid in the decision making of those who would participate in the structuring and operating of our schools, whether these be decisions of broad educational policy or in the selection of a specific curriculum. Decisions at all levels affect our schools' graduates—what they believe, how they think, and what they do—and the society in which they will live. If we are to create a society based on cultural pluralism, if our educational system is to support this ideal, or, and perhaps this is the more urgent question, if we are intelligently to decide whether this ideal is worthy of adoption, we must clearly understand what it means and what it entails. Thus, this book is written for policy makers, administrators, program directors, curriculum developers, and classroom teachers. It should also be of interest to boards of education and lawmakers as they function as overseers of schools and to an informed public, which supports the schools and has children who will be affected most by them.

Our analysis is broad and sweeping. We ask what a culturally pluralistic society will look like: What forms of social organization will exist? How will the relationships between and among groups be characterized? And how will the answers to these questions be reflected in American education? Our responses must be of two different kinds. One response will be descriptive and objective in nature. It will focus on a theoretical understanding, as theory operates in the sciences. It will be a description of what has happened, what is now happening, and what is likely to happen in the future. It will not be a statement of what we ought to do. Rather, questions of what we ought to do will compose the second inquiry. They will entail an ideological investigation, an investigation of values. What kind of a society do we want? On what basis do we want to meet each other as we live out our lives? What role do we want the schools to assume within our idealized conception of society? How should individuals and groups be identified and treated within the schools? What should our children be taught?

When one understands the climate out of which the contemporary concerns of cultural pluralism have grown, it becomes easier to appreciate the forcefulness of these questions. A brief historical perspective is also useful to fully understand the concerns, issues, and alternatives that face people in the field today. Thus, as an introduction to our inquiry we turn to a sweeping historical synopsis of cultural pluralism and multicultural education.

HISTORICAL BACKGROUND

It is sometimes thought that the roots of cultural pluralism in the United States can be traced to the political democratic pluralism envisioned by the framers of the Constitution. However, their concern was with building and maintaining a notion of one dominant culture from the many political and economic factions represented in the original thirteen states. Though diversity existed, the cultural stock of America in the last quarter of the eighteenth century remained predominantly British, and only the most perceptive individuals could have envisioned the significance of the mass immigration movement that was to follow. Thus, as originally conceived, pluralism in the United States was concerned with liberty and equality and not with promoting the historic identities of non-English subcultures.[5] Though the legal framework was established with the adoption of the first ten amendments to the Constitution, cultural pluralism as an ideal to protect ethnic and cultural diversity evolved much later.[6]

Historical antecedents of the contemporary ideal may be traced to the period between 1880 and 1920 when the massive immigration from Eastern and Southern Europe occurred. Although Chinese immigration took place mostly in the preceding decades and was brought to a halt in 1882, most of the Japanese, Koreans, and Filipinos also immigrated during this period.[7] Altogether an estimated 30 to 40 million people entered the country, and the total U.S. population went from 50 million to over 100 million.[8]

This massive influx of humanity was accompanied by industrialization, urbanization, and the rise of large-scale corporations. These developments in turn created severe social problems including overcrowded urban ghettoes, increasing crime and political corruption, violent labor conflicts, and growing discontent among the working-class poor.[9] Even Asian immigrants who had settled in the still developing Western states failed to escape these problems.[10]

Fueled by the evident strains on social stability, the flood of immigrants was viewed with great alarm by the dominant, native-born White-Anglo-Saxon-Protestants (WASPs) and triggered the reactionary Nativist Movement. Starting in the late 1800s, this movement reached its zenith during and after World War I; it was directed primarily at white ethnic groups of Eastern and Southern European origins and resulted in widespread violence against these groups.[11] In a related fashion, the "Yellow Peril" Movement on the west coast produced devastating consequences for Asians.[12]

Nativism was aided and abetted by the so-called Americanization Movement, whose adherents wished to quickly and forcibly assimilate the millions of new immigrants into the mainstream of American society. The public schools played a major role in this movement through their intensive efforts to "Americanize" children of immigrants. They imposed a strongly Anglocentric curriculum on these children, punished them for using their mother tongues, and often denigrated the cultural traditions and values of their parents.[13]

During this era, IQ testing was started on a massive scale. Almost 2 million military draftees were subjected to IQ tests during World War I. Since average IQ scores of immigrants were 10 to 15 points below those of native-born WASPs, the claim was advanced that persons of Eastern and Southern European origins were genetically inferior in intelligence.[14] These findings were later used to argue for the passage of the National Origins Quota Act of 1924, which restricted further immigration from the countries of Eastern and Southern Europe. Inasmuch as Asians were considered not only racially inferior but also unassimilable, the law also halted further immigration from Asia.[15]

As a result of the Nativist and Americanization movements, millions of white ethnics were traumatically acculturated into the American mainstream. The severe disruption of the cultural identities of many of these groups, which are only now being painfully revived, testifies to the brutal effectiveness of these movements.[16]

Sadly, only a few voices were raised in protest against the demand for cultural assimilation on the part of the new immigrants. One of them was that of the philosopher Horace Kallen, who in arguing for a more democratic alternative to Anglo conformity was among the first to articulate the philosophy of cultural pluralism.[17] The protests of Kallen and other pluralists were overwhelmed by the powerful forces of Americanization and the burgeoning industrial corporate state.[18] Anglo conformity, often thinly disguised in the "melting pot" metaphor, became the dominant ideology and has strongly influenced the shaping of our social institutions, particularly schools, to this day.[19]

During the past two decades, however, the philosophy of cultural pluralism has experienced a strong revival, largely as a result of the social upheaval of the 1960s. Until this time, many social scientists seemed to accept the so-called immigrant analogy, which viewed racial minorities as simply the last of the ethnic groups to migrate to the cities. They predicted that it was only a matter of time before these minorities would assimilate and gain upward mobility, as did the white ethnic groups that preceded them.[20]

Most Americans were unprepared for the outbreak of the urban riots in the 1960s and were shocked by the militant, ethnically conscious movements by Blacks and other minorities that followed. Ensuing conflicts in the field of education over such issues as school desegregation and community control forcefully called attention to the deplorable state of schooling for minority children and to functionally racist practices that prevailed in most urban inner-city schools.[21] As a result of their involvement in these struggles, many minorities became aware of the pervasiveness of the Anglo-conformity bias in the schools and increasingly concerned about the damage this bias was inflicting on the minds of their children. Such concerns led to demands by various minority groups for ethnic studies as an alternative to the existing Anglocentric curriculum of the schools.[22]

In the early 1970s, two developments gave further impetus to the eventual development of multicultural education. One was what Michael Novak has called the "rise of the unmeltable ethnics "—the rising ethnic consciousness of white groups, predominantly from working-class backgrounds, that had been subjected to the Americanization process described earlier.[23] These groups reacted against the condescending attitudes of many middle-class WASPs toward working-class white ethnics and called for the establishment of white ethnic studies as a way of reinstilling ethnic pride.[24]

The second, almost simultaneous development was the women's movement. Feminist activism was not new, but this movement was broader based and more militant than past efforts to combat sexism in American society. Many issues raised by feminists, such as sex discrimination and the low self-expectations of women, were not unlike those raised by white ethnic groups and minorities. In the field of education women began calling for the institution of women's studies and the elimination of sex-role stereotyping in schools.[25]

Some have characterized the white ethnic and women's movements as backlash reactions caused by resentment toward the gains made by minorty groups.[26] While this charge may have some validity, it would be a mistake to view these movements simply in those terms.

They have deeper causes, and there are important reasons for includ-ing their concerns in any conceptualization of cultural pluralism or multicultural education. Moreover, these movements must be credited with calling attention to the many components of American schools that reflect class bias and sexism and for adding their voices to the growing demand for alternative and pluralistic approaches to education.

Within the context of this milieu of conflict and change, current conceptions of cultural pluralism and multicultural education have gradually evolved. As some advocates see it, all these movements of minorities, white ethnics, and women basically seek the same ultimate goal: a more democratic society in which there will be greater equality in all spheres of life. There is also a growing realization that the persist-ent problems of racism, sexism, and class inequality cannot be under-stood, much less solved, by treating these movements as separate phe-nomena affecting each victimized group in isolation; these problems can be understood only by studying the interrelationships of groups in society—minorities, white ethnics, women, and perhaps most impor-tant, dominant WASPs—by viewing them as related phenomena tied to the social structure and culture of the society as a whole.[27]

But if this is a popular conception, it would be a mistake to consid-er it universal or even to believe that there is agreement among its adherents. There is still considerable disagreement over which group should be considered in political and educational policy, which strategies are likely to be most effective, and even over goal interpreta-tion. The development of cultural pluralism and multicultural educa-tion may be at a critical juncture. While the current thrust in the field, combined with other social and political movements, could develop into a significant force for fundamental educational and social reforms, there have been and will undoubtedly continue to be many attempts to "water it down" into innocuous forms that would necessitate only cosmetic changes in the existing educational systems, thereby ultimate-ly serving to perpetuate the status quo. In order to help prevent such cooptation, which has been the fate of so many other reform efforts in education, we must understand the issues, conflicts, and alternatives and strive to form an adequate educational response.

The remaining pages of this chapter put these questions directly before us. Before continuing, however, readers with a low tolerance for conceptual exploration and a high need for closure or absolute answers are warned to fortify themselves. The questions we are considering are complex, and answers are not easy. Much confusion exists about the ideas we are considering. In addition, the ideological alternatives from which we must choose can be supported in various degrees. In con-sidering cultural pluralism, there are no clear rights and wrongs, goods or bads. There are instead, defensible options, each capable of providing guidelines for social development and interaction.

UNDERSTANDING CULTURAL PLURALISM

What Makes a Group?

The first area of confusion in our current understanding of cultural pluralism centers on what groups are to be included in the diversity implied by pluralism. Richard Pratte makes an important point when he agrees that "human groups do not exist in nature, or rather, the part of difference that exists because of nature is unimportant."[28] "Whenever distinctions are made and groupings result, it is we who make them."[29] There seems to be no end to human ingenuity in thinking of characteristics by which to group people: Sex, age, skin color, beliefs, heritage, language, physical handicaps, and sexual preferences are but a few. Diversity signifies a decision on somebody's part to single out different factors in the group. In this respect every society is diverse. Conversely, we say that a particular group is homogeneous when the differences between group members are unimportant or irrelevant to our particular concerns. Which set of criteria do we apply when assessing the diversity to be included under the ideal of cultural pluralism?[30] Authors have variously argued that the focus should be on ethnic pluralism (American ethnic groups such as Blacks and Hispanics); on cultural pluralism (all U.S. cultural groups, even though they may not be based on ethnicity, e.g., Amish, Appalachians); on social pluralism (ethnic and cultural groups but also social minority groups such as homosexuals, women, communists); or on democratic pluralism (all special-interest groups including political groups, environmentalists, and labor unions); but even the narrower focus of ethnic pluralism is not without its difficulties. Contemporary discussions of ethnicity vary considerably, expanding from distinguishable classifications of "white" and "people of color" to the common classifications of Black, Hispanic, Native American, Asian, and white ethnic groups and, finally, to classification into groups such as Texans and Mormons.[31]

It is crucial to recognize that the problem of identifying groups is not merely semantic. There are consequences to the legitimate recognition of a group—access to social rewards, power, and claims to social equity and opportunity hinge on the decision. The decision dictates which groups have a legitimate claim to protection under the law, to federal and state funding, to affirmative action, to autonomy and control, to representation in school programs and curricula, and so forth. Clearly such decisions cannot be arbitrary. This is one of our concerns in Chapter 3.

What Form Should Cultural Pluralism Take?

A second area of confusion focuses on the form pluralism will take in society. Most position papers on cultural pluralism argue strongly for its adoption and are generally agreed that we must begin to focus on cultural diversity, that certain behaviors such as discrimination and exploitation based on cultural differences cannot be tolerated, and that we should reject ideologies of assimilation and amalgamation. But beyond these general notions, either it is not clear what cultural pluralism entails or agreement as to specific goals, purposes, and procedures quickly fades. Indeed, much of the earlier writing supporting pluralism relies heavily on rhetoric and emotional pleas, and functions as slogans designed to arouse interests, incite enthusiasm, and achieve a unity of feeling and spirit.[32]

Cultural Pluralism as a Slogan

When we label something a slogan, it usually has a disparaging effect. That is, the word "slogan," applied to a would-be serious argument, carries the connotation that what is being said is hollow and useless. But this view of slogans may follow from our tendency to judge slogans according to models taken from other linguistic domains when such models may not be appropriate.[33] Slogans do serve a purpose. In this sense, they may be the beginning of a more complex and systematic prescriptive argument. But before we move to this point, we should take a more careful look at what a slogan is and at some examples from the literature on cultural pluralism.

In addition to their ability to arouse interest and incite enthusiasm, slogans have other distinguishing features. For one thing, like generalizations, they tend to summarize assertions not explicitly stated in the general statement. For example, the slogan "no one model American" may summarize such assertions as "Americans may come from many different backgrounds," "no one set of beliefs, values or life style is exclusively American," and "we should tolerate a plurality of life styles and people in the United States." But, unlike generalizations, slogans always contain a prescriptive element and are by their nature systematically ambiguous until the ambiguity is eliminated through an arbitrary process of delimitation. There are several points in this last statement, and we should look at them one at a time.

First, in regard to their prescriptive nature, slogans do not merely describe practice but recommend, advise, exhort, hint, or suggest that certain practices should be followed and other practices avoided.[34] Thus, in the slogan "no one model American," as in slogans like "education for cultural pluralism" and "cultural pluralism, a mandate for change," we find a general appeal for equality, cultural sensitivity, the recognition of diversity, and a general plea for change. While they may also summarize other descriptive assertions, which may be included as part of a larger statement or article— for example, the U.S. population is culturally diverse, conflicts exist between different cultural values and learning styles, there exists a disproportionately high failure and dropout rate among minority students in our schools, and schools reflect white middle-class values and experiences—these are included to support the prescriptions for which the slogan stands. That is, these facts are relevant only because some desired proposal or outcome that the slogan supports is unfulfilled, in this case greater sensitivity to and recognition and support for cultural, racial, and ethnic differences.

A second distinguishing feature of slogans is their systematic ambiguity. It is important to recognize that while in general an appeal is set forth, no specific set of proposals or actions *logically* follows. Between the generalized slogan and its application to a particular case stands a somewhat arbitrary act of interpretation. In the examples above, we know that we should not discriminate on the basis of cultural differences, but we do not know the form pluralism should take. Do we work for greater integration or segregation? Would bilingual programs be transitional or emphasize enrichment? Will educational funding be identical for all groups or disproportionally distributed based on some criterion of "need"? On which groups do we focus? Advocates of pluralism take conflicting positions on each of these topics as well as many others, and all these positions are consistent with the general appeal for cultural pluralism. This is what we mean when we say slogans are systematically ambiguous; it is not that they have no reference but that they are embarrassingly rich in this commodity. In this sense, to say that a slogan is meaningless is to say that no attempt is made to restrict the great diversity of possible expressions.[35]

We should interject here that slogans are not limited to short phrases like the examples given above. Indeed, they are commonly developed into more lengthy prose and presented as an argument in an article or essay. Though space limitations prohibit the analysis of a lengthy example, several short ones may help illustrate the point. Consider the following statements:

1. It is our view, then, that the school in the American setting, and the educational process more generally, must adapt to cultural conditions. Given the existence of varying cultural traditions, and assuming that a setting's institutions are formal and enduring manifestations of local culture, then the school and the educational process must formally adjust to extant pluralism, if they are to retain their institutional character.

Moreover, not only must education itself adapt to cultural pluralism, it must educate the young for cultural pluralism. This latter task necessarily involves revision of not only educational technology and organization, but the ideology as well.[36]

2. Cultural pluralism involves the mutual exchange of cultural content and respect for different views of reality and conceptions of man. Pluralism assumes that ethnic groups have the right to preserve their cultural heritage and to contribute to American civil life.[37]

3. The concept of cultural pluralism must include basic ideas of equal opportunity of all people, respect for human dignity, and the power to control the significant environment and psychological forces impinging on people.[38]

These statements have common features that correlate with the conditions we have set forth for slogans. They clearly intend to focus our attention on matters related to cultural diversity. Moreover, if adopted, they will logically exclude certain behaviors, namely, discrimination and exploitation based on cultural differences, and will reject assimilationist ideology (where assimilation is understood to mean Anglo conformity). Nevertheless, while some alternatives are logically excluded, the statements are systematically ambiguous inasmuch as they do not define a specific form of pluralism or specific actions the schools must take.

Slogans need not remain ambiguous. Through a process of delimitation they can become associated with a particular set of proposals. Thus, we can associate cultural pluralism with a form of social organization where secondary levels of interaction (e.g., economic, political, and civic relations) are highly integrated but primary levels (intimate) tend to be confined within a particular group; where desegregated schools concentrate on the skills and knowledge that promote successful interaction at the secondary levels and at the same time are careful not to undermine the home culture. Notice, however, that this act of delimitation is both deliberate and largely arbitrary. Some person or group actually makes the slogan mean this or that. This is arbitrary in the sense that the interpretation is not the only one that *logically* follows from the slogan statement. Any number of other possible actions *could* follow from it. That is, "they *give* the slogan this interpretation. In a sense, they are legislating or establishing a rule for the interpretation of their slogan."[39]

Through this process, slogans may become connected or attached to a more or less clearly specified group of proposals together with definitions and empirical evidence used as arguments in favor of the proposals. When developed fully, slogans become known as philosophies or ideologies. Hence we talk about the philosophy of cultural pluralism or cultural pluralism as a new ideal. And it is when this state of development is reached that the ideal has the potential to serve as a guide for social development and educational prescription.

Cultural Pluralism as an Ideal

Much of the educational literature on cultural pluralism in recent years has been directed toward developing earlier slogans into ideological positions by which past and present educational practices can be evaluated and their future directed. What has evolved is not one ideology or philosophy but many, which at times conflict with one another. Though empty emotional slogans are not as prevalent as in the past, we still do not have a clear ideal capable of guiding our actions.

This is frustrating because we do not know how to select among alternative positions, but it may in fact turn out to be a blessing. As a matter of fact, one of the premises underlying the writing of this study is that while we must clearly understand the concepts, arguments, and proposals surrounding the general notion of cultural pluralism, we may want not one ideal conception of cultural pluralism but several. Or perhaps more accurately stated, we need a concept of cultural pluralism broad enough and flexible enough to accommodate several alternative expressions.

This position can be supported on the basis of the diverse nature of existing social-cultural situations to which our social institutions must address themselves. The culturally different populations with which our political, economic, and educational systems come in contact cannot just be characterized as poor minorities structurally isolated from the affluent mainstream of society. Although some individuals and groups wish to attain greater structural assimilation, others do not, and it may well be appropriate that they do not. What is "ideal" for some Blacks may not be "ideal" for others. What is "ideal" for Blacks in general may not be "ideal" for some Hispanics, some groups of Native Americans, some Chinese Americans, or members of other groups. The problem is compounded by the fact that our institutions reach into areas geographically, socially, and culturally isolated from the rest of society, such as remote areas in Alaska and the trust territories.

The value of this study need not rest on the acceptance of this position, for even if one believes that one ideological position of cultural pluralism is desirable for all, the fact remains that several exist, and the selection and implementation of one will hinge on the clear understanding of available alternatives. Thus, the central purpose of this study is to clarify the meaning of *cultural pluralism* in its various forms so that it may better function to direct educational policy.

Cultural Pluralism as a Theory

Though our discussion up to this point has been concerned with the adoption of cultural pluralism as an ideal, it is sometimes the case that we talk about the *theory* of cultural pluralism. This provides our third area of confusion.

In ordinary language we often use the term "theory" to refer to any systematically thought through position. Thus, one may hold a theory of education in the sense that he or she has a philosophy of education; or one may have a theory explaining the occurrence of some phenomenon, where the theory is intended to be an objective scientific explanation. The distinction between these two different usages of "theory" and the adoption of a more narrow use of the term is important to our later discussion and understanding of cultural pluralism. We wish to separate theories of cultural pluralism that seek to objectively and scientifically understand and explain pluralism in the United States from ideological statements that prescribe the course pluralism ought to take.

Theory, as seen by the sciences and as we use the term here, refers to "a set of related propositions that may explain how a phenomenon has arrived historically, how it works or what its meaning is empirically, and, under given circumstances, what we may expect in the future."[40] At the simplest level, theories reveal relationships between different parts of experienced reality. They purport to *describe*, as objectively and neutrally as possible, some phenomenon. As tools of science, theories are subject to the principle of replication and, by their nature, are testable.[41] That is, different individuals ought to be able to reproduce experiments and independently test a theory and arrive at the same conclusions.

In contrast, an ideology, as we use the term here, is a "set of ideas that explain or legitimate social arrangements, structures of power, or ways of life in terms of the goals, interests, or social position of the groups or social collectivities in which they appear."[42] In a word, ideologies attempt to *prescribe* what ought to be and contain a distinguishable evaluative, judgmental element. We have seen that they may develop out of slogans and may serve to interpret and direct the past, present, and future.

It would be a mistake to characterize ideology and theory as sharply separate and distinct. In fact, most theories depend on underlying assumptions, values, and biases, which often add up to an ideology.

For example, most Marxist economic theories are based on a conflict view of society, whereas most capitalist economic theories are based on a consensus view of society. Because of their different underlying ideological bases, different theories can take the same empirical data and arrive at different interpretations and conclusions. Thus, at times, theory and ideology may be so inextricably bound that the line of demarcation between the two is not always clear.[43] Nevertheless, by focusing on purpose and function, distinctions between the two can be made. Theory and ideology can also be distinguished by the means in which each is verified and supported: Theory ultimately relies on empirical, publicly verifiable data; ideology ultimately rests on an appeal to certain values and philosophical argumentation.

Pluralism has been written about from the perspectives of both theory and ideology; indeed, as suggested above, the two are often mixed. But even so, it is possible and desirable to distinguish between them. Theorists have attempted to explain what has actually happened, what is happening now, and what we can expect in the future. Such information in itself cannot tell us how to respond to current social concerns, but only with this information, as well as a guiding ideal, can we intelligently respond to social demands. Social policy, if it is to have any chance for success, must be related to empirical realities. That is, we must know what is happening and why, and what is likely to happen under certain conditions if we are to plan for the future. To confuse an ideological position with theory, then, would be most undesirable because it would debase the objective nature of the theory and its descriptive and predictive value. Under such circumstances, we would run a very high risk of being fooled into believing in some social phenomenon that in reality is a myth. This is what happened in the past with melting pot and assimilation "theories". Currently, this may be happening in our assessment of the kinds of intergroup relationships we can hope for if the ideal of cultural pluralism is adopted. In particular, how will cultural pluralism affect intergroup conflict?

CULTURAL PLURALISM AND CULTURAL CONFLICT

Strife has existed between cultural and ethnic groups in this country since its beginning. Starting with the early encounters between indigenous populations and European immigrants, a history of conflict has evolved through the importation of Black people from Africa as slaves, the arrival of waves of immigrants from Europe and Asia, and the Spanish conquests of territory that now makes up a large portion of the southwestern United States. Over the decades, the composition of the nation has changed, as have the circumstances in which various groups have met one another. Yet cultural conflict endures.

Most advocates of cultural pluralism believe that cultural conflict results from some dysfunction in society and that, to the extent that the ideal becomes operative, conflict between groups will decrease. They believe that conflict will fade as society becomes more democratic, fair, and equitable and as ethnocentrism, prejudice, and discrimination decline. If we attain a better balanced distribution of social rewards in economics, politics, and education; if we teach our children to tolerate and respect ways of life different from their own; if we adopt an enlightened multicultural curriculum—then understanding and appreciation will be cultivated, and greater harmony among different people will result.

Cultural conflict is often a result of some imbalance or dysfunction in society. But as a general explanation of strife between culturally different populations, this view may be exaggerated. Social theorists have begun to think of society in a dynamic sense and are examining the idea that conflict is a permanent feature of modern societies that may even serve a positive function. Because it contributes to a dynamic social equilibrium of change and consensus, conflict is being viewed as a functional part of the natural process of development of a culture. Thus, in our study of intergroup relationships, we recognize that, although it may be possible to reduce violence, we must look more carefully at the likelihood of eradicating or significantly reducing cultural conflict.

Lest the reader conclude that accepting the thesis that cultural conflict is inevitable weakens the commitment to address the ills of society, a brief digression is in order. If we should discover that cultural conflict comprises a permanent and at times functional component of society, it still follows that we should attempt to right wrongs, balance inequalities, and cultivate pluralistic values and attitudes. These efforts can be justified by higher ideological principles, such as humanism and justice. Although pragmatic considerations hold a privileged status in our highly systematized technological culture where cost efficiency is often the main consideration, an appeal to the sense of right and wrong should still carry considerable weight. Equal opportunity in employment, housing, and education may not spell an end to cultural conflict, but it can be justified and should be pursued simply because it is the right and humane way to treat human beings.

THE SCOPE OF THE STUDY

Our analysis of cultural pluralism in this study focuses on six central concerns. In Chapter 2 we explore the theory of cultural pluralism in an attempt to better understand the concept and just what is taking place. In Chapter 3 we take a careful look at alternative ideological positions of cultural pluralism. This analysis clarifies both the issues and the available options that will need to be addressed by agencies involved in cultural pluralism. Chapter 4 outlines the current ideological trend of pluralism in the United States as it has been defined by the courts. While theorists explain pluralism as a social phenomenon and various ideologies argue for support, decisions are being made out of practical necessity that are in fact shaping the course pluralism will take. In Chapter 5 we tackle the question of the proper ideal for the United States. An assessment is made of the diverse groups found in our society and their respective needs and desires. In Chapter 6 cultural conflict is explored. We consider the probability that strife between diverse groups will be a permanent feature of pluralism. The conflicts to be expected, the conditions under which they will likely arise, and some of the possible outcomes are presented. Finally, in Chapter 7 we turn to our school system. Key policy issues are examined. Curriculum recommendations are offered, as well as suggestions to make our schools more functional and responsive to a pluralistic society.

NOTES

1. This position is stated very matter of factly by William Greenbaum, "America in Search of a New Ideal: An Essay on the Rise of Pluralism," *Harvard Educational Review* 44 (1974): 440–41. It is also supported by Nathan Glazer and Daniel Moynihan, eds; *Ethnicity: Theory and Experience* (Cambridge, Mass.: Harvard University Press, 1975); and Henry J. Perkinson, "Education and the New Pluralism," *Review Journal of Philosophy and Social Science* 1, no. 1 (1976): 1–14.
2. Greenbaum, "America in Search of a New Ideal," p. 433.
3. Richard Pratte, *Pluralism in Education* (Springfield, Ill.: Charles C Thomas, 1979), p. 52.
4. James Banks, "Pluralism and Educational Concepts: A Clarification," *Peabody Journal of Education*, January 1977, p. 73.
5. Richard Pratte, "The Concept of Cultural Pluralism," *Philosophy of Education, 1972: Proceedings of the Twenty-Eighth Annual Meeting of The Philosophy of Education Society* (1972), p. 62.
6. The remaining portion of this historical section was written, with the exception of minor editing, by Bob H. Suzuki as a section of a larger paper entitled "An Asian-American Perspective on Multicultural Education: Implications for Practice and Research," ERIC ED 205 633, November 1980, pp. 3–10. The material is published with the author's permission.
7. Lowell Chun-Hoon, "Teaching the Asian American Experience," in *Teaching Ethnic Studies, 43rd Yearbook*, ed. James A. Banks (Washington, D.C.: National Council for the Social Studies, 1973).
8. Mark M. Krug, "Cultural Pluralism: Its Origins and Aftermath," *Journal of Teacher Education* 28 (May–June 1977): 5–9.
9. Oscar Handlin, *The Uprooted: The Epic Story of the Great Migrations That Made*

the American People (New York: Appleton-Century-Crofts, 1973); Joel H. Spring, *Education and the Rise of the Corporate State* (Boston: Beacon Press, 1972).

10. Chun-Hoon, "Teaching the Asian American Experience."

11. John Higham, *Strangers in the Land: Patterns of American Nativism, 1860–1926* (New York: Atheneum, 1974).

12. Roger Daniels, *The Politics of Prejudice* (Berkeley: University of California Press, 1962); Alexander Saxton, *The Indispensable Enemy* (Berkeley: University of California Press, 1971).

13. Higham, *Strangers in the Land*; Maldwyn A. Jones, *American Immigration* (Chicago: University of Chicago Press, 1960).

14. Thomas F. Gossett, *Race: The History of An Idea in America* (New York: Shocken Books, 1965); Thomas Sowell, "Race and I.Q. Reconsidered," in *Essays and Data on American Ethnic Groups* ed. Sowell (Washington, D.C.: Urban Institute, 1978).

15. Daniels, *Politics of Prejudice*.

16. Michael Novak, *The Rise of the Unmeltable Ethnics* (New York: Macmillan, 1971).

17. Horace Kallen, "Democracy Versus the Melting Pot," *Nation* 100 (February 1915): 190–94, 217–20; idem, *Culture and Democracy in the United States* (New York: Boni and Liveright, 1924).

18. Seymour W. Itzkoff, *Cultural Pluralism and American Education* (Scranton, Pa.: International Textbook, 1969).

19. Milton Gordon, *Assimilation in American Life* (New York: Oxford University Press, 1964); Edgar Epps, ed., *Cultural Pluralism* (Berkeley: McCutcheon, 1974).

20. Robert Blauner, *Racial Oppression in America* (New York: Harper & Row, 1972); Meyer Weinberg, "A Historical Framework for Multicultural Education;" in *Teaching in a Multi-cultural Society*, ed. Dolores E. Cross et al. (New York: Free Press, 1977).

21. L. L. Knowles and K. Prewitt, *Institutional Racism in America* (Englewood Cliffs, N.J.: Prentice-Hall, 1969); Charles E. Silberman, *Crises in the Classroom* (New York: Random House, 1970).

22. James Banks, ed., *Teaching Ethnic Studies, 43rd Yearbook* (Washington, D.C.: National Council for the Social Studies, 1973).

23. Novak, *Rise of Unmeltable Ethnics*; Murray Friedman, ed., *Overcoming Middle Class Rage* (Philadelphia: Westminster Press, 1971).

24. Peter Schrag, *Out of Place in America* (New York: Random House, 1970); Friedman, *Overcoming Middle Class Rage*.

25. Robin Morgan, ed., *Sisterhood Is Powerful* (New York: Vintage, 1970); Rose Tremain, *The Fight for Freedom for Women* (New York: Ballantine, 1973); Women on Words and Images, *Dick and Jane as Victims: Sex Stereotyping in Children's Readers* (Princeton, N.J.: Central New Jersey Organization for Women, 1972).

26. William J. Wilson, "The Role of Ethnicity in American Life," *Proceedings of the Conference on International Role of the University in the 1970's* (Amherst, Mass.: University of Massachusetts, 1973); Peter Rose, *They and We: Racial*

and Ethnic Relations in the United States (New York, Random House, 1974); Toni Cade, *The Black Woman* (New York: Signet, 1970).

27. William A. Newman, *American Pluralism: A Study of Minority Groups and Social Theory* (New York: Harper & Row, 1973); Bayard Rustin, "Black Power and Coalition Politics," *Commentary* 42 (September 1966): 35–40.

28. Nathan Glazer and Daniel P. Moynihan, *Beyond the Melting Pot*, 2nd ed. (Cambridge, Mass.: MIT Press, 1970), p. xiv; as quoted by Pratte, "Concept of Cultural Pluralism," p. 4.

29. Ibid.

30. Edward Spicer and Raymond Thompson, eds., *Plural Society in the Southwest* (New York: Interbook, 1972).

31. Nicholas Appleton, "Cultural Pluralism: Must We Know What We Mean?" *Philosophy of Education 1976: Proceedings of the Philosophy of Education Society,* (Urbana, Ill.: University of Illinois, Spring 1976), pp. 159–68.

32. B. Paul Komisar and James E. McClellan, "The Logic of Slogans," in *Language and Concepts in Education,* ed. B. Othanel Smith and Robert E. Ennis (Chicago: Rand McNally, 1971), p. 195.

33. Ibid.

34. Ibid, p. 198.

35. Ibid, pp. 200–201.

36. Thomas Hogg and Marlin McComb, "Cultural Pluralism: Its Implications for Education," *Educational Leadership* 27 (1969): 237.

37. Edgar Epps, *Cultural Pluralism and Education* (Berkeley: McCutcheon, 1974), p. 177.

38. William R. Hazard and Madelan D. Stent, "Cultural Pluralism and Schooling: Some Preliminary Observations," in *Cultural Pluralism in Education,* ed. Madelan Stent, William Hazard, and Harry Revlin (New York: Appleton-Century-Crofts, 1973), p. 15.

39. Komisar and McClellan, "Logic of Slogans," p. 202.

40. Newman, *American Pluralism*, p. 501.

41. Ibid, p. 52.

42. Ibid.

43. I am indebted to Bob Suzuki for clarifying this point. The point is further clarified in the beginning of Chapter 2. For a more scholarly and enlightening analysis of this point, see William E. Connolly and Glen Gordon, *Social Structure and Political Theory* (Lexington, Mass.: D. C. Heath, 1974).

2

The Theory of Cultural Pluralism

The rediscovery of ethnic consciousness has been accompanied by a renewed interest in understanding and explaining the phenomenon as
well as a careful look at the concept of cultural pluralism that seems to
support it. In their pure form, unlike slogans with their ambiguous
appeals, these theoretical analyses aim at precision and clarity and at
the formulation of testable hypotheses; and unlike the prescriptive
nature of ideological arguments, they intend merely to describe.

We say "pure form" for two reasons. First, research questions are
not value free. Affecting the formulation of a topic of inquiry are values
that influence the interests of the researcher. Research problems and
hypotheses are not plucked from the air; they are grounded in what is
perceived as an important topic of inquiry, which in turn is grounded
in the interests and values of individual researchers and the collective
societal interest radiating from some social context. This can be seen
operating in the renewed interest in researching ethnicity and pluralism
in general, as well as in the way specific theorists approach the problem.

Also, even the most carefully constructed scientific investigations
ultimately are tied to some view of the world and some value system.
At rock bottom every researcher must make certain unprovable
assumptions about the nature of the world (e.g., its order, the relationships of its parts if it is characterized as having parts, or how knowl-

edge is attained). These assumptions affect how research problems are constructed, the data that will be collected, the means by which data will be collected, and the manner in which data are organized into an explanatory theory. For example, as we have briefly noted, some social scientists characterize the natural state of modern societies in terms of consensus, stability, and order; others see conflict and change as society's natural state. Researchers from both schools of thought may focus on and agree to descriptions of the same empirical data; they may accept the same factual description of some phenomenon, say, the unequal distribution of social rewards. Because of their different orientations toward the nature of society, however, their explanation of the facts and predictions about the future may be dramatically different. Even more important, the adoption of one theoretical description over another often has the consequence of supporting certain social policies and values over others. For example, if conflict and change are accepted as givens, efforts are likely to be channeled toward transforming potentially destructive conflicts into a more functional expression. If, on the other hand, conflict is seen as a temporary state of instability, efforts are likely to be directed at eradicating conflict and restoring stability. The point is that "to adopt a particular theory . . . is to maintain that certain ideals cherished by some are simply unattainable, that other ideals would impose heavy costs on wide segments of the society if implemented, and that still others are attainable in ways that are at least moderately fulfilling to most of the inhabitants."[1]

The second reason for qualifying the objective-descriptive conditions of theory is that writers tend to support an ideological argument on a theoretical base. There is a tendency to analyze a problem in a descriptive, value-neutral fashion (as our understanding of theory dictates) but then to connect the theoretical statement with an ideological position that the author advocates. In such cases it is logically possible, and indeed desirable, to separate the two arguments, since their merits must be evaluated by different criteria. Theoretical statements must be evaluated by their ability to account for and/or predict various phenomena accurately. Ideological positions, on the other hand, must ultimately be judged on the basis of some value structure and on their ability to guide and direct human activity.

The focus of this chapter, then, is on the development of a better theoretical understanding of cultural pluralism. We do not explore what ought to be done—these considerations are discussed in Chapters 3 and 5; rather, we investigate as objectively as possible the conceptual and empirical nature of cultural pluralism. We ask: (1) What are we talking about when we talk about cultural pluralism? and (2) just what is taking place? We begin with conceptual considerations.

WHAT IS PLURALISM?

The Concept of Cultural Pluralism

Concepts like "cultural pluralism" are tools that we, as human beings, use to describe and understand the world. They are constructs that summarize certain experiences, states of being, or sets of qualities. For example, "chair" is a word that stands for or summarizes the attributes of a set of items that have common characteristics that can be distinguished from the characteristics of other things—say, tables, sofas, and beds. Often, however, we use concepts without being consciously aware of that which they summarize. This is complicated by the fact that concepts seldom have one precise meaning; as dictionaries show, words often have multiple meanings. And so it is with the concept of cultural pluralism.

Philosophers have long recognized the importance of the language and ideas we use in trying to understand the world around us. Consequently, a great deal of philosophic discourse has been directed at "dissecting" concepts and "discovering" their logic. By focusing on the use of terms in ordinary language, philosophers have been able to provide useful insights into complex and puzzling problems. Through this approach it has been possible to distinguish between three general applications or meanings of the concept of cultural pluralism.[2]

One application refers to the political-economic sense of the concept; here we mean to acknowledge the existence of a particular kind of democracy where multiple political and economic interest groups compete in and contribute to government in its various forms. It is characterized by the view of large, well-integrated groups in society representing significant divisions of political and economic interests and values.[3] The individual is seen as actively involved with groups that promote a diversity of experiences and interests and enable him or her to affect government in a variety of ways. It is also possible for new groups to form and articulate new perspectives and preferences that eventually will reach the decision-making process and contribute to the balance of power. It is this political-economic pluralism that the founding fathers had in mind in structuring our government with democratic representation and a balance of powers.

The second meaning is anthropological-sociological. Here the emphasis is on the existence of diverse cultural or subcultural groups. The membership of each group is based on a set of common cultural characteristics; these groups are generally thought to be more enduring and more defining than groups formed solely on the basis of political or economic interests. The characteristics defining the membership of the various groups may include language, race, ethnicity, religion, values, or life styles. These groups may function at times as political or economic interest groups, but this is not the basis of their existence. Also, the anthropological-sociological concept of cultural pluralism does not imply any particular relationship among or between groups. They may or may not interact; they may or may not share equal status or power. The test for this form of cultural pluralism is the determination whether a diversity of cultural or subcultural groups is present.

The political-economic sense of cultural pluralism has been most common in descriptions and analyses of the development and functioning of American politics; the anthropological-sociological sense of the concept has been useful in acknowledging and understanding the heterogeneity of our society. But both fail to articulate the subtleties implied in the everyday use of the term "cultural pluralism." Ordinary language has a way of capturing distinctions in the world that we find important but that nevertheless often elude us because of our closeness to them. A more careful look at the way we use terms and the subtleties implied therein can make us consciously aware of that which we subliminally acknowledge. Stop to think for a moment of what a model society characterized by cultural pluralism would look like. By looking at these model cases and contrasting them with those that seem to fall short of the concept, we are able to get a clearer picture of what conditions we ordinarily require in our collective experience to say that some society is culturally pluralistic. It is by means of this strategy that we identify the third sense of the concept.

Perhaps the first and most obvious characteristic of a model society characterized by cultural pluralism is that of cultural diversity. There must coexist groups with different values, races, religion, ethnicities, geographic backgrounds, subcultures, and so forth. Clearly a homogeneous society does not qualify, nor does a society where diversity is based solely on economic and political interests, age, height, sex, recreational interests, and the like. Rather, we think of a situation where different racial, ethnic, religious, and subcultural groups exist side by side, each retaining its historic identity and generally reflecting a certain cultural life style in ways such as special eating habits, attitudes, style of interaction, or family ties.

But if cultural diversity is necessary for cultural pluralism, it is not equivalent; we do distinguish between "cultural pluralism" and such terms as "culturally different." Not every culturally diverse society is a model of cultural pluralism. Why? There are several factors, but the key can be found in the nature of the relationships between and among the different groups. For example, we do not tend to apply the label of cultural pluralism where the different groups think of themselves as being distinct political entities and/or have little or no collective interests or interaction. Thus we do not think of the Common Market in

Europe as cultural pluralism because each member is considered to be a separate and independent entity. Minimally, the different groups must be considered (and consider themselves) as part of a common politic; they must be active members of the same society.

Now consider a situation in which different cultural groups are active members of the same society but the relationship between the groups is characterized by slavery, caste, or dominance and exploitation. We would not say the antebellum South was a model of cultural pluralism, nor would we apply the label to contemporary South Africa. We can see that for a society to be called culturally pluralistic, members of the constituent groups must possess roughly equal legal status and enjoy some equality of opportunity.[5] It is important to note that this does not require that each and every member of any particular group achieve parity with members of all other groups but that the range of opportunity should be about the same for each group and that no group should be discriminated against as a group.

Our model culturally pluralistic society, then, based on our application of the concept in ordinary language, is beginning to take shape. It is a society that boasts a diversity of racial, religious, cultural, or ethnic groups that coexist and interact as roughly equal members of a common politic. Now consider one final point. Given the above to be true for a particular society, suppose one or several of the groups desired to terminate their relationships with the other groups and become independent political entities. Alternatively, consider the effect if the goal of the society was to assimilate or amalgamate the diverse groups into one primarily homogeneous culture. If either were the case, we would no longer consider the society to be a model of cultural pluralism. The missing ingredient would be the commitment to and acceptance of the value of cultural diversity. The concept of cultural pluralism is, by its nature, an *evaluative* term. First, it is generally *positive*. We apply it to situations we approve of and find favorable. Second, it entails the value of continued diversity: the belief that cultural diversity is desirable. Thus, in cases where groups wish to dissolve their pluralistic relationship either by withdrawing from interaction and attaining political independence or by dissolving cultural differences, the label is withheld.

Our purpose in analyzing the concept of cultural pluralism—in identifying its different uses and making explicit the social conditions required by the concept as it is ordinarily used—is neither to support nor to condemn these uses and conditions; rather, it is to get a clearer picture of what we are talking about. Through such clarification, our discussion of the merits of the concept should become much more fruitful.

Up to this point we have identified three different meanings of the concept, one of which must be specified in a particular context as the subject of discussion if people are to be discussing the same thing. We have also identified conditions of the ordinary use of the concept that may, for the most part, heretofore have been implicit in discussions but beyond the conscious consideration and evaluation. We have said that cultural pluralism generally implies (1) cultural diversity, (2) membership in a common politic and some minimal interaction between and among groups, (3) relative parity and equality between and among the groups, and (4) a perceived value for the continuance of diversity. We have now made explicit the implicit criteria for determining the degree to which a particular society is culturally pluralistic.

The central focus and concern of most contemporary theorists of cultural pluralism is with the ordinary use of the term as discussed above, and we will use this meaning. We are concerned with the extent to which the four conditions we have uncovered have been met, are currently met, and will be met in the future and with the particular form these conditions might take in social organization, in political and economic institutions, and in education. Let us stipulate, then, that unless otherwise indicated in the remainder of this study, it is the ordinary use of the term cultural pluralism as discussed above to which we refer. This will help us avoid the confusion caused by slipping into either the political-economic or the anthropological-sociological senses of the term unknowingly.

Kinds of Cultural Pluralism

While we are now clearer as to the conceptual meaning of cultural pluralism, there still exist considerations we must face for the sake of clarity. One consideration addresses the nature of the structural and interactive relationships the groups will have with one another. That is, what will society look like in terms of the proximity of the various groups to one another and the level and frequency of their interaction? Currently, Chicago has the largest population of people of Polish ancestry outside of Warsaw. People of Mexican ancestry reside primarily in the southwestern states, and Black Americans tend to be concentrated in the inner-city areas of large metropolitan complexes. Is this the way our pluralistic society is to be? Are these patterns to continue, or will we find a greater or lesser proportional distribution across the country? Will we expect people of different social, ethnic, and cultural backgrounds to enter with greater frequency or less? These are a few of the questions we must try to answer.

Thomas Green offers a model that helps answer these questions.[6] He begins the model by acknowledging a distinction made in the social sciences between primary and secondary relationships. Primary relationships are characterized by informal relationships where one's total personality is involved. They tend to be intimate in nature and are generally thought to exist within families, between friends, and within social clubs, recreational groups, and the like. Secondary relationships are more formal, tend to be task oriented, and involve only a limited portion of one's personality. One typically interacts in a fashion designed to complete some transaction. Commercial and business relationships tend to be this way; one is not expected to confide in or become overly friendly with a salesclerk, official, or stranger asking for directions.

On the basis of these different relationships, Green constructs three ideal types of social organization between different cultural groups. (It should be clear that "ideal type" is not meant to have any value import but is used in the Weberian sense to imply model.) The first type, which he calls *insular pluralism*, is used to identify a social organization in which both primary and secondary relationships are confined to individuals who are members of one's own cultural group. One's playmates and friends, and certainly any prospective spouse, will be of the same group, as will individuals met during the course of the business day. An example of individuals living in a state of insular pluralism in the United States would be Native Americans living on reservations, the Amish and other relatively segregated religious groups, and perhaps a number of individuals living in "ethnic" communities such as Chinatown in San Francisco or Little Tokyo in Los Angeles or a Mexican American barrio in the Southwest who confine most of their interactions to their ethnic group. Thus, I may be born of Chinese American parents in Chinatown, go to a school with a predominantly Chinese American student body, work in a small Chinese business within the community, and marry someone and confine my friends to people of similar background.

The second ideal type Green calls *halfway pluralism*. Here the primary relationships are kept within the particular cultural group, but the secondary relationships are between different groups. Thus, one's intimate relationships—friends and family—are within the same group, but one ventures outside the group for economic, educational, and political pursuits. For instance, children may attend an integrated school and in the course of the educational day may interact with teachers and other students from groups different than their own; but they may play with or develop close friendships with only members from their original group and, upon going home, return to a culturally "pure" environment. As an example, consider the Chinese American counterpart of the person above who, while living in Chinatown, works in the city with Anglos and people of other ancestry. The interaction with these people for the most part remains businesslike. But when the workday is over, the individual returns home to his Chinese family and friends.

The third ideal type offered by Green is *structural assimilation*. Here, both primary and secondary relationships cross cultural lines. One's cultural background, in effect, is irrelevant to all forms of interaction. The result is an open society in which friendships and courting, as well as more formal interactions such as business transactions, are negotiated on an individual basis and not on group affiliation. What we typically think of as a metropolitan person falls into this category. Such a person would not think of himself or herself in ethnic terms and would choose friends on the basis of shared interests, common concerns, and similar likes and dislikes. While communities or schools based on this model would be integrated, this fact probably would go unnoticed because this ethnicity would be irrelevant.

In application, Green's model provides a continuum with three main junctures that serve as reference points for understanding the theoretical range of possible group relationships within a culturally plural society. At one extreme is insular pluralism, where there is almost no interaction between the different groups. In halfway pluralism there is interaction between groups at the level of secondary relationships but not primary relationships. At the other extreme is structural assimilation, where cultural differences become irrelevant in group relationships and interaction between groups takes place at both the primary and secondary levels.

Insular Pluralism	Halfway Pluralism	Structural Assimilation

FIGURE 2.1

Now, on the basis of the necessary conditions for cultural pluralism we established earlier, it may be possible to eliminate extreme cases at either end of Green's model as inconsistent with cultural pluralism. Recall, for example, that the diverse groups must interact at some minimal level (e.g., the political level) for the label to be applied. It will not do, then, for groups to be so isolated that they in effect become independent entities. Thus to the extent that a group withdraws from society, pluralism will not exist. As for the other extreme, we noted in our analysis that a value for continued diversity is also entailed by the concept of cultural pluralism. It may be that structural assimilation, with its emphasis on the irrelevance of group differences, implies a lack of value for continued diversity and so too would fail to count as cultural pluralism. Indeed, Green wants to argue that halfway pluralism comes the closest to meeting the requirements of the concept of cultural pluralism. He eliminates insular pluralism because interaction between groups and individual mobility across group lines is so severely restricted. Thus, while group freedom and autonomy exist, individual autonomy and freedom do not. If society was structured so that all groups lived in a state of insular pluralism, an individual would not be free to associate with members from other groups on any significant level. He eliminates structural assimilation for precisely the opposite reason. Because ethnicity is completely irrelevant, diversity, for all practical purposes, ceases to exist. The resulting organization will be an open society and not pluralism at all.

This is not to say that either end of the continuum is undesirable as a model of social organization—we are not concerned with the ideological merits of models here—but that both extremes contradict the meaning of cultural pluralism. In principle, there is no problem in opting for one extreme or the other, but if we do, we must realize that it is not cultural pluralism that we desire but something else. The point is that even in spite of the questionable ability of insular pluralism and structural assimilation to count as cultural pluralism, the model does show a wide range of options that theoretically meet the conditions and may serve as a way of classifying the kinds of cultural pluralism found in a society.

This same advantage for classification purposes can be gained by way of another structural distinction made on the basis of relationships between groups: This is between *segregated pluralism* and *integrated pluralism* and refers to the geographic proximity of one group to another. William Newman describes segregated pluralism as "a society in which there are many different groups, but in which each group inhabits its own geographic area."[7] In contrast, integrated pluralism "refers to a society in which there are many different groups that are also geographically intermixed."[8] The key to this distinction is that it refers to the geographical distribution of different groups on a *grand scale* and to the patterns of social contact and interaction between group members resulting from that distribution. It does not refer to *residential* integration or segregation. Thus integrated pluralism is not meant to imply that social groups become integrated in every sense; it does not mean that residential areas are highly integrated. Rather, it means that diverse groups live in relatively close proximity (e.g., within the same city), as opposed to being relatively confined to distinct geographic areas. Switzerland is an example of segregated pluralism where the country is divided into four distinct cultures. Each culture has a corresponding language—German, French, Italian, and Romansh—and is found primarily in one geographic area. The German part of Switzerland comprises approximately 70 percent of the population and includes all of the northern and eastern cantons (political units similar to our states). The French-speaking Swiss live mostly in the western part and comprise about 21 percent of the population. Italian is spoken by about 8 percent and is found primarily in the south-central portions of the country; Romansh is spoken by only about 1 percent of the people, mostly in the high Alps. The United States, with a few notable exceptions, repeats a pattern of cultural diversity in city after city. Blacks, for example, can be found in every major city in the country. And although Mexican Americans tend to be concentrated in the Southwest, southwestern cities report a similar pattern of heterogeneity including Anglos and, to a lesser extent, Asians and Native Americans. In the present terminology, then, the United States represents integrated pluralism.

The purpose of noting this distinction, as with insular pluralism, halfway pluralism, and structural assimilation, is to become aware that cultural pluralism as a concept can accommodate a number of organization structures and that these different structures describe different styles of interaction among groups and individuals within a society. The kinds of daily "in the street" interaction between different groups in a society characterized by integrated pluralism, and the issues and problems associated with this arrangement, will be different from the kinds of interaction in a society characterized by segregated pluralism, where groups have infrequent and peripheral contact.

One other set of distinctions might be made regarding the cultural pluralism that can exist conceptually. This has to do with the way groups are perceived and treated officially by governmental institutions. Milton Gordon makes the distinction between the two ideal types (i.e., models) of *liberal pluralism* and *corporate pluralism*.[9] Liberal pluralism "is characterized by the absence, even prohibition, of any legal or governmental recognition of racial, religious, language, or national origins groups as corporate entities with a standing in the legal or governmental process, and a prohibition of the use of ethnic criteria of any type for discriminatory purposes, or conversely for special or favored treatment."[10] That is, government would take an absolutely neutral stand—a position of noninvolvement—toward ethnic groups. This is not to say that members of ethnic groups could not receive governmental benefits as members of some other general population, for example as poor people, but that they could receive no benefit solely on the basis of their ethnic group. The pluralistic nature of society, within this model, would exist voluntarily as an unofficial societal reality in communal life. The transmission of ethnic cultural traits, heritage, and identity would remain in the private sphere and be the responsibility of each group. On the other hand, public institutions such as the public schools would respect the diversity within society and accommodate it as much as possible. Equalitarian norms would emphasize equality of opportunity and the evaluation of individuals on the basis of universal standards of performance.

In contrast to liberal pluralism, under *corporate pluralism* racial and ethnic groups would be formally recognized as legally constituted entities with official standing in the society. Economic and political rewards, whether in the public or private sector, would be allocated on the basis of numerical quotas, which in turn would rest on relative numerical strength in the population or on some other formula emanating from the political process.[11] In a word, government would officially recognize and subsidize the pluralistic nature of society. Social institutions would be expected to treat groups differentially, supporting the maintenance and survival of each. Public schools, for example, might include ethnic studies programs designed to facilitate ethnic cultural transmission or might be parochial in nature, with individual schools catering to specific groups. Equalitarian norms would emphasize equality of condition rather than equality of opportunity. That is, we would expect to find a relative parity among the different groups and not concentrate on individual mobility. We would expect under this arrangement to find sharper distinctions being made between groups, and a greater sense of identity within a group would exist than with liberal pluralism.

In liberal pluralism and corporate pluralism we have two models that conceptually fit the notion of cultural pluralism. Before proceeding with theoretical considerations of cultural pluralism, it may be helpful to review what we hope to have accomplished by making these distinctions. Cultural pluralism, first and foremost, is an idea, a way of distinguishing certain social relationships in a society from other forms. But, like many popularly used ideas, it is not always clearly understood just what particulars cultural pluralism represents. In order to take the greatest heuristic advantage of the concept, it is important to make its meaning(s) as clear and explicit as possible. Hence, we noted the different uses of the term, took what appeared to us to be most relevant to our investigation, and clarified the conditions that seem logically to be entailed by that application of the concept. Thus, we noted the political-economic and sociological-anthropological meanings of the term, dismissed them as not capturing the main thrust of the movement, and focused on the characteristics of a model culturally plural society. We sought further clarification by analyzing the range of social organizational structures attributable to the concept and found that the range includes varying degrees of interaction between diverse groups, insular pluralism, halfway pluralism, and structural assimilation, and at least two kinds of social arrangements in which it may take place: segregated pluralism and integrated pluralism. We further determined that society may consistently support the concept in at least two ways—one where government plays a neutral role (liberal pluralism) and one where government plays an active role (corporate pluralism). Yet we also found that the range is not limitless, and at some point we move beyond the conceptual boundaries of cultural pluralism altogether. Thus, to our question, "What is cultural pluralism?" we can conclude that, at least as implied by the ordinary use of the term, it includes a range of structural and political relationships within a society characterized by cultural diversity, some minimal level of interaction between the diverse groups, relative equality of opportunity between the groups, and a perceived value for the continuance of diversity within the society.

THEORIES OF AMERICAN PLURALISM

Attempts have been made to describe theoretically the dynamics of American ethnic groups and their place within the larger social order. These theories have sought to explain what is happening to ethnic groups and what is likely to be their future. Three theories— assimilation, amalgamation, and cultural pluralism—stand out as the most widely discussed. We consider these first, indicating some of their limitations as theoretical descriptions, and then turn to more sophisticated analyses.

Assimilation

Assimilation is a theory of conformity to the majority. It holds that, through time, ethnic minority groups become more and more like the dominant majority until finally all are part of one common culture patterned after the dominant group. Schematically, the theory can be formulated as $A + B + C = A$, where A, B, and C represent different social groups and A represents the dominant group.[12] In the American experience, the theory has been called "Anglo conformity,"[13] with A representing the Anglo-Saxon Protestant dominant culture in the United States and B and C representing various immigrant groups. It has been predicted that the eventual outcome will be for the different immigrant groups to conform to the mores, life styles, and values of the Anglo-Saxon Protestant majority.

As Milton Gordon points out, this may occur on two different levels.[14] One level is what Gordon calls behavioral or cultural assimilation and refers to the absorption of the cultural behavior patterns of the dominant culture. Here the focus is on the acceptance of common values and styles of life. The technical term for this process is acculturation. The second level is what Gordon calls structural assimilation and refers to the entrance of the minority group into the social cliques,

organizations, institutional activities, and general civic life of the receiving society (i.e., the dominant culture). The emphasis here is on
the increased participation and incorporation in the structural features
of society. It should be noted, then, that a minority group may adopt
the values and life style of the dominant culture but may choose not to,
or not be allowed to, participate in the institutions and group associations of the mainstream society. The members remain structurally
segregated. Blacks, for the most part, have been forced into this position in the United States. Similarly, a minority group may be integrated
into the structural features of society while retaining some behaviors,
values, or beliefs significantly different from the dominant majority.
Homosexuals are an example of a behaviorally different minority
group, and religious minorities such as Jews and Mormons are examples of integrated groups with differing beliefs. The point is that for
assimilation to take place in the fullest sense it needs to occur both
structurally and culturally.

There is some evidence that the theory of assimilation accurately
describes the experience of American ethnic groups. Where the first
generation of American immigrants tended to form ethnic enclaves,
studies of the second generation tend to show the opposite. As "ethnic
groups were able to obtain a higher social class position, their members
often moved out of the old ethnic neighborhoods, changed or Anglicized their names, and generally established new patterns of social relationships, breaking the old European pattern of extended families."[15]
Women acquired a greater degree of autonomy, fathers' traditional position of authority was eroded, and families became more child-centered.
Similarly, studies have suggested that ethnic intermarriage is taking
place and that ethnic churches are a thing of the past.[16]

But if evidence supports the hypothesis that American ethnic
groups are becoming assimilated, there is also evidence to the contrary.
Assimilation at the structural level depends on the dominant group's
willingness to accept minority groups into its fold and on the desire of
minority groups to become assimilated. The presence of these conditions for some groups is very questionable. Prejudice and discrimination have worked to create and maintain group distinctiveness and
solidarity. Indeed, there is substantial evidence that while the development and operation of public education in the late nineteenth century in
the United States were designed to culturally assimilate and control
lower-class natives and immigrants, the function was also to reinforce
the class structure. That is, the fathers of our public educational system
wished to develop the values, attitudes, and behaviors of the dominant
group in the poor and uneducated masses and at the same time avoid
structural assimilation. Schools served as one means of sorting individuals into their approximate status and power positions in the social

structure.[17] The explanatory value of assimilation can also be challenged in the observation that where many second-generation ethnics seemed intent on assimilating, the third generation seems equally intent on reviving ethnic identity. Regardless of causes, it is clear that American ethnic groups have not lost their foothold, though perhaps they have changed. Cities in the United States can still be characterized as a "mosaic of segregated peoples." Indeed, even the suburbs, once thought to be monotonous, homogeneous, and middle class, reveal ethnic, religious, and class pluralism.[18] It would appear that while a significant amount of behavioral assimilation has taken place, structural assimilation has not been as extensive as first thought. This is particularly true for the intimate primary relationships.

Assimilation theorists, of course, can always argue that enough time has not passed for the process to be complete; it is still taking place and will be accomplished in the future. But in view of the fact that some groups well into their fourth generation continue to be distinct, we have good reason to question this assertion. It is more realistic to believe that, while behavioral assimilation has taken place to a greater or lesser extent for many groups, the theory does not capture the essence of experience of ethnic groups in American life. It depicts a linear, one-way movement toward Anglo conformity and, as such, fails to account for the contemporary resurgence in ethnic identity as well as an enduring ethnic cohesiveness within some groups.

Amalgamation

Amalgamation is a theory that predicts the development of a unique new cultural group resulting from the amalgam or synthesis of previously existing groups. It can be represented by the formula $A + B + C = D$, where A, B, and C represent different social groups and D represents the new distinct group.[19] Another name for this theory is the "melting pot," though care must be taken not to confuse this with assimilation. Often the melting pot is used to mean the melting away of ethnic characteristics, eventually leading to Anglo conformity. This is not the meaning, however, as it was first understood in Israel Zangwill's famous play or as it is used here. Rather, different cultural groups move toward each other, forming a common American culture from a combining of their different features. Thus Western Europeans and Southern and Eastern Europeans would, through time, combine and give rise to a hybrid American culture different from that of any one specific group. Presumably, given enough time, this process would also include Blacks, Hispanics, Native Americans, and other American ethnic minorities.

Though the notion that America has been a great melting pot has been popular, there is only marginal evidence that the process has actually taken place. We do have a Spanish architectural influence in the Southwest; include Italian, Greek, and Mexican dishes in our diet; and celebrate St. Patrick's Day. But beyond these superficial displays little support can be found. There are several reasons for this. First, as with assimilation, for amalgamation to take place the dominant group must be willing to make a place and share its power with the minority group. This has rarely been the case in the United States. Second, both the dominant majority and the minority groups must be willing to give up certain features of their culture to form an amalgam with other groups. While this requirement is more likely to be met than the first, ethnocentrism works against it, and it is rare. Third, where amalgamation has taken place, it has usually been limited to a small number of groups and has involved long periods of time and geographical isolation, conditions not found in pluralistic societies like the United States.* While some degree of amalgamation does occur in culturally diverse societies, manifestations of assimilation and cultural pluralism are much more common.

Classical Cultural Pluralism

In presenting a theory of cultural pluralism, it is necessary to distinguish between two different formulations: classical cultural pluralism and modified cultural pluralism. Classical cultural pluralism as a theory of group relationships sees diverse groups living together as common members of a society with each maintaining its cultural distinctiveness and identity. It can be formulated as $A + B + C = A + B + C$, where A, B, and C represent different social groups that through time maintain their uniqueness.[20] The theory can be understood to hypothesize a state of peaceful coexistence following some period of adjustment. The diverse groups, as we saw in our earlier discussion of the concept of cultural pluralism, must have some common bonds and interaction. It is probable, then, that cultural distance between the groups will decrease as individuals adopt common political values, share languages, and exchange ideas through the media and other institutions. It is important, however, to keep the emphasis on group distinctiveness and autonomy.

Some evidence can be found to support the theory of classical cultural pluralism for the United States. When immigrants first arrived in America, it was common for them to settle in ethnic enclaves and establish community, political, and educational organizations. Though

---

* Mexico is an example of amalgamation. The process began following the conquest of Cortez and involved an amalgam of Spanish and Indian populations and, in smaller numbers, Indians and Blacks and finally the two mestizo groups.

there seems to have been interim movement toward assimilation, today many ethnic groups still tend to collect into ethnic communities and seem to be reasserting their ethnic identities. In addition to this general phenomenon, a number of relatively small groups in the United States have effectively isolated themselves for the most part from the rest of society and maintain a high degree of insularity. The Amish, Hutterites, Hasidic Jews, and some Native American groups are examples of this form of pluralism.

But if ethnic identity is still important and if a few small groups maintain insular pluralism, it should be clear that the high degree of distinctiveness and autonomy required by this theory does not describe the general state of affairs in the United States. Group boundaries have not been and are not now as rigid as classical cultural pluralism demands. Over time there has been some degree of assimilation and the development of a common American culture shared by most members of society. Thus, while classical cultural pluralism can explain aspects of the American experience, it falls short, as have the other theories, of giving an accurate general account.

Modified Cultural Pluralism

The theory of modified cultural pluralism is similar to that of classical cultural pluralism in that groups maintain a degree of distinctiveness and identity; it departs from the classical theory in its emphasis on the development of a common culture and a higher degree of interaction among the different groups. It can be represented by the formulation $A + B + C = A_1 + B_1 + C_1$, where A, B, and C represent different groups and A_1, B_1, and C_1 represent groups distinct from one another but also different from A, B and C.[21] The subscript on each letter designates qualities of a common culture the groups now share, the result being a so-called hyphenated-American. For example, Italians, Greeks, and Mexicans, through interaction with the dominant American culture and the process of acculturation, change and become Italian-Americans, Greek-Americans, and Mexican-Americans. Each group in its own time and place becomes a collective entity serving as a source of individual identity as well as a platform to pursue political and economic interests. In a typology of theories of ethnicity in the United States parallel to the one we are developing here, Andrew Greeley equates our modified pluralism with a perspective he calls "acculturation but not assimilation."[22] As he describes the process, immigrant groups absorb large numbers of cultural traits from the dominant majority, with the dominant group picking up a few traits from the immigrant groups. The result is the emergence of a relatively large common culture that all groups share. But the process of acculturation stops short of total cultural assimilation, and each group maintains cultural traits that distinguish it from the others; in particular, the groups maintain some distance from one another in the private spheres of their lives (i.e., in primary relationships).

The theory of modified cultural pluralism comes much closer than any of the other theories we have considered in its ability to account for what seems to be happening in the United States. It acknowledges both assimilation and pluralism as being active social processes that function to maintain group distinctiveness while contributing toward the building and maintenance of a common culture. It allows for the change of groups over time without being committed to their ultimate demise. Thus, Italian, Greek, and Slavic Americans, who in their first generation exemplified social relationships characteristic of classical cultural pluralism, have become decidedly more "American." Yet they still can be found living in ethnic enclaves and, at least on some issues, making demands on the basis of their ethnic distinctiveness. The same is true for Blacks (Afro Americans), Hispanics (Mexican Americans), and Asian Americans. But as effective as the theory of modified cultural pluralism is, it still fails to capture certain features of American ethnic groups. Groups change and develop in directions that cannot be explained solely on the basis of traits inherited from their past or from the characteristics of other groups. Similarly, some groups may be completely assimilated, while other groups that previously did not exist come into being. Greeley, recognizing these dynamics, hypothesizes a theory that attempts to combine and supplement the other four.

Ethnogenesis

The theory of ethnogenesis, as Greeley describes it, views ethnic groups as dynamic flexible mechanisms that can grow and change and have integrity, as ethnic groups, that is not necessarily threatened by the change.[23] But before we look at the changes, it is important to consider the characteristics of the groups prior to any interaction between them. Often at the time that diverse groups come in contact, there will already exist various common characteristics between them. These characteristics are part of the original cultural system of each group. For example, many European groups immigrating to the United States shared part of a broad Western cultural inheritance. Upon their arrival in the United States most of the Irish spoke English, for example, and understood something of the English political style of the eighteenth and nineteenth centuries that strongly influenced the politics of the day. It should of course be recognized that the initial degree of similarity between a minority group and the dominant group will vary, some having many common features and some having few. These qualities may range from cultural or religious similarities to socioeconomic characteristics to race or skin color, and it is probable that these will influence the dynamics that develop between the groups. Initially, then, diverse groups exist but usually with some common feature. This is represented in Figure 2.2. The lower portion of the figure represents qualities that are uniquely characteristic of the immigrant group. The middle portion is that set of qualities that the two groups have in common at the beginning of their interaction with one another.* Note that the characteristics of each group represents that group's original cultural system, that is, its culture at the time interaction between the group begins.

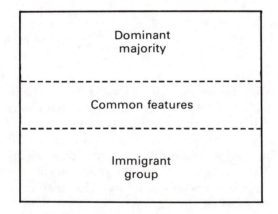

FIGURE 2.2   Original cultural system.

Under the influence of interaction, acculturation, and other experiences in American society, both at the time of immigration and subsequently, the common culture grows larger. As time passes, immigrants become more like the dominant culture and the dominant culture may become somewhat like the immigrants. Certain immigrant characteristics persist along with a modified group identity. This is the process we described in the theory of modified cultural pluralism and is represented in Figure 2.3.

While the process of adaptation works to bring diverse groups together and build a common culture, it also works in the other direction. Under the impact of American life, some traits become more rather than less distinctive. Certain aspects of the immigrant heritage

* There are only two groups depicted in the diagram, the dominant majority and one immigrant group. This is only for purposes of simplification. In actuality, a number of different groups may be present. The differences and similarities of each could be assessed in relation to each of the others.

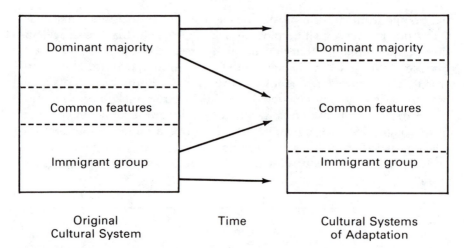

FIGURE 2.3

are emphasized and developed in response to the challenge of American society. What evolves is a cultural system that is a combination of traits shared with other groups and traits that are distinctive to its own group. For the ethnic group, then, the mix of traits and the emphasis within the cultural system are different from those of their immigrant predecessors. They share more with the common culture than they did to begin with, but in some respects they also may be more different from the descendants of the dominant majority than their ancestors were from the dominant majority upon their (the immigrant group's)

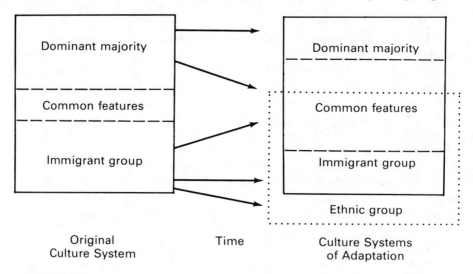

FIGURE 2.4

arrival.[24] This growth beyond any of the original characteristics of either the dominant or the immigrant group is expressed by the dotted lines in Figure 2.4. It can be seen that the dotted line moves back toward the original cultural system as well as expanding out to new horizons. At times an ethnic group reasserts and recovers aspects of its cultural heritage previously lost to acculturation. Thus, ethnogenesis is not unidirectional. A group may consciously revitalize itself and reestablish past ways, reversing the process of acculturation.

To test this theoretical model, data would need to be gathered in a systematic manner. On the surface, however, the model seems to have considerable validity. We see that ethnic groups have undergone change over past generations; in many respects they have been assimilated, yet they are still with us politically, culturally, and residentially. They are not the same as they were, but nevertheless they are viable and in some respects more unique than in the past. "When Poles prove more likely on Election Day to vote than Americans of any other ethnic group and also more likely to vote Democratic, they are manifesting a Polish ethnic culture trait, which probably has far more to do with the experience of the Polish-American collectivity than anything in the Polish ancestral past."[25] While Mexican Americans cannot be characterized as simply being displaced Mexicans, neither can they be described as simply being Anglicized. The Navajo are not the same people they were 50 or 100 years ago, but neither are they "white men." They are distinctly Navajo but in different ways, some of which have been borrowed from the white man, some of which are traditional Navajo, and some of which are products of the unique circumstances in which they find themselves. The same is true for other American ethnic groups, such as Blacks, Chinese, other Asians, and Europeans.

This dynamic evolutionary process continues over time. Though our diagram does not show it, the process operates for the dominant culture and all other groups. To capture the complexity, we would need to develop a diagram for each group in relation to all other groups. In addition, our diagram does not illustrate how new social groups, previously not in existence, can form out of interests in the more established groups. Some of these "new" groups may be considered to be ethnic in nature depending on what criteria for ethnicity are used (consider the Mormons, for example), some may be considered subcultures (e.g., Appalachians, religious cults), and some may be social minority groups (e.g., homosexuals, handicapped people, women). Nevertheless, the important point is that ethnic groups, as well as other social groups, tend to change and grow over time—some traits being lost while others evolve, some groups passing from the scene while others are created—and that all contribute to the continued pluralistic nature of the United States.

Ethclass

There is yet another theory addressing the evolutionary nature of ethnic groups in the United States. While the theory has certain short-comings shared by the first four theories presented, it introduces a new set of variables that can enrich our understanding of the complex nature of an ethnic group. The theory, presented by Milton Gordon,[26] describes the development of an *ethclass*.

In general, Gordon sees an ethnic group as involved in a process of assimilation involving a number of variables. The main distinction, however, is between behavioral or cultural assimilation and structural assimilation. As noted, behavioral assimilation refers to the absorp-tion of the cultural behavior patterns of the dominant culture, and structural assimilation refers to the integration of a minority group into the institutions of the dominant group at the levels of both primary and secondary relationships. Gordon argues that while behavioral assimi-lation has taken place on a relatively broad level, structural assimilation has not and will probably never be complete, particularly in primary re-lationships. He attributes the lack of structural assimilation to pre-judice, discrimination, conflict between groups, and the desire of some groups to maintain their ethnic distinctiveness.

He sees society, then, as being segmented and including a number of different social groups. The groups, however, can no longer be char-acterized simply on the basis of past ethnic characteristics. He sees race, religion, and national origin intersecting with social class to pro-duce groups he calls ethclasses. He believes that differences in each of these variables produce significant differences in the nature of the group. Thus, a lower-class Protestant Black is, in important ways, different from an upper-middle-class Protestant Black. The same would hold true for a lower-middle-class Polish Catholic contrasted with a lower-middle-class Irish Catholic. Other examples of ethclasses would be Mexican American Catholics and middle-class Chinese Christians. As Gordon sees it,

With a person of the same social class but of a different ethnic group, one shares behavioral similarities but not a sense of peoplehood. With those of the same ethnic group but of a different social class, one shares the sense of peoplehood but not behavioral similarities. The only group which meets both of these criteria are people of the same ethnic group *and* same social class. With these birds of our feathers we truly share a sense of . . . 'consciousness of kind'—with these particular members of the human race and no others we can really relax and participate with ease and without strain.[27]

The point of acknowledging Gordon's ethclass concept is to note that the adaptation of immigrants to American society is more complex than simple acculturation. A number of variables operate in the defining of an ethnic subculture, and these may be important in analyzing and understanding the dynamics of a pluralistic society. The heuristic value of the concept of ethclass still needs testing. Data need to be collected to determine the extent to which groups have functioned as ethclasses in the past and the extent to which ethclasses are evident. For example, do middle-class rural Mexican Americans living in mining towns in the Southwest perceive issues, their position in society, and the means of negotiating conflict differently from lower-class rural Mexican American agricultural workers in the Southwest? Or is it more accurate to characterize these two ethclasses as belonging to the same ethnic group as they come into contact with the dominant majority? It is possible that one grouping will be more appropriate in some situations, while others are more appropriate in different situations. These questions need to be explored in more detail.

Gordon's general theory of behavioral and structural assimilation does have explanatory limitations. As with theories of assimilation and amalgamation, it is unidirectional and linear in nature and fails to explain reversals in the process. It is also restricted in its ability to account for groups that remain behaviorally and structurally insulated from the dominant society and to explain higher frequency and increased intensity of ethnic groups to reassert their identity and function as special-interest groups.[28]

It may be useful to pause and recapitulate this section of the chapter. We have been looking at theories that purport to explain what happens to an ethnic (immigrant) group in the United States. That is, how can the process of adaptation of the minority group to the dominant majority be theoretically conceptualized? We have looked at several common theories and found assimilation, amalgamation, classical cultural pluralism, and modified cultural pluralism to be wanting in varying degrees of explanatory value. The theory of ethnogenesis has been presented and seems to be the most complete in its ability to include the variety of ways ethnic groups have adapted. In addition we have introduced the notion of ethclass as a possibly useful way of further classifying changes in ethnic groups.[29]

But if we have been exploring changes in ethnic groups as they attempt to adapt to a dominant majority, we have largely ignored the nature of ethnic groups and the role ethnicity is likely to play in modern cultures in the future. Indeed, an example of how ethnicity varies over time can be seen in the increase in activity of ethnic groups today. The resurgence of ethnic consciousness has reached proportions that few theorists would have predicted a decade or two ago. There has been a pronounced and sudden increase in tendencies by people in many countries and in many circumstances to insist on the significance of their group distinctiveness and identity and on new rights that derive from this group characteristic.[30] This has particularly been the case in the United States. Sometime after the Black civil rights movement, the number of ethnic groups demanding recognition, legitimation, and equal or special treatment has proliferated. Indeed, Americans seem to have become fascinated with ethnicity, with the phenomenon finding its way into television programming, congressional lobbies, and public evaluation. Given this trend, we would be justified in asking what is taking place and why? What is behind the rediscovery of ethnic identity?

THEORIES OF ETHNICITY

The Characteristics of Ethnic Groups

A good deal of our discussion has been directed at the dynamics of ethnic groups. In the next chapter, discussions of cultural pluralism are not limited to ethnic groups but include a number of different social groups. Yet the theories just discussed clearly point out that the central concern of American pluralism is with what we generally consider to be ethnicity. But even while this is true, it is not altogether clear who or what comprises an ethnic group. The terms "racial," "cultural," and "ethnic" are often used interchangeably with reference to minority groups, and religious groups being common. Because of our interests in the persistence of ethnicity and the resurgence of the perceived relevance of ethnicity in the United States today, it may be useful to consider what the characteristics of an ethnic group are.

The starting point in delineating the nature of ethnic groups can be found in the fact that various people within a society recognize differences among themselves and have names for themselves and others based on these recognized differences.[31] These names are an important feature of a group's identity and symbolize the group's conception of itself in relation to all other groups. When terms such as Black, Chicano, Polish, Italian, and Anglo are used within a particular society, then, it is evident that the members of the various groups associated with these terms perceive relevant differences between themselves and the members of other groups. The labels serve as an instrument employed by a group for the expression and reinforcement of its sense of distinctiveness and common identification. While the intensity and meaning of the label may vary among groups and among individuals within a particular group, the content of the differences implied by the labels revolves around three components: cultural content, historical experience, and group image.[32] That is, members of a group sense a difference between themselves and members of other groups in regard to cultural behaviors, such as norms, customs, and religious practices;

experiences as a group historically, such as enslavement, colonialization, and exploitation; and ideas of who they are as a people, for example, honest, hard-working, brave, "chosen people," and the like.

Wsevolod Isajiw has tried to capture the essence of an ethnic group in a formal definition. "Ethnicity," he states, "refers to an involuntary group of people who share the same culture or to descendants of such people who identify themselves and/or are identified by others as belonging to the same involuntary group."[33] If we look at this definition carefully, we can see the features outlined above, as well as other important points. We can see that ethnicity has to do with group identification. It evolves out of a desire of some group to distinguish itself from other groups in society. As the definition suggests, the desire to make a distinction may emanate from the particular ethnic group or may result from the imposition of a distinction by some other group. That is, a population may define themselves as different from other members of the society, or they may find themselves the object of a distinction that they heretofore had not found relevant. Regardless of the source, the result is the same: A group image and sense of identity evolve.

The sources of the distinctions made between the groups, according to Isajiw, are cultural. Ethnic groups perceive themselves as being a different people in respect to norms, customs, traditions, life style, and the like—that is, at least different in origin. Isajiw includes the important observation that cultural differences need no longer exist. Group identity may be based on a select set of real differences or on a select set of differences thought to exist in the past of the particular group of which the members are descendants. A group's image, then, may evolve from both contemporary cultural patterns and a sense of history. This is particularly relevant for white ethnics in the United States. While third- and fourth-generation Italians, Greeks, Poles, and Slavs may display only a limited degree of contemporary cultural distinctiveness, the tradition from which they are descended provides the basis for their ethnic distinctiveness.

Of particular importance to Isajiw's definition of ethnicity is the fact that it is involuntary. The idea of common ancestral origin (i.e., sharing the same cultural traits or being of the same descent) indicates that a person is born into a group and acquires the traits through socialization. There is, of course, no choice as to the specific cultural group into which one is born and which provides for one basic process of socialization. This feature distinguishes ethnic groups from other associations in which one has a choice of membership (e.g., special-interest groups). Persons are identified by others as belonging to one or another ethnic group even if they no longer actively share cultural patterns with that ethnic group as long as a link to their ancestors can be made. Identification by others in turn usually stimulates self-identification. The result is that ethnicity is a matter of a double involuntary boundary, a boundary from within maintained by the socialization process and a boundary from without established by the process of intergroup relations.[34] It is the involuntary nature of the ethnic group, Isajiw believes, that is connected with the affective ties that tend to develop among group members—the feelings of sympathy and loyalty toward members of one's own ethnic group.

In the sense that we have been discussing the term, we are all ethnic—that is, we all belong to some ethnic group. But not all ethnic groups nor all individuals within a particular ethnic group function or identify themselves the same with respect to their ethnicity. James Banks and Geneva Gay have developed a typology that allows us to capture some of these differences and assess the degree and type of ethnicity a group or individual may display.[35] They emphasize that their typology represents ideal types (in the Weberian sense) and that in reality no actual ethnic group represents a "pure" type. Rather, the categories should be thought of as a continuum.

The three main variables in the typology are cultural traits, a shared sense of economic fate, and a shared sense of political interests and interdependence. A group that is culturally ethnic is an ethnic group that shares a common set of values, experiences, behavioral characteristics, and linguistic traits differing substantially from those of other ethnic groups within the society.[36] An economic ethnic group is an ethnic group that shares a sense of group identity and sees its economic fate tied together. Individual members of the group feel that their economic fate is intimately tied to the economic future of other members of the group.[37] A political ethnic group is an ethnic group that has a sense of shared political interests and a feeling of political interdependence. The group responds to political issues collectively and tries to promote public policies and programs that will enhance the interests of its members as a group.[38] Banks and Gay point out that political ethnic groups are usually economic ethnic groups also. When such is the case, we can refer to the group as an eco-political ethnic group. Finally, when all features are present, we have what Banks and Gay call a holistic ethnic group. This is an involuntary group of individuals who share a sense of peoplehood and an interdependence of fate, a common sense of identity, and common behavioral characteristics. Its members respond collectively to economic and political issues and try to promote public programs and policies that will further the interests of the group as a whole.[39]

In applying the typology to the United States, Banks and Gay conclude, as we have, that every American is a member of an ethnic group, with some individuals and groups being more "ethnic" than others. As groups, for example, Afro Americans and Mexican Americans closely approach holistic ethnic groups. Within a particular group, say that of Afro Americans, a lower-class Black individual who lives in an all-Black community, speaks Black English, and is active in Black political and economic activities is more "ethnic" (i.e., more ethnically Black) than the highly acculturated Black who tries desperately to avoid any contact with other Blacks. The same can be said for a counterpart in the Mexican American ethnic group. In general, white ethnic groups, such as Poles, Greeks, Italians, and Slavs, are less "ethnic" in respect to the intensity of each of the three variables than either Blacks or Mexican Americans. Nevertheless, and noting the individual variability within each group, cultural, economic, and political qualities exist, with a recent renewed emphasis on the cultural. Anglo Americans as a group are a cultural ethnic group who, for the most part, do not organize politically and economically as a group. Other groups, such as Native Americans, Chinese Americans, Japanese Americans, Puerto Rican Americans, or Cuban Americans, and individuals within these groups, can be similarly placed on an ethnic continuum. An important feature of this typology that should not be overlooked is that the degree to which a particular cultural, national, or racial group is ethnic varies over time, in different regions, with social class, with mobility, and with the pervasive sociopolitical conditions within the society.

The Permanence of Ethnicity as a Social Factor

Social scientists generally predicted that the force and significance of ethnicity would diminish and that surviving cultural and ethnic allegiances would be budged by cooperation, respect, and interdependence to form a harmonious and stable social order. These prophecies have not come to pass. Recent history and current events, in both the United States and the world at large, show strong, even revitalized emotional ties to ethnic and cultural symbols, as well as continued conflict among different cultural groups. Today there remain 892 definable ethnic groups in the world,[40] with many countries having more than 5 major ethnic groups.[41] Moreover, ethnic differences are the single most important source of large-scale conflict within countries. Since World War II, the most common cause of violence involving nations has been internal ethnic conflict,[42] *not* external wars.

One likely reason for the gap between predictions and actual events is that the theories of ethnicity on which the predictions were based are inaccurate. Called developmental theories, the common view has been that societies advance through developmental stages toward modernization by means of trends inherent in human civilization.

Using postindustrial societies like the United States as models, developmental theory assumes that humankind, through reason, science, and organization, will transform nature and adjust societies to meet new conditions. One outcome of this process will be the weakening of primordial bonds, superstitions, fatalism, and other prerational sentiments and a shift to more sophisticated social and political organization.

Ethnic identification is seen as a prerational sentiment, and it is predicted that ethnicities will become less important to the individual when such concerns as occupation, education, income, and legal rights come to define one's identity. Thus, according to this view, ethnicity is seen as a primitive form of political organization, believing that ethnic groups begin when individuals band together to further their common interests or meet some need. Group identity and cohesiveness develop as a result of the association. Common experiences and struggles with groups strengthen the sense of group identity and emphasize a "we/they" relationship. In time, myths develop to explain the group's existence in the world, and as succeeding generations are initiated into the ways, beliefs, and myths of the group, a strong sense of identity and allegiance develops. As societies modernize, however, and as industrialization develops and greater cooperation and division of labor are required, the ethnic group loses its effectiveness as a political organization because it is less functional. Individuals begin to identify themselves as members of a larger society, and common interests, once defined in a relatively narrow social framework, are now considered in the broader contexts of class or nationality. In the end, ethnicity remains only as a fond remembrance of one's heritage, with folktales, dances, foods, and customs passed along only as ties to the past and as continuing traditions.[43] Thus, as societies become increasingly modern and sophisticated and as they become economically and technologically developed, people begin to organize and define themselves on the basis of political, economic, and social interests. One's accomplishments become more important in determining status than do ascribed traits with which one was born. Presumably, even nationalism will give way in time to broader forms of political identification.

Many students of human behavior have begun to rethink this view of ethnicity. Some political scientists who once supported the developmental view now believe that we may have underestimated the importance of ethnicity in meeting human needs. Individuals, they hypothesize, may have a need to explain who and what they are beyond mere political and economic associations. That is, ethnicity in advanced modern societies might be a result of a human need for a basis of social relationships more enduring and less instrumental than those associated with modern political and social development, and that is why cultural identity survives long after its traditional functions have been taken over by increasingly impersonal social groups. In particular, these political scientists point to what seems to be a human need "to revive myths as metaphors to enclose the spaces of their own lives";[44] people need a greater sense of purpose and of being; they need something to help make sense out of the day-to-day affairs of ordinary life and provide an enduring continuity. Ethnic identification, particularly in its association with religion, has traditionally served this function. Close associations, common experiences, and a well-known network of religious and cultural traditions have provided psychological and cosmological homes of reference for human experience. Individuals find comforting support and order among others like themselves.

With respect to the United States, in comprehending the revival of ethnic consciousness it is important to realize that as the discussion above suggests, ethnicity never really ceased to be an important aspect of the American social fabric.[45] Although ethnic differences remained behind the scenes in the decades immediately following the Second World War, they never became irrelevant. Ethnicity has continued to play a role in American politics, with the practice of creating ethnically and religiously "balanced" slates of candidates, especially on state and local levels, remaining a major feature. Ethnic communities, too, have persisted. Most major urban areas contain several distinguishable ethnic enclaves; ethnic parishes in the Roman Catholic church, though their total numbers have perhaps declined, are as strong today as they were fifty years ago; even the suburbs, once thought to be the epitome of American homogenization, are characterized by religious, ethnic, and social-class differences creating a diverse mosaic. Thus, as noted, theories of assimilation and amalgamation do not accurately describe the ethnic experience in the United States. While some ethnic groups have become politically and economically enfranchised, a significant cultural and structural pluralism remains. Indeed, far from declining, ethnic pluralism has become institutionalized. It has become "an underlying aspect of America's social, political, and economic matrix. As such, ethnic consciousness became a residual ideological resource which, given certain conditions, could easily once again become a controversial social issue."[46]

To return to the question, why has this ethnic pluralism again made itself known in the proportions it has today? A number of hypotheses have been advanced. One analysis views the phenomenon as part of a larger movement of individuals to form groups for self-protection. Henry Perkinson believes that a feeling of powerlessness and a consciousness of victimization has driven people together into groups of similarly situated "victims," forging them into liberation movements.[47] According to Perkinson, this trend extends far beyond the traditional group lines of race, sex, ethnic origins, and age. While Blacks, women, Italians, and the elderly have all organized to protect themselves, others, such as employees in the public service (e.g., police officers, firefighters, sanitation workers, teachers), consumers, prison inmates, individuals seeking to protect a way of life (e.g., conservationists, hunters, hippies, pacificists, antinoise and antipollution groups), and ad hoc groups formed to protect against a specific threat have united as well. Once formed, these groups use governmental and extragovernmental means to protect themselves. They use the courts, lobby in the legislatures, and appeal to government agencies. In addition, they engage in bloc voting during elections, sign petitions, employ boycotts, demonstrate, and advertise. They create organizations that engender militancy; publish their own journals, magazines, and newspapers; and issue admonitary warnings to would-be oppressors.[48]

Thus, for Perkinson, we are in the presence of more than simply a revival of cultural pluralism. The movement is much larger, and many more groups are involved. The purpose of the movement is not the preservation or extension of group differences—certainly this is not what women, consumers, and senior citizens want—rather, what every member of every group wants is protection against victimization.

Perkinson is not alone in his analysis. William Newman[49] and Glazer and Moynihan[50] came to similar conclusions. Newman sees the pluralistic ethnic revival resulting from inner-group conflict—conflict over social resources, status, power, and values. He also sees it as involving more than groups defined as ethnic; he includes all minority groups, such as homosexuals, women, handicapped persons, and countercultural groups. With specific regard to the rise of white ethnic consciousness in the 1970s, he hypothesizes that it arose as a response to the claims of other groups for a larger share of the social pie. As the pie was divided into smaller pieces, and in the face of a slumping economy, white ethnics perceived a real threat to their newly established positions in society.

In their analysis, Glazer and Moynihan too recognize the strong tendency of ethnic groups to function as special-interest groups. They see the movement in the United States as being part of a worldwide phenomenon and argue that whereas in the past conflict between ethnic groups was likely to emphasize culture, language, and religion *as such*, today the emphasis has shifted to focus on the broadly defined interests of the members of the group. That is, ethnic conflicts have become one form in which interest conflicts between and within states are pursued.[51] As a partial explanation of this development, Glazer and Moynihan point to the tendency of socialist and democratic governments to become crucial and direct arbiters of economic well-being and political status and the benefits that flow from it. In such a situation, it is not usually enough to assert claims on behalf of large but loosely aggregated groups such as "workers" or "white-collar employees"; such claims are too general to have a significant and lasting impact. A smaller, more cohesive group, such as an ethnic group, is much more effective because significant concessions are possible and direct gains can be attached to the concessions made. Thus, in the United States it is easy, for example, for a mayor doing something for the Polish community within a city to both allocate resources for this restricted population and see the potential benefits on election day; in contrast, it would be much more difficult and have much less impact to make some concession to workers in general. Because of the nature of our political system, then, and because of the identifiable nature of ethnic groups, the two become a utilitarian complement, each contributing to the advantage of the other. The net result, the strengthening of the tendency of individuals to assert their demands as ethnic collectives, in turn results in the strengthening of ethnic ties.

Other variables Glazer and Moynihan see as explaining why ethnicity has become a focus for political mobilization include social stratification, where group conflict is generated from a struggle over egalitarianism and the adoption of social norms; an ever-increasing cultural diversity brought about by continued immigration; and the sharpening of our awareness of ethnic conflict fostered by worldwide mass communication. But while economic, political, and value conflicts certainly contribute to the resurgence of ethnic identity, Glazer and Moynihan believe there is more. They argue that one reason ethnicity becomes an effective means of advancing interests in the modern world is that it involves more than interests: It combines an interest with an affective tie.[52] They are not willing to go as far as theorists who associate ethnicity with a primordial force in humankind, which when suppressed will always rise again.[53] Yet the affective element is important and distinguishes the ethnic group from other human collectives formed to secure some economic or political advantage or security. Identification as a people plays an important role both as a political instrument and as a source of individual identity.

This combining of individual identity with group interest has a profound consequence. According to Milton Gordon, because individuals define themselves, at least in part, in terms of the group, they come to view their personal interests as the interests of the group.[54] In a manner of speaking, individuals come to perceive themselves as extensions of the group and their personal interests as extensions of the group's interests. This phenomenon accounts for the widespread presence of ethnocentrism and the tendency of an individual to perceive an injury to the ethnic group as a personal injury. Thus, the intensity of the passions engendered by ethnic conflict becomes comparable to that engendered by threats to oneself. In Gordon's words, "... man defending the honor or welfare of his ethnic group is man defending himself."[55] Contemporary ethnicity, then, can be understood in terms of group conflict, but its full meaning can be appreciated only when one recognizes that the affective ties within the ethnic experience transpose a threat to the ethnic group into personal threat. In grasping this notion, it is easier to comprehend why ethnic conflicts tend to be so intense.

To our question, "What is behind the rediscovery of ethnic identity?" we have advanced several interrelated and complementary hypotheses. Each probably contributes to an accounting of the phenomenon, but they are only hypotheses tentatively stated, and as Moynihan and Glazer concede, little in this field has been resolved. We are all beginners here. What does seem to be certain is "that there is a phenomenon here that is, in ways not yet explicated, no mere survival but intimately and organically bound up with major trends of modern societies.[56]

SUMMARY

We set out in this chapter to get a clear theoretical (as opposed to ideological) understanding of cultural pluralism and ethnicity. We began with a close conceptual look at cultural pluralism and discovered several distinct uses of the term. Concentrating on the ordinary language sense, we established four necessary conditions of society for the concept to apply: (1) cultural diversity, (2) membership in a common politic and some minimal interaction between and among groups, (3) relative parity and equality between and among the groups, and (4) a perceived value for the continuance of diversity.

We further discovered that these conditions could be met by several different organizational structures within a society. On the basis of whether primary and secondary relationships remained within a particular cultural group or whether they were allowed to develop across group lines, we distinguished between insular pluralism, halfway pluralism, and structural assimilation. We noted that the extreme forms of insular pluralism and structural assimilation both failed to meet the required conditions for cultural pluralism. On the basis of geographic proximity of one group to another, we distinguished between integrated pluralism and segregated pluralism. And on the basis of the role government assumes in maintaining the pluralistic nature of society, we distinguished between liberal pluralism and corporate pluralism.

We next explored theories that tried to explain the dynamics of American ethnic groups and their place within the larger social order. Beginning with the theory of assimilation and considering in turn the theories of amalgamation, classical cultural pluralism, and modified cultural pluralism, we found each to be wanting in descriptive accuracy. The theories of assimilation and amalgamation were linear and unidirectional and failed to account for the resurgence of ethnic activity in the United States; those of classical and modified cultural pluralism tended to be too restrictive in their ability to account for the changing nature of ethnic groups. The theory of ethnogenesis proved to have the greatest heuristic value in understanding the directions in which ethnic groups might evolve. We supplemented this theory with the introduction of the concept of ethclass as a possible way of classifying different ethnic groups.

Turning to ethnicity, we sought a clearer definition of an ethnic group. We first acknowledged that the content of an ethnic group focused on cultural traits, group image, and historical experience. Next, we reviewed the features of ethnicity presented in a definition. We noted that it is an involuntary association based on a select set of cultural traits existing in either the past or present. We also reviewed a typology of different ethnic groups and how it functions in the United States. Ethnic groups may emphasize either cultural traits, common economic interests, common political interests, or some combination of these in varying degrees.

Finally, we made a brief inquiry into the possible reasons for the revival of ethnic consciousness so prevalent today. It appears that a number of variables have contributed: First, ethnic distinctiveness in the United States has never really vanished; second, there is a tendency for people to band together for mutual economic and political security and benefit; third, the tendency of governments to distribute economic and political well-being has strengthened ethnic consciousness; fourth, the ethnic group provides for individuals a source of identity and belonging not easily provided by other social factions of society.

NOTES

1. William E. Connolly and Glen Gordon, *Social Structure and Political Theory* (Lexington, Mass.: D. C. Heath, 1974), p. 8.
2. Richard Pratte, "The Concept of Cultural Pluralism," *Philosophy of Education 1972: Proceedings of the Twenty-Eighth Annual Meeting of the Philosophy of Education Society* (1972), pp. 61–77.
3. Ibid., p. 64.
4. Ibid., p. 69.
5. Ibid., p. 70.
6. Thomas Green, *Education and Pluralism: Ideal and Reality* (Syracuse: School of Education, Syracuse University, 1966).
7. William A. Newman, *American Pluralism: A Study of Minority Groups and Social Theory* (New York: Harper & Row, 1973), p. 54.
8. Ibid.

9. Milton Gordon, "Toward a General Theory of Racial and Ethnic Group Relations," in *Ethnicity*, ed. Nathan Glazer and Daniel Moynihan (Cambridge, Mass.: Harvard University Press, 1975), pp. 105–6.
10. Ibid., p. 106.
11. Ibid.
12. Newman, *American Pluralism*, p. 54.
13. Andrew Greeley, *Ethnicity in the United States* (New York: Wiley, 1974), p. 304.
14. Milton Gordon, *Human Nature, Class, and Ethnicity* (New York: Oxford University Press, 1978), p. 203. R. A. Schermerhorn, using the terminology differently, also makes this distinction; see *Comparative Ethnic Relations* (New York: Random House, 1970), p. 80.
15. Newman, *American Pluralism*, p. 75.
16. Ibid., p. 76.
17. See, for example, Michael B. Katz, *Class, Bureaucracy, and School* (New York: Praeger, 1975); Michael B. Katz, ed., *Education in American History*, (New York: Praeger, 1973); and Clarence J. Karier, ed., *Shaping the American Educational State* (New York: Free Press, 1975).
18. Bennet Berger, *Working Class Suburbs*, 2nd ed. (Berkeley: University of California. Press, 1970); Herbert Gans, *The Levittowners* (New York: Pantheon, 1967); Gans, *The Urban Villagers* (New York: Free Press, 1962).
19. Newman, *American Pluralism*, p. 63.
20. Ibid., p. 67.
21. Ibid., p. 79.
22. Greeley, *Ethnicity in the United States*, p. 306.
23. Ibid., pp. 308–10.
24. Ibid., p. 309.
25. Ibid., p. 310.
26. Milton Gordon, *Assimilation in American Life* (New York: Oxford University Press, 1964).
27. Ibid., p. 53.
28. Gordon does recognize some of these limitations and addresses them in "Toward a General Theory of Racial and Ethnic Group Relations," in Glazer and Moynihan, *Ethnicity*.
29. It should be emphasized here that we have not by any means surveyed the entire field of theories attempting to explain majority-minority relationships in the United States. We have not looked, for example, at the theories that concentrate on prejudice and discrimination in race relations or at theories of social conflict. Our reluctance to consider these is not because they are unimportant or because they lack explanatory value— indeed a number are quite insightful—but because our interest is with the transformation of ethnic groups. For theories that explore the relations between majority and minority groups, the reader is referred elsewhere. See Glazer and Moynihan, *Ethnicity*; Newman, *American Pluralism*; H. M. Blalock, *Toward a Theory of Minority Group Relations* (New York: Wiley, 1967); Schermerhorn, *Comparative Ethnic Relations*; B. Sizemore, "Shattering the Melting Pot Myth," in *Teaching Ethnic Studies*, ed. J. Banks (Washington, D.C.: National Council for the Social Studies, 1973), pp. 73–101; P. L.

Van den Berghe, *Race and Racism: A Comparative Perspective* (New York: Wiley, 1967).

30. Glazer and Moynihan, *Ethnicity*, p. 3.
31. Edward Spicer and Raymond Thompson, *Plural Society in the Southwest* (New York: Interbook, 1972), p. 22.
32. Ibid., pp. 22–30.
33. Wsevolod Isajiw, "Definitions of Ethnicity," *Ethnicity* 1, no. 2 (1974): 122.
34. Ibid.
35. James Banks and Geneva Gay, "Ethnicity in Contemporary American Society: Toward the Development of a Typology," *Ethnicity* 5 (1978): 238–51.
36. Ibid., p. 244.
37. Ibid., p. 245.
38. Ibid.
39. Ibid.
40. George Peter Murdock, *Ethnographic Atlas* (Pittsburgh: University of Pittsburgh Press, 1967).
41. Abdul A. Said and Lewis R. Simmons, eds, *Ethnicity in an International Context* (New Brunswick, N.J.: Transaction Press, 1976), pp. 10–16.
42. Martin O. Heisler, "Ethnic Conflict in the World Today: An Introduction," *The Annals of the American Academy of Political and Social Science* 433 (September 1977): 1; Walker Cannor, "The Politics of Ethnonationalism," *Journal of International Affairs* 27, no. 1 (1973): 1–21.
43. David E. Apter, "Political Life and Cultural Pluralism," in *Pluralism in a Democratic Society*, ed. Melvin Tumin and Walter Plotch (New York: Praeger, 1977), pp. 58–91.
44. Cynthia H. Enloe, *Ethnic Conflict and Political Development* (Boston: Little, Brown, 1973), pp. 261–274. Also see Apter, "Political Life and Cultural Pluralism," pp. 61–67.
45. William Newman, "A Revival of Ethnic Consciousness: A Look at America's Rediscovered Pluralism," *Journal of Current Social Issues* 10 (1972): 12–18.
46. Ibid., p. 15.
47. Henry Perkinson, "Education and the New Pluralism," *Review Journal of Philosophy and Social Science* 1, no. 1 (1976): 1.
48. Ibid., p. 5.
49. Newman, *American Pluralism* and "Revival of Ethnic Consciousness."
50. Glazer and Moynihan, *Ethnicity*.
51. Ibid., p. 8.
52. Ibid., p. 19.
53. For this position, see Harold Issac, "Basic Group Identity: The Idols of the Tribe," in Glazer and Moynihan, *Ethnicity*, pp. 29–52.
54. Milton Gordon, "Toward a General Theory of Racial and Ethnic Group Relations," in Glazer and Moynihan, *Ethnicity*, pp. 84–110.
55. Ibid., p. 92.
56. Glazer and Moynihan, *Ethnicity*, p. 26.

3

Cultural Pluralism and Ideology

Earlier we suggested that the United States is about to adopt the new social ideal of cultural pluralism. We also suggested that ideals have the potential to serve an important function in society in that by relating belief to action, they justify and guide social action. That is, as idealized conceptions of what ought to be, they act as guideposts for formulating and evaluating social policy. But the ability of ideals to guide social action in a consistent and coherent manner is only as strong as the ideal is clear. To the extent that an evolving ideal remains at the ambiguous level of a slogan, it can arouse interest and recruit a following but cannot effectively guide social action. In the beginning, this was the case with the ideal of cultural pluralism. In the early stages of sloganeering, general appeals were made for the recognition and legitimization of cultural diversity: Discrimination on the basis of racial, cultural, or ethnic grounds was not acceptable; and toleration, respect, and equal opportunity became the new catchwords. But it remained unclear what specific goals followed from this general appeal. What forms of social organizations did it entail? What was to be the role of various social institutions? How were public schools to respond in terms of organization and structure, programs, and curriculum?

In some contexts, "cultural pluralism" is still used in a broad and ambiguous manner as a label and functions as a slogan. Sometimes this is intentionally done to keep the discussion on a general level; sometimes it results from careless use or from an inadequate understanding of the complexity of the concept. But in response to the initial systematic ambiguity and the need to formulate social policy, serious efforts have been made to develop for cultural pluralism a more mature ideological position, a position associated with behavioral prescriptions. As a consequence, not one but many ideologies have developed, some of which seem appropriate for one social context but not for others. It is the purpose of this chapter to review these different ideological alternatives and their implications for public schooling.

IDEOLOGY

Before looking at the ideological positions themselves, it might be helpful to look briefly at what an ideology is and how it functions. It will be recalled from our discussion in Chapter 1 that ideologies attempt to prescribe what ought to be and contain a distinguishable evaluative element. Richard Pratte, in analyzing the logic of ideologies, suggests that ideologies grow when a group of individuals desire to secure certain benefits in society and so come together to form an interest group intended to bring about certain desired results.[1] The cementing of the interest group and the development of some common group identity centers on a set of beliefs, values, and empirical claims. Thus, with regard to the formation of the general ideal of cultural pluralism, individuals have coalesced around beliefs that society is not treating culturally different populations fairly, that these people do not have equal opportunities in society, and that minority populations have a legitimate claim to the benefits of society. Further, agreement was reached on the value of diversity, the value of equal opportunity, and the idea that society should provide different cultural groups with a means of access to existing social institutions. There is also agreement regarding certain empirical claims, such as that a disproportionately high number of minority students fail in school; that minorities are not equally represented in positions of power, status, and economic well-being; and that either there has been a failure to include minorities in the history and culture of the society, or when they are included, they are presented in a prejudicial and disparaging manner.

In this way, the basic elements of the ideological structure are formed. For the sake of cohesiveness and strength, individual disagreements and differences among the interested parties are overlooked. Slogans, metaphors, analogies, and the like that capture the essence of the broad areas of agreement are generated and used to promote unity, stability, and common purpose. The persuasion is emotional, and positions are simplified and presented in extremes. The intent, of course, is to rally support for the desired outcomes and to move the group to action. "Hence, problems that really inhere in group factions are side-stepped, and policy decision (what to do) is disengaged from policy principle (what to believe.)"[2]

In the beginning a guide for specific actions is missing, but more specific goals and actions are forthcoming as the ideology develops. These are not derived from the ideological position and claims themselves but become attached to or associated with them through a process of delimitation. Broad and ambiguous statements are interpreted to mean a certain set of results intended to be achieved. As these desired results are explicated, empirical data are generated that support them and show the means by which they can be achieved. Thus, belief is connected with action. The net result of the entire process is a full-blown ideology capable of interpreting a portion of the world around us and guiding social behavior. It is composed of a set of beliefs and values directed toward or interpreted in a particular context, which becomes associated with a particular set of goals to be achieved and a means to achieve them. The relation of the goals and the means by which they are to be accomplished is supported by empirical data.

Looking at the developing ideologies of cultural pluralism, we can see a set of beliefs regarding the values of democracy, equal opportunity, cultural diversity, and an equitable distribution of social rewards; a set regarding the inherent worth of different cultures and the equal abilities and capacities of individuals from all groups; and a set regarding the past discrimination and exploitation of minority groups in the United States, the unresponsiveness of social institutions (such as the public schools) to the needs of minority groups, and the presence of an assimilationist polity (ideology) that has governed the treatment of culturally different groups in the United States. These sets of beliefs have been applied to the status and position of minority groups in the United States and have been used to interpret both past and current practices. Slogans like "unity and diversity," "Black is beautiful," and "viva la Raza," as well as more elaborate yet general appeals for cultural pluralism, respect, tolerance, and an elimination of prejudice and discrimination, have developed to express the emotional element and generate cohesiveness and commitment. Gradually, more specific goals have been articulated, such as equal representation of minority members in positions of power and status, a more porportional success rate of minorities in the public schools, the legitimization of culturally different populations, and the recognition and inclusion of their contributions to American culture and history. Finally, though substantial variation exists in this area, specific social policies have been advanced as tactics for achieving these ends. Desegregation of the schools, multicultural education, bilingual education, and affirmative action in all levels and areas serve as examples. These policies are supported as viable tactics for achieving the intended outcomes by empirical data from the social sciences, data showing that current inequities and failures result from past and present discrimination and suggesting that the reversal of this trend will result in substantial improvement of the situation.

Our general description portrays an ideology as a consciously derived system of which we are all aware. When we look at the development of the ideal of cultural pluralism, which, it should be recognized, is still in the process of formation, this is the case. But it is extremely important to realize that most of the ideologies governing our lives are not like this; they remain part of our unquestioned view of reality, serving as the paradigm by which we interpret the world around us. In essence, they construct reality for us, and until they are deliberately shaken, they go unquestioned and unrecognized. In this respect, Pratte points out that "the test of strength of any ideology is the extent to which its basic assumptions remain not merely unquestioned but literally unrecognized. The more the assumptions appear to be simply a part of the fabric of fact, the stronger the intellectual hold of the ideology they support and the greater the difficulty of changing the practices and policies arising out of it."[3] The ideology of cultural pluralism seems clear, since it is directly before us, but it should be remembered that it took a good many years to question the ideology of the melting pot and realize that what was subsumed within the ideology was not taking place. The ideology of male supremacy, to use another example, is only now being recognized for its dominance in Western culture in general and American politics in particular. One need only thumb through the elementary reading books of a few years ago to find little girls neat and clean in their pretty dresses, terrified of snakes and dirt, while their brothers climbed, explored, and built things. Mothers typically could be found in the kitchen while fathers read their newspapers. As an ideology, the power of such portrayals is not merely in their socializing effect but as an unquestioned view of reality. Simply, this is the way things were (are), beyond question or justification.

The point is that while ideologies are useful in directing our social behavior, they are also very powerful. In themselves, they don't describe the world in the manner that theories do; rather, they legitimate certain practices as being right while others are wrong. In this sense, ideologies are not right or wrong or true or false but are social conceptions of reality that support one set of prescriptions over another. In the context of our present discussion, it appears that previously held ideologies—assimilation and amalgamation—have been challenged and are being abandoned in favor of the new ideology of cultural pluralism. But as a new ideal, the general notion of cultural pluralism is still being refined into a specific set of goals, or intended results. There is still disagreement in this area, particularly in respect to specific policies and strategies. The result has been, predictably, the generation of a number of competing ideologies (or interpretations) of the more general and broad notion of cultural pluralism.

CRITICISMS OF CULTURAL PLURALISM

Prior to the descriptions of competing ideological alternatives within cultural pluralism, it is important to recognize that many individuals in our society do not view the ideal of cultural pluralism as desirable. In particular, critics argue that cultural pluralism reinforces the existing class structure, that it restricts equal opportunity and individual autonomy, and hence that it is a threat to the democratic ideal. These criticisms cannot be dismissed by attributing them to racist or politically backward people, for this is not the case; many are highly respected and influential people in politics, business, education, and academia. Because of the seriousness of these claims and the arguments supporting them, an analysis of the concept would not be complete without their careful consideration. It is to these criticisms that we now turn.

Democracy and Cultural Pluralism

The strongest challenge to the ideal of cultural pluralism is that it is in conflict with the democratic ideal. Because of the nature of this claim and the fact that many advocates of cultural pluralism think the two ideals are complements, a slight digression into democracy and its relationship to pluralism is in order.

Historically democracy has assumed a number of ideological interpretations.[4] Flowing from the context of democratic liberalism, contemporary democracy in the United States has been highly influenced by the conception that democracy is a way of life. To quote John Dewey:

Democracy . . . means voluntary choice, based on an intelligence that is the outcome of free association and communication with others. It means a way of living together in which mutual and free consultation rule instead of force, and in which cooperation instead of brutal competition is the law of life; a social order in which all the forces that make for friendship, beauty and knowledge are cherished in order that each individual may become what he and he alone, is capable of becoming.[5]

This conception of democracy incorporates three primary ideals:

1. Each individual personality is unique, is to be held in high regard, and is worthy of development. A corollary of this is that

the individual is nothing fixed, given, or ready-made; rather, human beings are products of a dynamic interplay between their unique physiological makeup and their environmental experiences, both cultural and physical.

2. Cooperation and collective action are critical to the qualitative growth and development of individuals and the entire community. A corollary of this is that an organic relationship exists between the individual and society and that a pooling of resources will result in a far richer milieu than is possible at minimal levels of interaction.

3. The experimental method (Dewey's method of intelligence) is the ultimate source of authority. Here unrestricted public inquiry, the free play of intelligence, and continuous testing and evaluation, based on the consequences of actions upon social conditions, become the sole basis for establishing authority.

As we have seen, cultural pluralism also has a central core composed of conditions that must be obtained for the concept to apply: (1) Cultural diversity must be present within the society; (2) there must be some minimal bond or interaction among the diverse groups (e.g., a common politic); (3) the coexisting groups must share approximately equal political, economic, and educational opportunity; and (4) the society must value cultural diversity and hold cultural pluralism as an ideal.[6]

Several theorists writing in support of cultural pluralism treat pluralism and democracy as complements. Francis Villemain, for example, in describing the norms and values that ought to govern social relationships in and among cultural groups, argues that "... what is of ultimate worth is the fullest possible development of each person—the realization of whatever potentiality there may be for excellence."[7] For Villemain, this principle at once justifies a pluralistic arrangement and governs the groups allowed to exist and how they interact. Within this context, cultural variety or diversity becomes a potential resource providing alternative frames of references, value structures, and life styles in which an individual may choose his or her identity. It is also this diversity that enriches the quality of cooperation and collective action by providing alternative perspectives and social arrangements: the worth or value of the various social arrangements being ultimately tested by their contribution to the whole.[8]

We can see, then, that one of the primary emphases of a democratic pluralistic society is providing an opportunity for individuals to choose who and what they will become.[9] In this context we would expect relaxed and fluid social boundaries among diverse groups. We should withhold labeling and ascribing status, position, and mem-

bership to a particular individual by virtue of some other's socially derived perceptions of that individual and thereby allow the individual
to freely choose a role in society.

In the same manner diverse social-cultural groups must be allowed
to form and flourish free from the oppression of other groups. This is
true for two reasons. Perhaps the most obvious reason is that it will be
from the resulting group diversity that an individual's alternatives will
be derived. As Villemain points out, "[t]he pervasive qualities of life
we name Mexican, Chinese, American or Irish are then competing
candidates for use and possible modification. The point being that the
qualities are most assuredly objects of assessment with a view to their
being adopted, repudiated, or conjoined."[10] And not only do groups
provide alternatives from which an individual could choose his identity, they also provide the means. The reliance on cooperation and collaboration within a democracy is based on the realization that, for the
most part, individuals can not go it alone and that the overall quality of
available alternatives is greatly enhanced by a pooling of individual resources. Thus, we depend on our associations with others to free us
from rudimentary life-sustaining activities and provide us with the
availability and opportunity to pursue an otherwise higher quality of
life.

Criticisms

In the recognition of the interdependence between the individual and
groups we first encounter a possible conflict between pluralism and
democracy. If it is true that a diversity of groups enriches a democratic
environment and that groups play a major role in the development and
actualization of individuals, there is also the potential for groups to
restrict an individual's opportunities and autonomy. Francis Hsu, a
psychological anthropologist studying American culture, argues that
this is particularly true in the United States where group membership
is extensively used as a means of demonstrating and securing self-
reliance and status.[11] In order to maintain relatively high status positions in our stratification system, groups demand conformity from their
own members and discriminate against "undesirable" individuals and
members of competing groups. When this principle is applied to a society in which cultural diversity is considered important, we encounter
a further complication: We introduce race and ethnicity as a criterion for
group membership and consequently ethnic conformity and discrimination. That is, to the degree that ethnicity and race are important in
determining identity, they will tend to be used as relevant variables in
the determination of one's position in the stratification system.

Orlando Patterson addresses this consequence when he criticizes cultural pluralism for being in conflict with the democratic ideal. Arguing for a return to the cosmopolitan ideal—his term for amalgamation—Patterson warns: "Ethnicity, and the spurious philosophy of pluralism that rationalizes it, are the new dangers to individuality and personal autonomy."[12] He believes that pluralism, with its tendency to see humans in need of group and cultural identity, promotes ethnicity and parochialism and the tendency to see other human beings in terms of tribal blocks—Jews, Gentiles, Blacks, honkies, females, WASPs—rather than as unique, autonomous beings.[13]

These are strong claims, but Patterson finds several contributing factors that support them. One is the tendency of pluralists, influenced by anthropology, to apply the doctrine of cultural relativism to ethnic and racial groups in the United States. In essence, relativism asserts that each culture, or subculture, must be treated on its own terms because of the basic premise that the values, attitudes, and prejudices of each group are determined by that group's own peculiar form of conditioning. Human values, in short, have no absolutes, and those belonging to one group can be taken as no better or worse than those of another.[14] Within relativism one might objectively describe the moral structure of a cultural group other than one's own, but as soon as one passes judgment on that structure one has acted ethnocentricly, that is, one has used his own cultural reality to judge another.

Patterson concedes that relativism is often supported by pluralists as a means of encouraging a liberal sense of tolerance toward other people; it disarms those who would dogmatically impose their way of life on another group as the best. But, to Patterson's mind, if relativism can be liberal, it can just as easily be associated with a reactionary view of the world and can be used to rationalize inaction, complacency, and even oppression. It is easy for those who would maintain the status quo or absolve themselves of any responsibility for poverty and inequality to support their actions on the grounds that they are protecting a valuable and legitimate subculture and life style. Thus, one might accept the poverty, poor nutrition, high infant mortality rates, and despair often found on Indian reservations, in Mexican American barrios, or in Black ghettoes as tolerable by-products of a chosen and valued way of life. Similarly one need not be concerned with equal educational opportunity where formal education is not valued, or with achievement and advancement where competition, future orientation and materialism are not valued. Thus, in a patronizing and self-serving way, we, as a society, can "protect" and preserve the ways of life of ethnic minority groups and thereby perpetuate the existing class structure under the label of cultural relativism.

Relativism does present the opportunity to reinforce existing inequalities in society by both well-meaning liberals and self-serving

bigots. It is likely that the problem is exaggerated, however, particularly as it applies to the United States. There is bound to be some modera-
tion of the tendency to relativism by the pervasive effects of industrial-
ism, technology, the mass media, the U.S. Constitution, and most
important, by the fact that most people are within the mainstream culture,
at least with respect to secondary relationships, and clearly work to
share in many of the benefits it has to offer.[15] The undesirable potential
of relativism may also be avoided by shifting away from a paternalistic
relationship with ethnic minorities in favor of group autonomy and
shared power. The danger to freeze groups in their present state exists
where the dominant culture views itself as the guardian or caretaker of
subordinate groups and as having legitimate power over them. In such
cases the dominant group determines the desires of the subordinate
group and what is best for them. Presumably, in the ideal pluralistic
society, the dominant group will no longer retain this favored position.
Rather, each group will determine which of its values and life styles are
desirable and to be preserved and then, when conflicts arise with other
groups, will negotiate these determinations with shared power.

It may be argued that the adoption of these conditions will result
in the continuing poverty of minorities through neglect. If the dominant group is no longer in a guardian relationship to minorities, it is
freed from any legal or moral responsibility for helping that group
achieve parity and thus is justified to adopt a position of neglect. This
does not necessarily follow. Should minority groups opt to participate
in mainstream society, as most will, the responsibility of the dominant
group to support them, particularly in the light of historical treatment,
will remain. What will change will be that the decision for inclusion,
and presumably at what levels and by what means it will take place,
will now rest, at least in part, with the subordinate group.

A second consequence of pluralism seen by Patterson as limiting
the opportunity of individuals is the inevitable focus on race that it
produces.[16] By drawing attention to cultural distinctions, pluralism
lends credibility to the concept of racial distinctiveness and tends to
sharpen racial conflict, prejudice, and discrimination. In effect, it encourages people to view one another as members of racial groups,
legitimates attention to racial differences, and thereby makes race a
relevant factor in the daily interaction of individuals. The racial stereotyping and prejudice that results inevitably stands in contradiction to
the cosmopolitanism of an open democratic society. In Patterson's
words, "when several ethnic groups can be united on the basis of a
more inclusive racial category and played off against one or more
smaller, expendable groups, pluralism becomes an irresistable weapon
for the ruthless, who see in it a chance to build new 'majorities' of the
middle and the petty that are anything but silent in their prejudices
and viciousness toward the unincluded."[17]

Patterson is correct. The recognition of racial and ethnic distinctiveness, particularly in a society (such as ours) that is extremely conscious of social stratification and emphasizes competition and achievement as prescribed social norms, will heighten intergroup competition and, thus, prejudice and attempts at discrimination. He is also right that we should be particularly concerned with race because race, unlike ethnicity and culture, is a biological distinction to which unalterable inherited genetic qualities are easily attached. Whereas ethnic and cultural characteristics are learned and therefore modifiable or rejectable, racial attributes are thought to be permanent, enduring features of one's physiological being. Similarly, ethnic and cultural stereotyping can be challenged on the grounds that an individual associated with a particular heritage may be historically and behaviorally far removed from that group; race, with its biological association, cannot be escaped. Race, then, encourages the tendency to attach ability, capacity, and behavior to immutable biological determinants and therefore justifies differential treatment. This tendency can be seen in the treatment of Blacks in the United States from the unloading of the first slave ships to contemporary debates over IQ and native intelligence.

The concept of race will present real difficulties if it is allowed to operate as a legitimate variable in a pluralistic society. Its destructive force and use as an ideological weapon has been well documented by psychologists and sociologists.[18] And in spite of the fact that it has no objective or scientific basis (i.e., biologically the concept of race cannot be supported in any systematic way), it will probably continue to play a role in the United States whether pluralism is adopted or not. Indeed, the past record of other ideologies has fared very poorly with regard to neutralizing racial exploitation, and there is little evidence that the contemporary movement toward pluralism has in any way heightened racial conflict or awareness. In fact, the new interest in pluralism probably grew out of the racial awareness created by the civil rights movement, which in turn was at least in part a response to continued social inequality. To help neutralize its damaging potential we must clearly distinguish between race as a label for cultural and ethnic qualities and race as a label for biological characteristics. The danger lies in the latter. To the extent that the concept of race is used synonymously with that of ethnicity—for example, Blacks are viewed as an ethnic, cultural or special-interest group and not as a biological subspecies—it will be no more dangerous than other differentiating constructs within the pluralist ideology. To keep the concept of race on this level may prove difficult, for there is a strong historical and cultural tendency in the United States toward the biological interpretation. Nevertheless, through a constant vigil this goal may be attained.

Patterson offers yet a third way in which pluralism threatens personal autonomy and thereby the democratic ideal. He claims that the greater the diversity and cohesiveness of groups in a society, the smaller the diversity and personal autonomy of individuals in the society. He explains this phenomenon on the basis of two sociological observations.[19] First, the strength of a particular group is a function of the degree to which individual members share a common set of norms and aspire to a common set of ideals. The strength and cohesiveness of an ethnic group, then, is bought at the expense of the individuality of members of that group. Second, the greater the number of ethnic groups in a society, the greater the tendency toward cohesiveness within each group. This follows from the tendency of ethnic groups to become special-interest groups competing for a limited quantity of social rewards. In order for ethnic groups to compete successfully, they must maintain a high level of cohesiveness, and since ethnic cohesiveness implies increasing conformity, Patterson concludes that group diversity is antagonistic to individual diversity and autonomy.*

This is an important challenge to pluralism and deserves to be considered further. But first let us look at another potential conflict between individual and group autonomy. Where Patterson sees restrictions emanating from constraints imposed on individuals by groups in order to enhance their ability to function as special-interest groups, Thomas Green describes restrictions resulting from the processes of enculturation a group relies upon to pass on cultural traits and commitment from one generation to the next.[20] Cultural transmission is most effective and cultural diffusion is lowest when intergroup associations and individual mobility between groups is lowest. As intergroup associations and individual mobility increase, so does cultural diffussion, threatening the cohesiveness and survival of the group. Thus, Green describes a process whereby we must choose between the strength and preservation of the group, at the expense of individual free association, or individual free association at the expense of the group. To the extent that free association for individuals is the goal, ethnicity needs to become increasingly irrelevant as a variable influencing social interaction at both the primary and secondary levels. Therefore, as we move toward an open democratic society where free association for individuals is at its highest, we move away from a culturally pluralistic society where identity and group membership are defined in ethnic terms.

One way to avoid the conflict that seems to be developing between the ideal of democracy and cultural pluralism is to conceptualize plural-

* Bob Suzuki has pointed out in a critique of this manuscript that one phenomenon unrecognized by Patterson is that when ethnic consciousness heightened during the 1960s, it led to increased expressions of individuality on the part of many people. For example, when Blacks began to sport Afros and wear dashikis, others felt freer to be nonconformists, and we began to see a wide (and often wild!) variety of hairstyles and clothing. Increasing ethnic consciousness thus can lead to greater individuality as well as greater conformity.

ism so as to minimize the importance of ethnicity and race as a means of locating an individual in society. For example, though we may accept the existence of diverse ethnic groups, we may understand cultural pluralism to mean that these groups *will not* serve as a basis for group competition or for placement in the stratification system. They will remain irrelevant in such matters, deferring to other variables such as achievement, occupation or wealth. Indeed, this seems to be the position of Andrew Greeley. In response to Patterson, Greeley rejects "a false pluralism which 'pillorizes' a country and forces individuals into an artificial framework of a 'mosaic society.'"[21] He equates this pluralism with that advocated by Horace Kallen and some of the more militant spokesmen for minority groups. As we shall see more clearly later in this chapter, Greeley agrees with other contemporary pluralists who believe that the emphasis of cultural pluralism is not on the preservation and maintenance of ethnic groups but on the opportunity for individuals to determine to what extent they wish to remain members of a group and partake of its cultural offerings or, alternatively, to venture out and participate in or adopt other cultural ways. (See the section on voluntary ethnic choice in this chapter.) For those who accept this view, if traditional ethnic groups undergo significant evolution and modification, there is no need for concern as long as the process is a result of autonomy and choice of individual group members and not the ethnocentric domination of another group.

Pluralism, then, might be seen as an ideology to free individuals from social impositions based on ethnic heritage. If adopted, it would be illegitimate to coerce individuals to give up their ethnic cultural traditions and life style, to discriminate against individuals who did not give them up, or conversely, to force individuals into an ethnic identification they wish to abandon. Within this conception of cultural pluralism, the condition that cultural diversity must be valued would be understood to mean that we, as a society, would not be hostile to the continuance of ethnic groups—we would not actively seek assimilation or amalgamation. The condition of relative equality and opportunity would entail that we do not discriminate against individuals on the basis of their ethnic heritage, nor do we impose any such heritage upon them. We may wish to think of this conception as emphasizing freedom *from* various restraints and constraints.

Such a conception may even be possible without fully realizing the consequences projected by Green. It will be recalled that Green hypothesized that optimum free association for individuals would exist in a state of structural assimilation, that is, in an open society, where ethnicity and cultural diversity would be irrelevant. While behavioral (i.e., cultural) diversity would indeed be minimized under these conditions, it would still be possible for individuals to perceive an ethnic heritage relevant to determining their personal identification. Even though an individual may avoid reference to an ethnic background when in contact with others during the course of the day, one's heritage may still be relevant in the way one thinks of or defines himself or herself. That is, in defining one's identity an individual may include Hispanic, Catholic, and Spanish speaking, as well as female, mother, doctor, runner, competent person, outgoing, and so forth. In fact, even while the ethnic qualities of this set may remain totally irrelevant for most of one's personal and social life, there may be instances in which they are central, for example at family reunions, a religious worship, or a trip to the land of one's grandparents. They will probably also remain relevant in the shaping of one's beliefs, values, and life style.

Let us stop to summarize the ground we have covered in response to this last criticism. Patterson claimed that pluralism would lead to competition between ethnic groups and that this competition would encourage groups to demand greater conformity and cohesiveness of their members, thereby limiting individual autonomy. Green further argued that groups must retain strong controls over their members and limit intergroup interaction if they were to limit cultural diffusion and maintain their unique identities over time. In order to avoid the criticism that pluralism limits individual autonomy, some theorists, suggesting that Patterson has misunderstood what pluralism is all about, have defined the concept in such a way that group identity and preservation is secondary to individual autonomy. Thus, to Greeley, pluralism is a means to remove the restraints and constraints that have historically combined to place individuals in one role or another on the basis of ethnicity. Furthermore, we have suggested that it may be possible to attain this outcome without completely destroying the significance of an individual's ethnic heritage.

There are two difficulties with this solution to the conflict between pluralism and democracy. First, the interpretation of pluralism offered by Greeley is not accepted by all. Some group spokesmen recognize the advantages of group solidarity and cohesiveness in political struggles and therefore wish to maintain a strong group identity. Still other groups emphasize the importance of the preservation of their group and are perfectly willing to limit the functioning of individual autonomy outside the group. If we accept these points, we must conclude that to conceptualize pluralism predominantly as a means to increase individual autonomy is too narrow.

The second difficulty with this solution presents, by extension, yet another juncture where democracy and pluralism may at times conflict. In order to function as an autonomous person in a democratic society, one needs to have more than the opportunities created by removing social restraints and constraints. An individual must have the knowledge, skills, and dispositions to act democratically (i.e., to participate in a democratic way of life). Such a way of life requires that individuals be aware of and able to exercise available alternatives. Further, they must be skilled in and committed to the experimental method; they must be able to keep an open mind and exercise their free choice and autonomy. Hence rational processes will play a major role in the identification of problems, in the forming of special interest groups, and in the resolution of problems. But it follows that these dispositions and skills will tend to destroy some subcultures that are voluntarily segregated and/or greatly deviate from the mainstream core culture. Consider the effect on such groups as the traditional Hopi residing in northeastern Arizona, who choose to maintain many of the "old ways" and live without electricity, running water, and other modern conveniences; and on such groups as the conservative Amish, Mennonite, and Hutterite religious orders.

The threat to the continued existence of some groups should be clear. To present individuals with real alternatives, thereby increasing individual autonomy, and to establish a disposition to rely upon the experimental method as a means of encountering the world, conceptualizing and solving problems, and selecting membership in interest groups, may run counter to the very premises on which the group is based, as well as threaten the process of enculturation. For example, because enculturation begins at birth and much of the foundation for beliefs, values, perceptions, and styles of interaction takes place during the earliest years of childhood before the individual becomes capable of the reasoning required for democratic participation, a significant amount of questioning and relearning will need to take place later in the individual's life. This will be particularly true where faith rather than reason, [22] or the perception of the universe based on a fatalistic mode rather than as controllable or manipulable, is an important feature in the teachings of the culture. In addition, some fairly common practices of enculturation, such as indoctrination and manipulation, may need to be reevaluated.[23] In the final analysis, we may find that as a result of democratic training, an individual may be prepared to participate in a democratic society but may not be prepared or inclined to assume complete membership in his or her subculture. As the Supreme Court recognized in a case involving the Amish, for some the preparation for participation in the larger mainstream society may not only threaten the continuity and survival of the group but the very salvation of those involved.[24]

To rephrase the conflict we are now considering between the ideals of democracy and cultural pluralism, it can be argued that within pluralism there is a danger that, through strict socialization practices, children may become imprisoned by strong subcultural communities.

The emphasis in the first potential hazards we discussed was on social barriers that restrict and constrain the interaction and mobility of individuals; the emphasis here is on restrictions emanating from a closed set of beliefs and experiences provided by the subculture, which restrict an individual from considering or participating in other life styles. It appears, then, that one must choose between democracy that maximizes individual autonomy or pluralism that protects the autonomy of the group.

It should be clear that we are not faced with a single choice between one ideal and the other; democracy and cultural pluralism are not at opposite ends of the continuum. The two function a good deal of the time as complements. The dilemma we have posed between the two can be significantly reduced if we interpret cultural pluralism to be a form of voluntary ethnic choice. But even by so doing we cannot escape the dilemma completely; a real problem exists that pluralists must take to heart. The enculturation practices of some groups will create beliefs, values, and intellectual habits that are incompatible with the experimental method of problem solving and inquiry required of the democratic citizen. In some cases, to foster the democratic method of intelligence will entail that individuals be encouraged to question (at the least) the traditional teachings and beliefs of their cultural heritage and (at most) be required to abandon them. Of course, some individuals would argue, as did Justice Douglas in his dissent in the Amish case, that the autonomy gained by the individual in such cases outweighs any threat to group stability. One might argue, for example, that as simple and romantic as the way of life of some of these groups appears, the fact remains that the children, because of the parochial nature of their education and the limited nature of outside experiences, lack the individual freedom and opportunity to choose beyond their culture and thereby suffer limited potentials as human beings—their destiny is chosen by their parents and an accident of birth.

It is also probable that democratic theorists will not be greatly concerned over any threats to groups that find it difficult to perpetuate their teachings without the use of guilt, fear, anxiety, or other manipulative techniques. But the point is not whether democratic advocates support these outcomes or not. Rather, to prepare an individual to participate fully in the larger democratic society will in some cases directly threaten group autonomy and stability in a way that undermines the ideal of cultural pluralism as it has traditionally functioned in the United States. Historically, the right of groups to maintain a way of life different from the larger society has been protected, providing these groups serve no threat to the well being of society. To actively prepare all children to live a democratic life may violate this ideal. The ideal of cultural pluralism may require that members of some groups do not become the democratic citizen envisioned by democratic theorists.

As noted, if one adopts the ideal of cultural pluralism in spite of the consequence of its conflict with the ideal of democracy, this in no way is a justification for one group to keep the members of another group in their place. There is the danger of actively pursuing the cultural diversity dimension of cultural pluralism and imposing cultural stagnation on another group as a paternalistic gesture to preserve or protect some romanticized way of life. There is also the danger of denying the opportunity of individuals to move out of their group because of treatment based on stereotypes, that is, the assumption that all members of a group think and act alike and have the same expectations and aspirations. Of course we need to avoid trapping individuals within existing and potentially limiting life styles. We must provide a means of mobility for those who choose to exercise it. We need to allow, perhaps even encourage, individuals to go beyond where they are. But this does not mean we are justified in forcing persons into new opportunities. There is the equal danger of assuming a missionary stance and attempting to save individuals from themselves or their cultures in the name of the democratic ideal.

IDEOLOGICAL ALTERNATIVES OF CULTURAL DIVERSITY

Nonpluralistic Ideologies

Assimilation. The ideology of assimilation can be expressed by the same formula we used to characterize the theory of assimilation presented in Chapter 2: $A + B + C = A$.

The group, of course, that the ideology of assimilation is designed to serve is the dominant culture; hence, it can be thought of as a majority ideology. This position holds that, over time, all groups will (and should) conform to the mores, life style, and values of the dominant group. In the United States, since the majority is generally thought to be representative of the Anglo-Sazon Protestant tradition, assimilation is often characterized as the ideology of Anglo conformity.

As Newman points out, the ideology of assimilation arose in American society after the first quarter of the nineteenth century. At this time, a sentiment appeared that a dominant culture existed and that incoming groups would be expected to conform to this majority culture. Supporting this sentiment and the ideology was the notion that the culture of the dominant group was in some way superior to the minority culture. Members of the dominant culture were viewed as honest, industrious, clean, and freedom-loving; newcomers were viewed as dishonest, poor, unclean, and politically subversive because of their allegiance to the Pope.[25] Another component of the ideology was the development of the myth of racial superiority, which helped legitimate the discriminatory practices of the dominant culture against minority groups. On the basis of racial superiority, the dominant culture felt justified in preserving its racial "purity" by demanding that "outsiders" conform to dominant ways and by excluding certain "inferior" racial groups altogether.

We are familiar with much of the strong impact of the ideology of assimilation on the school curriculum. Overall, it suggests a curriculum concerned with eliminating cultural diversity by making over the various cultural groups to conform with the dominant majority's attitudes and values.[26] As Pratte points out, there is no place in the curriculum for the teacher to attempt to put children of minorities in touch with their own history or literature.[27] Since the strategy is to make an "American," as defined by the dominant majority, out of everyone, examples are restricted to models of this group. When minorities are treated in the curriculum, they are portrayed as culturally inferior or backward, as a problem to be contended with or a hurdle to be overcome in the advancement of civilization and in the name of progress. The organization, methods, and activities of the school, too, reflect and reinforce the Anglo way of life. "Proper" language, manners, and general styles of interaction are demanded and violators punished. Conformity, self-reliance, punctuality, respect for "proper" authority, future orientation, and verbal prowess reflecting Anglo middle-class norms are expected. Students who learn their cultural lessons well and demonstrate a willingness to advance themselves are rewarded with success and gain entry into the more desirable positions of the social structure. Those who do not "mature" are screened out by the system, labeled problems or failures, and relegated to less desirable positions in the social structure or kept on its fringes.

In sum, the general flavor of the ideology of assimilation for the schools is one of "salvation." The children of minority groups must be freed from the narrow-minded influence and backward ways of their native culture. Change and Americanism are the buzzwords. Minority children must be stripped of their parochial ways and given the opportunities of the majority culture. Education must be compulsory, with a common Anglo-American curriculum for all. In a liberal context, integration and bilingual education may be used as means to enhance assimilation, but never will bilingual education be used to strengthen cultural affiliations. Where bilingual education is used, students are expected to make as rapid a transition to English as possible.

Amalgamation. Amalgamation can be represented by the formula $A + B + C = D$. The ideology of amalgamation, also known as the melting pot, holds that over time all the different groups will and should become Americans, a new group that is different from any of the original groups but is also a synthesis or combination of them. This ideology developed as a minority response to the chaotic and difficult times resulting from their cultural "uprooting." It was a way in which immigrants were able to impart positive meaning to an otherwise unpredictable situation. The idea of amalgamation was that the different cultures would eventually merge, creating a new social order, and thereby set a new path for human history better than the one that existed before. In contrast to the ideology of assimilation, which grew out of an interpretation of the present and future through the past, predicting the continued dominance of the majority culture, amalgamation forecast a new future for the nation and, particularly, for immigrants severed from their past.[28]

Important to the ideology of amalgamation is the belief that the new culture will represent only the "best" qualities and attributes of the different cultures that contribute to it. As with the ideology of assimilation, there is the underlying assumption that cultures have distinguishable positive and negative qualities. Contrary to assimilation, no group would remain the object of prejudice; rather, all groups would be able to acknowledge their positive and unique contributions to the new culture, which would be a sum of all the desirable attributes of the different groups. Thus, an individual could embrace America and become an American without accepting the idea of assimilation.

The ideology of amalgamation as reflected in schooling would be directed toward eliminating cultural diversity but, in this case, cultural homogeneity would be achieved by cultivating a unique American citizenry. As Pratte conceives it, the curriculum, especially literature and history, would focus on the wide range of cultural groups in order to point out or demonstrate the "best" or "preferred" elements that should be kept in the new amalgamated type.[29] Teachers would emphasize in both subject matter and style cooperative problem solving, where one's own class and group interests would be submerged in the free play of critical inquiry. Democracy as a social way of life and as a means of problem solving would be cultivated, underscoring the value of change and the unprejudiced weighing of all points of view. Emphasis on the need to search for the "common interest" by all contending parties of any social conflict would be stressed. "Hence, there would be a social side of schooling that would be emphasized. Cooperation, the search for common interest, and good temper in defeat are all happy conditions basic to this position."[30]

Schooling would be compulsory and, as near as possible, integrated. Cultural differences and conflict would be minimized and interpreted in the light of the evolution of a unique culture. Old ways and group associations would be discouraged as American nationalism replaced ethnic identification. "American" values, manners, and life styles would be cultivated and transmitted by the school. In this sense, the aim of public education, through what it taught and how it taught, would be to facilitate the evolution of and commitment to the development of a unique America based on a pooling of its rich and varied cultural resources.

Open Society. In Chapter 2 we distinguished between insular pluralism, halfway pluralism, and structural assimilation in describing different kinds of interaction between diverse groups in a culturally plural society. It will be recalled that structural assimilation as an ideal type describes a society in which interaction among and between members of diverse social groups takes place in both primary and secondary relationships. That is, individuals are as likely to interact on an informal personal basis and on a formal task-oriented basis with individuals coming from cultural, racial, or ethnic groups other than their own as they are with members from their own group. Cultural background, in effect, is irrelevant to social interaction.

When this type of social relationship ceases to function as a logical construct and becomes a model for the way societies should function, it becomes an ideology. As an ideology, it advocates an open society where social participation and mobility are potentially open to all individuals and are determined by individual achievement and not ascribed on the basis of cultural background or affiliation. The ideology can be expressed by the formula $A + B + C = O$, where A, B, and C represent different groups and O represents no relative advantage or disadvantage to be had by anyone in the society as a result of affiliation with a group.[31]

The ideology of the open society relies heavily on a sense of democracy that places the individual at the heart of the social order. There is the belief that all individuals are capable of making a positive contribution to the well-being of society and that each person and the ideas of each person should be evaluated on the basis of individual merit and relevance to a particular situation. While group associations play a role in the social and political framework of society, these groups are not based on ethnic criteria. Rather, groups form and dissolve on the basis of like interests and concerns; they are completely voluntary in nature, being open to anyone who would like to become associated with the interests of the group. Conversely, when group goals are met or when individuals determine that the group no longer serves their best interests, they are free to disassociate themselves. In this ideology, ethnic associations are believed to be primitive forms of political organizations that give way to more sophisticated alternatives as societies develop and modernize. Ethnic associations that continue to exist are seen as remnants of the past and are generally considered to be troublesome and a nuisance.[32]

The ideology of the open society, then, assumes a secular society in which traditional ethnic, racial, and religious differences no longer count in social relationships. It is important to recognize that this does not mean that society is hostile to ethnicity; instead, ethnicity is irrelevant in social interaction. Ethnicity may still be very important for individuals in the development of personal identities; in this respect, it will be a private matter functioning in much the way religion does for many Americans today. For example, it is not uncommon for individuals who consider themselves religious and who gain sustenance from their religious beliefs and practices to engage in both primary and secondary relationships in the social world in such a way that their religion remains undetectable. An individual's employer and personal friends may simply be indifferent to the individual's private religious life.

In contrasting the ideology of the open society with the ideologies of assimilation and amalgamation, we may consider assimilation and amalgamation to be antipluralistic ideologies and the open society to be a nonpluralistic ideology. While there is no active attempt to destroy diversity within the open society, as there is in the first two, it is also not legitimate to recognize or support it in any fashion. The emphasis is on individual achievement and mobility, with diversity celebrated only in personal and private life.

A school curriculum consistent with the ideology of the open society would stress a participatory democracy. Students would learn of civic responsibility and acquire the skills needed to participate effectively in civic affairs. History would be taught in such a way as to stress the developmental nature of society and politics. Tribal societies and societies dominated by primordial bonds would be represented as primitive and undeveloped. Students would receive a wide range of educational experiences and ideas designed to free them from parochial or provincial attitudes. In this sense, they would be educated for upward mobility and instilled with a cosmopolitan view of the world. Both the content and structure of the school would emphasize individual competition and achievement. Students would learn that one gets ahead on one's ability—what one does—and not on the basis of ascribed qualities. Objective "fair" testing would be the means for establishing students' abilities, reward distribution, and placement in desirable positions. In the same way, students would learn to put prejudice aside when evaluating an idea or individual and to rely solely on objective merit. Thus, they would learn that race, religion, and gender are irrelevant to the social world.

Ideologies of Cultural Pluralism

Classical Cultural Pluralism.   Classical cultural pluralism can be expressed by the formula $A + B + C = A + B + C$. As an ideology it means that diverse cultural groups will and should, over time, live in peaceful coexistence while maintaining their unique identities. As with amalgamation, it is a minority ideology capable of giving meaning to the chaos and confusion created by mass immigration. Here, however, the hope for a stable future is based on preservation of the past.

Horace Kallen is credited with coining the term "cultural pluralism" and was probably the most influential in popularizing the ideology. Written in the first quarter of the twentieth century, his philosophy of cultural pluralism was primarily aimed at the majority ideology of assimilation and pure Americanism, but he also wished to refute the doctrine of the melting pot, which had gained popularity among liberal intellectuals of the day.[33] In Kallen's conception of democracy, assimilation was interpreted as a form of coercion that was subtly and psychologically exerted to make people conform to one pattern of Americanism. He argued that democracy implied the right of newcomers to retain their ethnic and cultural affiliations and that therefore they should not suffer any debilitating consequences from the exercise of this right.[34]

Kallen's conception of cultural pluralism was a federation of nations. Unconvinced that anything in the value systems immigrants brought with them was inimical to democracy, and believing that diversity was the natural state of humanity, he saw the United States as consisting of a number of nationalities federated to the larger nation, much as the states are united into one nation.

The form would be that of the federal republic; its substance a democracy of nationalities, cooperating voluntarily and autonomously through common institutions in the enterprise of self realization through the perfection of men according to their kind. The common language of the common wealth, the language of its great tradition, would be English, but each nationality would have for its emotional and voluntary life its own peculiar dialect or speech, its own individual and inevitable ethical and intellectual forms.[35]

Kallen's cultural pluralism, then, was a democracy of groups based on ethnic (i.e., national origin) inheritance. This ascribed inheritance would dominate primary relationships, but individuals might extend secondary (work) relationships across ethnic lines.

Several assumptions or beliefs serve as the foundation for the ideology of classical cultural pluralism. One is that ethnic identities are inherited and thus not voluntary. A corollary of this is that inherited ethnic identities endure over time; it is unlikely that even after long periods a person will forget that his or her family was once German, Italian, Jewish, or Irish. A second assumption is that the natural state of society is diversity. Uninfluenced by the powers of the state, people naturally tend toward social and cultural diversification. Third, each group is believed to be positive and to have something of value to contribute to society. Each of the diverse groups, then—their values, life styles, and traditions—must be considered equal to all.

There are at least two forms classical cultural pluralism might take in society. One way to achieve and maintain cultural distinctiveness and identity is through geographic separation. We might, then, have a society with segregated pluralism as a form of social organization (refer to Chapter 2). The various diverse groups would be associated with specific geographic areas within the country. For the most part, because of the geographic isolation from other groups, individual members of each group would have little daily interaction with individuals from other groups. The result would be close to what we described earlier as insular pluralism (refer to Chapter 2). Primary and secondary relationships would be confined to a particular cultural group.

Switzerland and French Canada are contemporary examples of segregated pluralism. We might note a departure in these two cases from what Kallen described in respect to language. Kallen saw the adoption of one language as the principal language of the nation, in which all affairs of state would be conducted. The "native" languages of the diverse groups would be maintained and reserved for personal, family, and community use. In contrast, the Swiss Constitution deals with the issue by recognizing four languages as "the national languages of Switzerland," and in Canada both French and English are recognized.

The second form classical cultural pluralism might take is an integrated pluralism that maintains residential segregation. This differs significantly from segregated pluralism in that patterns of cultural diversity repeat themselves over and over throughout the country instead of one group being associated primarily with one geographic region. That is, a number of diverse groups would exist within a given geographic area, say a metropolitan area, but would remain residentially segregated within that area. This pattern would be repeated from metropolitan area to metropolitan area across the country. The result would be a much higher level of interaction between group members at the secondary levels than in the insular pluralism associated with geographic segregation. Individuals from different cultural groups would come in contact as they engaged in formal social activities such as work and business. Nevertheless, relationships would, for the most part, remain within each cultural community, reinforcing a strong sense of identity and guaranteeing the transmission of the cultural life style from one generation to the next. We can see this pattern in many American metropolitan areas where Italian, Jewish, Black, Chinese, Puerto Rican, Mexican, and other "communities" can be readily identified. It is likely that this is the form of cultural pluralism that Kallen envisioned.

For both the integrated and segregated forms of classical cultural pluralism, racial and ethnic groups are formally recognized as legally constituted entities with official standing in the society. Economic and political rewards, whether in the public or private sector, are allocated on the basis of numerical quotas that in turn rest on the relative numerical strength of each group as they join in the political process. In this sense, cultural pluralism is similar to what Milton Gordon has called "corporate pluralism" (refer to Chapter 2).

Horace Kallen felt the public schools should play an active role in the development and maintenance of cultural pluralism. He was very critical of the way schools functioned at the time of his writing, believing they acted as levelers of ethnic diversity by indoctrinating and acculturating students.[36] He envisioned the schools as agencies reconstructed to promote cultural pluralism, to recognize the vast ethnic diversity of American culture and teach the worth and respect for different ethnic groups and the contributions they had made to society. Besides public schools, Kallen advocated the creation of ethnic schools[37] that could supplement the offerings of public schools and help compensate for past failure to teach mutual respect for ethnicity. Children could be taught about their ethnic traditions and values. The schools would be a means of rekindling ethnic identity.

The implications of classical cultural pluralism for contemporary schools would be similar to those outlined by Kallen, and it probably matters little whether segregated or integrated pluralism is adopted. We would expect the curriculum to include ethnic studies designed to enhance a positive sense of ethnic identity. Students would learn of their common history, ancestry, and culture and gain a sense of being a common people. Bilingual education would be common and would be based on a language maintenance model and not on a transition to the dominant cultural language. In structure and organization, schools would tend toward community ethnic schools. The contemporary policy of school desegregation would be reversed. Neighborhood schools composed of and staffed by individuals predominantly of one ethnic population would abound, with strong community influence and control. Indeed, should a group determine that schooling was not in their best interest, public schooling might be limited, as it is by the Amish. The essence of education would be the maintenance and support of each group's life style as determined by that group.

Modified Cultural Pluralism. Where the ideology of classical cultural pluralism designates a high degree of group distinctiveness, separation, and autonomy, modified cultural pluralism sees the development of a substantial common culture with a high degree of interaction between and among diverse groups. As indicated earlier, this position can be formulated as $A + B + C = A_1 + B_1 + C_1$, where the subscript attached to the letters representing the diverse groups designates a commitment to a common American culture and life style. The distinct cultural groups in society, then, through their interaction with one another and their adaptation to the American experience, become acculturated but nevertheless retain their separate identities. In this sense, each group becomes American but in some contexts functions as a distinct group; this is particularly likely to occur as groups function as political and economic groups, but it will also be evident in some personal, family, and community relations. Behind this description is the belief that ethnicity, albeit in changed form, will continue to be important for individuals, and that attempts to eliminate it will prove ineffective. The hyphenated American (e.g., Italian-American, Polish-American, Mexican-American, Afro-American) characterizes the resulting relationship.

The ideology of modified cultural pluralism would take a political form some place between the secular individualism of the open society and the closed partisan politics of classical cultural pluralism. Individuals would be encouraged to take part in a participatory democracy, but group associations would remain relevant in determining representation and the allocation of social resources and power. Government, while not directly playing an active role in the support or continuance of group diversity, would recognize and be responsive to group demands. Underlying this recognition and responsiveness would be the belief that all citizens, as group members, have an equal right to share in the powers and benefits of society. But also there would be the understanding that the general welfare of society supersedes the interests of any one group should a conflict arise.

The curriculum of a school system supporting the ideology of modified cultural pluralism would cultivate both a sense of nationalism—we are all Americans—and a sense of the importance and value of the diversity of the society. Multicultural education would be the theme. Each group would be shown historically to have contributed to the development of the nation. The significance of different events would be perceived and appreciated from a variety of different cultural perspectives.[38] Contemporarily the society would be represented as composed of a number of legitimate diverse groups of equal value. The narrow focus of the ethnic studies associated with classical cultural pluralism would give way to a more inclusive approach. Children would learn about the similarities of different groups as well as the special qualities that set them apart, and would learn to respect both. As far as the structure and organization of the school go, we could expect equal opportunity to be interpreted as meaning that each child and each group would be treated equitably. That is, each would receive the educational help and resources appropriate for success in school. The long-range goals for each group would, for the most part, remain the same, but the school would be expected to accommodate differences in learning styles, language, and background. A maintenance model of bilingual education would be appropriate for some groups but not all. Specific curriculum, then, might well vary depending on the needs of the group. Proof of the effectiveness of the school program could be seen in a proportional representation for each group in the different levels of school success. That is, we would expect a proportional representation of students from all groups to be going on to higher education and entering the professions. To the extent that imbalances persisted, affirmative action would be justified. Integration at all levels would be expected.

Given some latitude for variation, the ideology of modified cultural pluralism is the most popular in the United States today. Most advocates of cultural pluralism see ethnic identity and diversity continuing to play some role in society and believe this diversity should be recognized and accommodated by the public schools. Moreover, in the final analysis, most see a relatively high level of interaction between members of diverse groups as desirable, with one's group identity for the most part irrelevant for secondary levels of interaction (i.e., secondary relationships). Even with this general sense of agreement, there remains considerable variation and disagreement among advocates, much of it revolving around the role of government with respect to the schools' acknowledging and supporting ethnicity. For a clearer understanding of the ideological alternatives consistent with cultural pluralism, it may be helpful to sharpen some of our distinctions. The next three ideologies share some of the main premises of modified cultural pluralism but go beyond to advocate more specific conditions of social organization.

Cultural Pluralism as Voluntary Ethnic Choice. Freedom of choice and opportunity is a common theme among contemporary writers advocating the ideal of cultural pluralism. In view of past treatment of non-Anglo-Saxon Protestant populations in the United States, this emphasis is understandable. Opportunities and choices have often been available on the basis of ethnic variables rather than achievement. In condemning this past record, many proponents of cultural pluralism advocate greater freedom of choice for members of ethnic minorities.

Among the new freedoms advocated is the freedom to choose one's ethnic identity and determine how it will affect one's life.

The freedom to determine one's ethnic identity can be seen as an extension of contemporary democratic ideology. It is a broadening of one's ability to exercise alternatives in deciding who and what to be. Consistent with this democratic principle, William Newman, in the last chapter of his sociological analysis *American Pluralism*, states: "The essential meaning of social pluralism is choice both for the society and for the groups and individuals in the society. The challenge is to create a social environment in which groups and individuals may choose voluntarily the identities they wish to play out."[39]

Newman's appeal for more relaxed and fluid social boundaries among diverse groups follows from a sociological analysis that portrays the United States as a society with strong group distinctions and boundaries resulting from intergroup competition and conflict—a society in which groups are in a constant struggle for what appears to be a limited quantity of social resources and rewards. His appeal is to withhold labeling and ascribing status, position, and membership to a particular individual or group by virtue of another group's socially derived perceptions of that individual or group and thus to allow the individual or group to freely choose a role in society.

Michael Novak, too, envisions greater individual choice in the determination of ethnic identity. But where Newman wants to relax socially derived boundaries, Novak's emphasis is on freeing the individual from subconscious and unexamined primordial ethnic forces that can imprison one in the past.

Ethnicity is not to be conceived in our condition as a merely primordial, fateful, and tribal bond. On the contrary, it can be freely chosen, developed as part of a multi-cultural competence, and rooted rather in the socially aware individual than in the unthinking group. A self-conscious and freely chosen ethnicity is not the same as a merely inherited, inexperienced, and relatively closed ethnicity. We are in a position to make something new of ourselves as individuals, and of our nation as a multi-culturally aware society.[40]

Both positions—the increased potential for intergroup mobility expressed by Newman and the personal selection of values, beliefs, and life styles expressed by Novak—are set forth by Andrew Greeley and support his position that "the freedom to accept, reject or ignore ethnic identification is the goal of American pluralism. . . ."[41] Greeley supports his claim by appealing to two principles he holds for ethnic groups in the United States. The first principle, optional membership, is the belief that no one in the United States should be constrained to have an ethnic identification. To Greeley it would be ideal if Americans were free to be, and free not to be, whatever their skin color and religious heritage suggest. That is, "no person should be constrained either by his own group or by others to be part of a group."[42] The second principle, permeable boundaries, asserts that one should be able to move in and out of ethnic boundaries. That is, one should be able to choose to identify in different ways at different times in one's life and to choose one's primary ethnic identity from a number of different available alternatives.

While it is popular to equate the ideal of cultural pluralism with individuality and democracy, not all would agree that these are compatible. As we have seen, Orlando Patterson drew the opposite conclusion. (See criticisms of cultural pluralism in this chapter.) He argued, in effect, that because of the tendency of diverse groups to act as special-interest groups, pluralism would result in groups demanding greater conformity and solidarity of their members and thereby would limit individual autonomy and mobility. What Patterson described as the net result is exactly what advocates of pluralism argue will be alleviated by the adoption of the ideal.

It will be recalled that the apparent dilemma of having to choose between group autonomy and strength on the one hand and individual autonomy and mobility on the other may not present a real problem for Greeley. The emphasis of contemporary pluralism, in Greeley's mind, is not on the preservation and maintenance of ethnic groups but on the opportunity for individuals to determine to what extent they wish to remain members of a group and partake of its cultural offerings or, alternatively, to venture out and participate in or adopt other cultural ways. Thus, if traditional ethnic groups undergo significant evolution and modification, perhaps even to the point of dissolution, there is no need for concern as long as the process results from autonomy and choice and not from the ethnocentric domination of another group. This position is also reflected in the statements of Newman and Novak; each seems concerned that groups support individual growth and autonomy.

The preference for individual autonomy over group survival is also supported by theorists who believe that an individual need not select between mutually exclusive cultural alternatives but can enjoy the benefits of both worlds. Ramirez and Castaneda adopt this position under the label of cultural democracy.

The writings of many cultural pluralists have placed a major emphasis on the presentation of the language, heritage, and cultural values of the ethnic group. . . . The basic theme in our interpretation of cultural pluralism is not this preservation as such, but the ability to function in both cultural worlds, whatever their characteristics at any given point in time.[43]

This position assumes that by developing bicultural (or perhaps multicultural) competencies an individual can, by choice, successfully function in and contribute to two or more cultural worlds. The bicultural individual, then, has the ability and opportunity to consciously shift from one ethnic reality to another in response to the requirements of a particular situation. Thus, individuality and opportunity are enhanced and cultural pluralism can be seen as an extension of the democratic ideal.

If individual choice and mobility and not the preservation and cohesion of ethnic groups are at the heart of the new pluralism, Patterson's conclusion may not be correct. That is, if through pluralism we can remove the negative effects generally associated with membership in ethnic groups and make ethnicity an individual matter by emphasizing achievement as the determinant of position in the stratification system, ethnic groups may not become special-interest groups and divide society.[44] The emphasis will be on breaking down social and cultural barriers—group membership will become voluntary, and individuals will be encouraged to reflect upon the meaning of their ethnicity. But it should be apparent that the more voluntary groups become, the closer we move to the ideology of the open society, where cultural background becomes irrelevant in public interactions.

While advocates of free ethnic choice clearly move in this direction, they tend to stop short of adopting this ideology. One reason they do is because they accept the underlying premise of the ideology of modified cultural pluralism that ethnicity is important and will continue to be important to individuals in establishing their identity. Thus, while groups may change and some may even disappear, in the long run diversity will endure and will continue to be important in the lives of many individuals—given free ethnic choice, individuals will continue to choose to identify themselves ethnically.

The schools have the potential to play an important role in maximizing the autonomy and free choice of the individual in several ways. First, through content and example they will have to impart a sense that any attempt to restrain or constrain the opportunities or mobility of any individual on the basis of ethnic background is unjust. Toward this goal, students will learn that stereotyping is dangerous and that the identity of other individuals should be defined by those individuals. Similarly, students will be socialized to think discrimination on the basis of cultural background is wrong.

A second role of the school will be to teach that there are alternative identities and cultural life styles and that at least some of them are within the realm of choice for any given individual. In a word, the school will teach students that they are free to determine who and what they will be. To learn to exercise options, students will learn how to participate and succeed in a multicultural setting. This is what Ramirez and Castaneda have in mind when they speak of bicognitive development. Students learn how to function in both their native culture and the dominant culture without being forced to choose one over the other.

A third role of education will be to develop ethnically literate individuals. Michael Novak argues that if ethnicity is to be chosen and used creatively, individuals must become aware of the subconscious ways their ethnic backgrounds and upbringing affect them. Students, then, need more self-knowledge in order to understand and define themselves. They need to know how their backgrounds, beliefs, feeling, actions, and community life are similar to and different from those of people from other groups and, equally important, they need to know why.

Novak places some of the responsibility for the development of ethnic literacy on the home. But what the home does not or cannot do, the school should. In particular, Novak criticizes schools for offering no illumination to the Italian, Greek, Slavic, and other children concerning the different family patterns and emotional contexts out of which they came. Dick and Jane in the elementary readers are plainly white Anglo-Saxon Protestant in attitude, behavior, and image.[45] The school curriculum, then, should help students objectify their inner tendencies. It should help students understand the relationship between what they feel and believe and their cultural background.

Cultural Pluralism as Integration. The pursuit of a contemporary ideology of cultural pluralism has been fueled by the controversy over and the consciousness-raising effects of the twenty-five-year-old movement to integrate the public schools. For some, integration is critical if we are to meet the requirement of pluralism for equal opportunity.

Thomas Pettigrew, for example, believes that integration is a necessary condition for the eradication of white racism at both individual and institutional levels.[46] The integration Pettigrew has in mind refers to institutionalized biracial situations in which there is cross-racial friendship, racial interdependence, and a strong measure of personal and group autonomy.[47] He is quick to point out that this does not mean either assimilation or simple desegregation. The latter refers to institutionalized biracial settings that involve little cross-racial acceptance and, often, patronizing legacies of white supremacy; and in assimilation, minorities disappear. Pettigrew thinks of integration as a dynamic exchange; it involves the integration of whites as well as Blacks and thus liberates both to develop in creative ways. The long-term goal of integration, then, as Pettigrew sees it, is not a complete obliteration of cultural pluralism but the transformation of ghettoes from racial prisons to ethnic areas freely chosen or not chosen.[48] In this respect, the position is similar to cultural pluralism as voluntary ethnic choice.

Underlying integration as a strategy for achieving individual and group autonomy are beliefs that cultural isolation prevents each group from learning of beliefs and values shared with other groups and that isolation leads in time to the evolution of genuine differences in beliefs and values, making interracial contact in the future even less likely. That is, members of diverse groups kept apart come to view one another as very different; this belief, combined with racial considera- tion, causes each group to reject contact with the other; real differences develop, and these perpetuate racial stereotyping and discrimination. In short, separation is the cause of awkwardness in interracial contacts. On the more positive side is the belief that racism in American society can be effectively combatted by bringing different groups together in a setting where they have equal status; seek common goals; are cooper- atively dependent on one another; and interact with the positive sup- port of authorities, laws, or customs.[49]

Pettigrew sees two main strategies for achieving his integration ideal. The first is the complete attainment of integration in smaller com- munities and cities where racial separation exists. In these settings we would wish to promote a genuine interaction between individuals of the diverse groups based on understanding, cooperation, and respect. The second strategy is the enrichment of the inner-city areas of large metropolitan complexes where, because of current demography, in- tegration is impossible to achieve. But Pettigrew warns that we must be careful to ensure that proposed enrichment programs will not hinder later dispersal and integration. The enrichment programs he views as productive are effective job-training programs and reconstruction of the economies of the ghettoes. Both would promote future integration, since skilled workers would become more mobile and an economically sound city would attract businesses and workers from outside. The building of enormous public housing developments within the ghetto and the decentralization of public school districts into many small homogeneous school districts, on the other hand, would lead to the further concentration of minorities and would be counterproductive to later integration. In sum, Pettigrew believes that the attainment of a vi- able democratic nation free from personal and institutional racism re- quires extensive racial integration in all realms of life as well as vast programs of ghetto enrichment.

A second advocate of pluralism as integration is Nathan Glazer. Like Pettigrew, he is careful to distinguish integration from desegrega- tion and assimilation. For Glazer, integration implies an organic rela- tionship: Just as a personality may be integrated, so may a society. In this same sense, the term also implies a clear articulation of the parts, that is, there is some degree of identifiability of each part.[50] But unlike Pettigrew, Glazer's emphasis is not on the physical and social interac- tion of people, though this is perfectly consistent with his conception.

Rather, he sees as being in the best interest of both individual groups and the entire nation a form of cultural pluralism in which the emphasis on distinctive histories and cultures is integrated into a larger sense of American history and the American experience. That is, the diverse groups in society should perceive themselves and other groups primarily as being integral (organic) parts of American society; each group is but one element of the whole. Groups, then, should see one another as complements and not as separate distinct components existing in a state of competition.

The educational policies Glazer supports can serve to clarify his conception of integration. He believes the curriculum of the public schools should be designed around our conception of a desirable society. What we select to teach and how we teach should be guided not only by truth but also by our view of the future we want. The society Glazer views as desirable is one that is generally open both to those who have no interest in a background defined by their descent and no desire to maintain it or make claims for it and to those who take an interest in their background and wish to maintain it and instill it in their children.[51] Glazer argues that we are and should be engaged in the process of making a distinctive nation based not on the primacy of a single ethnic group yet with a defined history, character, and ideals. "In other words, we are still engaged, and must continue to be, in the making of Americans, since this is still a country of mass immigration with large populations still imperfectly integrated into a common nation, both for reasons of past prejudice and discrimination and current parochialism."[52]

Glazer's view of cultural pluralism as integration in the schools and society is that we should not support the creation of sharp differences. Ethnic studies should not teach resentment and antagonism or assume a position advocating ethnic identity and distinctiveness. Rather, ethnic studies should be integrated into those parts of the curriculum where they have a place (e.g., history, economics, sociology, social science, and literature). The achievements of a group should be sought insofar as they play a part in each subject. Should a culture or ethnic group be the focus of study, the enrollment in the course would not be limited to those of a given heritage, and qualification for instructing these courses would be based on knowledge of the subject matter and not on ethnic heritage. The underlying policy of public agencies such as the schools should be one of benign neutrality toward ethnic inheritance. All individuals and groups should be free to maintain whatever distinct identity or part of an ethnic heritage they wish as long as that does not transgress on the rights of others; this would be a private matter for the individual, family, or community. Glazer says that "we should still engage in the work of the creation of a single, distinct, and unique nation, and this requires that our main attention be centered on the common culture. Cultural pluralism describes a supplement to the emerging common interest and common ideals that find all groups in the society; it does not, and should not, describe the whole."[53]

The positions of Pettigrew and Glazer on integration can be summarized under the label of what Milton Gordon calls "liberal pluralism" (refer to Chapter 2). Recall that this form of pluralism is characterized by the absence of any legal or governmental recognition of ethnic groups as corporate entities with standing in legal or governmental processes and by the prohibition of the use of ethnic criteria for discriminatory purposes. While members of disadvantaged ethnic groups might receive benefits as individuals under social or educational programs, they would not be eligible directly because of their ethnic background. Pluralism under these circumstances would exist voluntarily as an unofficial societal reality and would be subject to the pressures toward conformity to general societal norms implicit in whatever degree of industrialization and urbanization was present in society. Schools would stress equality of opportunity and the progress of individuals on the basis of universalistic standards of performance.

To summarize, we see here an ideological statement that views pluralism as an integration of the diverse groups in society. Group identity and distinctiveness are played down in favor of commonalities and interrelationships. In a continuum with separation (insular pluralism) on one end and an open society (structural assimilation) on the other, this conception comes close to that of the open society. As in the conception of cultural pluralism as voluntary ethnic choice, the maintenance and survival of diverse groups is not as important as individual mobility and the opportunity of individuals to choose their own meaning of their ethnic heritage.

Cultural Pluralism as Separation. We have seen that to some, cultural pluralism means integration. Ironically, in reaction primarily to the integration (desegregation) movement following *Brown v. Board of Education*, another ideology of cultural pluralism developed based on racial separation.

Two different schools of pluralism as racial separation can be identified. The first, and by far the more extreme, views separation as an end in itself. This position was pioneered by the Black nationalists led by the young Malcolm X through the teachings of Elijah Muhammad, and it later spread to other radical minority-group spokesmen. Although very visible for a short period of time, this extreme form of separation managed to capture the interest of only a small following and is not our concern here. The second school of separation has been far more influential and consists of those who view racial separation as a means to the eventual inclusion of minority groups in society. This is the position on which we now focus.

Several individuals have argued for the adoption of the ideology of separation.[54] Most have been spokesmen from the Black community who have concluded that while true integration (i.e., inclusion in the mainstream of society) may be desirable in the long run, as a contemporary strategy it is bankrupt. This is based on the observation that white Protestants control the power and the economic and political resources of society and will never voluntarily share them. Any minority group that integrates under these conditions would be "functioning as an accommodation to white superiority."[55] For integration to work, the minority group must come from a position of strength that can be developed only in isolation from the dominant majority. As Ron Karenga, a Black leader in Los Angeles, put it, "We're not for isolation, but interdependence. But we can't become interdependent unless we have something to offer. We can live with whites interdependently once we have Black Power."[56] Again, as Carmichael and Hamilton point out, Black Power must come from within:

The concept of Black Power rests on a fundamental premise: Before a group can enter the open society, it must first close ranks. By this we mean that group solidarity is necessary before a group can operate effectively from a bargaining position of strength in a pluralistic society. Traditionally, each new ethnic group in this society has found the route to social and political viability through the organization of its own institutions with which to represent its needs with the larger society.[57]

The ideology of separation, then, is based on the view that because of the imbalance of power in society and the racism that serves to legitimate and reinforce this imbalance, a direct route to an integrated democratic and pluralistic society is impossible. If a truly integrated society is to be achieved, minority groups must separate themselves from the dominant majority—if not physically, at least socially and culturally—to develop a strong sense of unity and autonomy and then return when they are able to negotiate from a position of strength.

The ideology of separation is also consistent with the idea that minority groups are colonialized people. The dominant Anglo-Saxon Protestant majority has in effect conquered and subjugated such groups as Blacks, Hispanics, and Native Americans. In the modern world, colonies are expected to be freed so that they can find their own distinctive courses of political, economic, and cultural development. Thus, we would expect minority groups to separate and develop independently. The ultimate inclusion into the mainstream society would be as autonomous groups negotiating from a position of strength.

Barbara Sizemore has developed a model for this process.[58] Termed the "power-inclusion model for excluded groups," it is composed of five stages. The first is the *separatist stage* during which the excluded group defines its identity. This process includes the emergence of a sense of peoplehood where the in-group, "we the chosen people," is defined in juxtaposition to the out-group, "they." Race, religion, ethnicity, and culture are usually used as the bases for identity, which is also often associated with a territorial base (e.g., Africa, Latin American, Italy, or China). In the second stage, the *nationalist stage*, the excluded group intensifies its cohesion by building a religio-cultural community of beliefs around its creation, history, and development. The territorial base takes on a strong significance for group identity and provides the source for the beliefs, rituals, customs, and ceremonies that replace the rejected Anglo-Saxon Protestant ways. This intense nationalistic involvement increases separation and the rejection of others and intensifies group identity and group cohesion. It is here that the group emerges as Afro American, Hispanic, Polish American, and so on. At the third stage, the *capitalistic stage*, an economic base and mutual support system begins to develop or capture a segment of the labor force or economy. This can be seen in the domination of certain labor unions or industries (e.g., the garment industry) by particular ethnic groups and in the creation of economically viable ethnic communities such as San Francisco's Chinatown. The fourth stage is the *pluralistic stage*, during which the group utilizes its strong cohesion and sense of identity to form a political bloc on its economic base in order to thrust its interests into the foreground of the political arena. It is here that the ethnic group functions as a strong interest group able to form coalitions, engage in bloc voting, and make political and economic demands. The fifth and final stage is the *power* or *egalitarian stage*. In this stage, the economic and voting blocs and coalitions guarantee that the interests of the group have as much chance of winning as those of other groups at this level of participation. It is here that the groups function as equals, that a minority group can neutralize attempts at domination and exploitation by the majority, and that true integration is possible.

Education plays an important role in the separatist ideology, particularly in the early stages. If a sense of identity is to develop, the ethnic community must be able to protect itself from the debilitating racist ideology perpetuated by the dominant majority. The schools have traditionally functioned to transmit this ideology and reinforce the status quo. Thus, it is important for the schools to be controlled by the community. The curriculum of the schools would be designed to develop a strong sense of identity, that is, a sense of peoplehood, and to strengthen individual attachment and allegiance to the group. Ethnic studies programs would be taught by and for members of the particular ethnic group and would concentrate on the development of a distinctive sense of history and culture including language and literature, the group being presented in a positive light. The schools would also teach about capitalism, power, and conflict, arguing that, as a minority, they are in competition with other groups for power and social resources. Students would be taught how to compete and would be politically socialized to act as members of a special-interest ethnic group. Further, they would be taught that they, as members of a particular group, are in control and should remain in control of their own destiny.

Factions of some minority ethnic groups seem to have adopted, at least in part, the power inclusion model. The Black Power movement set the example and has been the most visible since the 1960s. But in recent years Hispanics and Native Americans have also shown an interest in this strategy. It is not uncommon to hear appeals for a strong sense of ethnic solidarity and brotherhood. Political and persuasive cohesiveness is strongly reinforced—one is first Hispanic, Black, or Native American. Control of one's education is paramount, and every opportunity should be taken to reinforce a positive sense of ethnic identity.

Beyond Cultural Pluralism

Our discussion of the ideologies of cultural pluralism, as would be expected, has centered on cultural, racial, and ethnic groups as sources of group organization and mobility and individual identity. One conception of pluralism, however, goes beyond cultural subgroups with their special interests and considers groups formed as a result of mutual concern over a problematic situation. The position as presented by Richard Pratte is termed "dynamic pluralism."[59] It begins with the existence of cultural subgroups that have a ready agenda of politics and values and then moves beyond this to the forming of factions through which people give expression to a multiplicity of different values.

In describing dynamic pluralism, Pratte recognizes the importance of ethnic groups in society and their roles as interest groups and as a source of identity for individuals. But Pratte believes that the ideology of cultural pluralism, with its emphasis on ethnic criteria as the basis for group association, is too narrow. Using Dewey's concept of community, Pratte cites two weaknesses of stressing ethnicity as the basis for group formation. First, cultural subgroupings are not always based on conscious, reflective action; they may be rather mindless. Second, the recognition of a common problem by a cultural subgroup is not necessarily based on a mutual concern for the common problems of society. Cultural groups may deny the existence of a common social problem or may perceive their own special interest as the justifiable basis for dealing with the problem. These two possibilities amount to shortcomings of ethnic group association, since in Dewey's mind, and presumably in Pratte's, the best possible society is one defined by common community interest (i.e., a common sense of community and commitment to the public interest) and the voluntary implementation of the method of intelligence (i.e., rationality as defined by the scientific method). To the extent that ethnic associations and the actions that flow from them are not carefully thought through in terms of the problems of others and with concern for public consequences, they are limiting. Moreover, to the extent that an individual limits personal commitments solely to ethnic group interests and fails to rally behind other communal interests, and to the extent that an ethnic group pursues its own interest in spite of what is best for the larger community, ethnic associations can be detrimental to the well-being of society.

This does not mean that ethnic associations are not recognized as filling an important role in society. Rather, they are looked at as the foundation for and the beginning of the development of other group associations. In order for individuals to commit themselves to some social interest and join in a social collective to achieve it they must first have some set of values and norms on which to base the commitment. These values and norms are initially rooted in the cultural subgroup in which one is raised. Thus, one's cultural group provides the foundation for the commitment to other ideals and the formation of other social groups in the future. It provides the normative base from which other social commitments arise. If such a value base did not exist, individuals could not be expected to perceive social situations as problematic in the first place or work toward their resolution.

Dynamic pluralism, then, recognizes the existence and role of cultural subgroups in American society, but the essence of dynamic pluralism is for individuals to move beyond these initial subgroups to the formation of communities of interests. During the course of social interaction, a multiplicity of different values come together and individuals come to recognize some aspects of society as being problematic. On the basis of some common concern or commitment, these individuals form a social collective to pursue their mutual interests. When the "community of interest" fulfills its function, it dissolves. Dynamic pluralism is thus continuously emergent insofar as each of the society's members must reinterpret shared concerns and goals in the context of ever changing social, economic, and political conditions. It is a process whereby individuals consciously and thoughtfully define a problematic situation, assess its relative pros and cons, and organize into communities of interest in pursuit of their perception of the common good. It can be seen, then, that unlike cultural, ethnic, and racial groups, the groups of dynamic pluralism are always formed out of the conscious reflective actions of individuals. Furthermore, they are formed around a perceived common community interest and are subject to the principles of intelligence (i.e., rationality).

In Pratte's view, the advantage of dynamic pluralism over other conceptions of pluralism is that it preserves the values of freedom of association and diversity in society. It is founded on the belief that a democratic society must afford room for many competing interests. The diversity of society, then, is maintained by the constant forming of interest communities. Not only is a multiplicity of points of view and life styles tolerated, it is encouraged as vital to a healthy society. In this light, groups are recognized as legitimate forms of representation in society. They have rights, are protected, and may at times compete with one another for prominence and social rewards. On the other hand, group membership is voluntary—individuals are free to associate themselves or not associate themselves with interest communities as they see fit. Their identities, loyalties, and commitments are chosen and not ascribed.

This description of dynamic pluralism sounds very similar to that of the open society. Pratte is careful to distinguish the two, however. Whereas both see cultural, racial, and ethnic subgroup affiliations as insignificant in directly determining individuals' participation in civic affairs, the open society goes much further and declares such affiliations to be totally irrelevant for all primary and secondary relationships. This society is composed of a collection of individuals who, as individuals, interact with one another to meet personal and common needs. Moreover, the open society views ethnic identity as a primitive form of group organization and as generally troublesome. In the open society one is an individual whose identity is based on achievements and social roles within a democratic society. For example, one may be a mother, a Ph.D., a professor, a Democrat, and a runner; one is not, at least for purposes of social interaction and special interests, Black, Hispanic, Jewish, Catholic, or Protestant. Though special-interest groups may form, the focus of identity remains on the individual and not on group membership.

In contrast, in dynamic pluralism the emphasis is on the person as a social being whose identity and personal needs are met through group associations. The individual is often defined and interacts as a member of a voluntary special-interest group. The importance of ethnic associations is recognized as the starting point for establishing these group associations; thus, they are important in the early socialization of the child and in adulthood as an identity point from which to launch one's social commitments. For example, one may be associated with the pro-life movement in the contemporary debate over abortion. The fact that one's position is founded in a background and belief system that is Catholic is relevant. Such a background is recognized as necessary, fundamental, and legitimate, and allowances are made for its continuance. It is important to recognize, however, that one does not support a pro-life position because he or she is a Catholic—one's position is not constrained because of a Catholic lobby—but because of a held set of beliefs. In further contrast to the open society, dynamic pluralism can accommodate the belief that one may belong to and identify with an ethnic community because of its contribution in providing a sense of purpose and of being and in providing the psychological and cosmological frames of reference that help enclose the spaces of our lives.

Dynamic pluralism also has features similar to our conception of pluralism as voluntary ethnic choice. Both emphasize the relevance of ethnicity and the voluntary nature of group membership. The big difference between the two can be found in the limited nature of pluralism as voluntary ethnic choice. This view concerns itself only with ethnic group membership, whereas dynamic pluralism goes well beyond into a more general theory of democracy. Another important difference between the two is that voluntary ethnic choice allows for interest groups based on ethnicity, the only requirement being that membership remain voluntary. Dynamic pluralism, on the other hand, views ethnic special-interest groups as potentially dangerous and unresponsive to the welfare of the larger community.

A school system supporting the ideology of dynamic pluralism would need to teach both the value of diversity and the importance of individual commitment and achievement. In regard to diversity, while schools would not honor inherited cultural values as good in themselves, they would take them into account in the curriculum. The contributions of the diverse groups to society would be taught, as would respect and understanding; but in teaching students to understand and appreciate their backgrounds and the backgrounds of others, the emphasis would be on this inheritance as a starting point for interaction in society and the formation of other groups. Thus, the stress on diversity would be on the acceptance and tolerance of different value perspectives on contemporary issues. Students would be taught critical thinking skills and to take stands on social issues. Teachers would know how to recognize, discuss, appraise, and resolve value conflicts in the classroom and would encourage students to do the same. In regard to individual commitment and achievement, schools would work to eliminate racial, ethnic, and cultural prejudice and discrimination. Students would learn to appraise an individual's achievements and not cultural or racial background. In order to support diversity and encourage individual choice in the matter, schools would provide alternative curricula, different career choices, and information on alternative life styles and would instruct students on how to make rational choices. Here, alternative values and interest choices would have to be fundamental enough to reflect truly different points of view, but the differences should not be so fundamental as to be nontransformable or nonnegotiable. That is, they should provide for a real pluralism, but should not be so sharp as to be devisive.

SUMMARY

Ideologies function to legitimate or prescribe social arrangements, power structures, or ways of life in terms of the goals, interests, or social positions of particular groups. They grow out of the desire of a group of individuals to secure or maintain certain benefits in society.

So it has been with cultural pluralism. Beginning with the rejection of the ideologies of assimilation and the melting pot, the contemporary ideology of cultural pluralism formed first around broad and general slogan statements. The slogans were systematically ambiguous and emotional in flavor, their main purpose being to arouse interest and develop commitment and solidarity among followers. Over time, more specific statements of goals and desired outcomes and the strategies for achieving these goals have become associated with cultural pluralism. Nevertheless, even though a set of common beliefs and values is the basis, the delimitation and explication of the broad and ambiguous appeals for cultural pluralism have led to not one but many conceptions of cultural pluralism. The net result has been the creation of alternative and competing ideologies of cultural pluralism. Our intent in this chapter was to make clear these different positions.

At the outset we acknowledged the criticism that cultural pluralism has the potential to limit the autonomy and freedom of indiviauals as it protects the interests of groups. Group conflict and competition, which are likely to be aggravated in a pluralistic society, contribute to this. To compete effectively, groups need cohesiveness and solidarity, and this, it is thought, leads to a greater demand for individuals to conform to group norms. In addition, identity with a group is likely to become more pronounced during group conflict; this sharpens group distinctiveness, which in turn is likely to lead to a rise in prejudice and discrimination. Thus, there is a tendency for individuals' choices to be limited by both the norms of their group and the discriminatory behavior of other groups. There is the further possibility that in a cultural pluralism characterized by a high degree of separation between groups, an individual may, through strict socialization practices, become imprisoned by strong subcultural communities. That is, by virtue of socialization such an individual would be unable to function in other social settings. The concern that an ideology of cultural pluralism will limit individual opportunities and autonomy is real and should not be dismissed too quickly. It should be kept in mind when evaluating alternative conceptions of pluralism, though it should also be recognized that other ideologies that have directed our social affairs in the United States have been inadequate in protecting individual autonomy. Perhaps the greatest protection against such outcomes is to be constantly aware of them and constantly work against them.

In our discussion of ideologies, we have identified three nonpluralistic ideologies that compete with cultural pluralism: assimilation, amalgamation, and the open society. Assimilation, a majority ideology, holds that eventually all groups will conform to the mores, life style, and values of the dominant group. Since the dominant group in the United States is that of white Anglo-Saxon Protestants, the ideology is alternatively called Anglo conformity. With this ideology, public schools would be used as instruments to make over the members of culturally different groups in conformity with the dominant culture's attitudes and values.

Amalgamation, or the melting pot ideology, holds that eventually all the different groups will pool their best features and form a distinct new group of Americans. Thus, a synthesis will take place with all groups sharing in a culture better than any individual culture involved in its creation. A school system supporting amalgamation would be directed toward the development of a new American common culture and cultural homogeneity. Old ways and group associations would be discouraged as American nationalism replaced ethnic identification.

The ideology of the open society holds that ethnicity is irrelevant to social relationships. One's cultural heritage should be neither celebrated nor condemned; rather, individual achievements and abilities should be stressed as the basis for social interaction, recognition, and reward. Ethnic associations should be viewed as primitive forms of political development that naturally give way to more sophisticated institutions as the country modernizes. Schools in an open society would stress individual achievement and objectivity, and students would learn to ignore ethnic qualities in others, believing they are remnants from historical associations and irrelevant to the present and future.

In our discussion of ideologies sympathetic to cultural pluralism, several species have been identified. The strongest form of pluralism is that of classical cultural pluralism, which envisions a federation of ethnic groups. The diverse groups, while members of the same nation, would remain relatively autonomous and separated, retaining much of their traditional native culture, traditions, and customs. Racial and ethnic groups would be formally recognized as legally constituted entities with official standing in society. The schools would be controlled by each respective group, one of their goals being to rekindle and transmit cultural identity. Students would learn of their common group history, ancestry, and culture and would develop a sense of peoplehood to be celebrated as a legitimate and identifiable component of the larger society.

A more moderate ideology is modified cultural pluralism. Whereas classical cultural pluralism designates a high degree of group distinctiveness, separation, and autonomy, modified cultural pluralism sees the development of a substantial common culture with a high degree of interaction between and among the diverse groups. As with classical cultural pluralism, though to a lesser extent, ethnic groups would be formally recognized in society and economic and political rewards allocated on the basis of numerical quotas or some other formula emanating from the political process. At the secondary levels of interaction, primarily in the world of work, ethnic associations would become increasingly less significant, with the focus shifting to individual achievements, resulting in a higher degree of individual mobility and intergroup interaction than with classical cultural pluralism. The schools would acknowledge the presence and contributions of the diverse cultural groups but would emphasize their similarities and common interests as integrated members of a common society. Ethnic groups would retain some influence in school affairs, but matters of national interest would have priority.

The greater interaction between and among groups and the greater degree of individual mobility make modified cultural pluralism popular among advocates of cultural pluralism. There remains considerable controversy, however, over the specific goals of pluralism and the role of government in recognizing and supporting ethnicity. Many see voluntary ethnic choice as the essence of the "new" pluralism. From this perspective, a government policy of "affirmative" ethnicity would be too strong; rather, government agencies and schools should recognize the relevance of ethnicity to American life but should not actively promote or reinforce ethnic associations, which should remain an individual and voluntary matter. In this perspective, individuals determine for themselves to what extent they wish to remain as members of a group and partake of its cultural offerings or, alternatively, whether to venture out and participate in or adopt other cultural ways. Schools would play an important role in this process by teaching students to respect and tolerate diversity; to develop understanding of their own ethnicity, as well as alternative life styles, values, and beliefs; and to decide for themselves how they wish to assert or accept their ethnicity or if they should do so.

A closely associated position of pluralism as free ethnic choice is cultural pluralism as integration, which is not to be confused with the desegregation of schools but refers to institutionalized biracial situations where there is cross-racial friendship, racial interdependence, and a strong measure of personal and group autonomy. What advocates of this position intend is not complete obliteration of cultural diversity but the transformation of ethnic ghettoes from racial prisons to ethnic areas freely chosen or not chosen. Government institutions, including the public schools, would adopt a position of benign neutrality toward ethnic inheritance; the schools would support the development of a common culture and would stress equality of opportunity and the evaluation of individuals on the basis of universalistic standards of performance.

But the ultimate goal of including ethnic minorities into society can lead to an ideology of separation as well as to the ideological position of free choice and integration. Some spokesmen for ethnic minorities have argued that for minority groups ever to be accepted in a pluralistic society, they must first separate themselves in order to develop unity and strength. Thus, this ideology argues for voluntary segregation until such time as the minority group can demand its fair representation in society and its share of social rewards. In the ideology of separation the schools would be controlled by each respective ethnic community, would play an important role in developing group identity and cohesion, and in preparation for the future would teach students about conflict and competition in a pluralistic and capitalistic society.

Finally, there is a position that began with cultural pluralism as a base but argued for a more liberal and expansive dynamic pluralism. While recognizing the importance of ethnicity to American life, advocates of dynamic pluralism thought cultural pluralism too narrow and restrictive and argued instead for a pluralism of groups formed around communities of interests, that is, groups of individuals who come together in response to some communal problem or issue. The ethnic group would remain important in the socialization of the individual, but individuals would go beyond the limiting interests of these associations to form others in the best interests of society. Schools would prepare individuals to take part in the dynamic pluralistic society by teaching respect and value for different positions, by encouraging students to rely on the scientific method for problem solving, and by fostering a commitment to the general welfare of society.

NOTES

1. Richard Pratte, *Pluralism in Education* (Springfield, Ill.: Charles C. Thomas, 1979), pp. 51–60.
2. Ibid., p. 56.
3. Ibid., p. 52.
4. For a discussion of these various interpretations, see Carl Cohen, ed., *Communism, Fascism and Democracy: The Theoretical Foundations* (New York: Random House, 1962).
5. John Dewey, as cited in "The Report of the Committee on the Function of Science in General Education," Commission on Secondary School Curricu-

lum, Progressive Education Association, *Science in General Education*, pp. 34–53. For a summary of other writings where Dewey describes democracy as a way of life see Cohen, *Communism, Fascism and Democracy*, pp. 668–89.

6. See Chapter 2.
7. Francis T. Villemain, "The Significance of the Democratic Ethic for Cultural Alternatives and American Civilization," *Educational Theory* 26, no. 1 (Winter 1976): 45.
8. Ibid.
9. Villemain makes these points, but they are also supported by others. See the statements by Greeley, for example, in the discussion of pluralism as voluntary ethnic choice.
10. Villemain, "Significance of the Democratic Ethic," p. 45.
11. Francis L. K. Hsu, "American Core Values and National Character," in *Psychological Anthropology*, ed. F. L. K. Hsu (Cambridge, Mass.: Schenkman, 1972), pp. 241–62.
12. Orlando Patterson, "Ethnicity and the Pluralistic Fallacy," *Change*, March 1975, p. 10.
13. Orlando Patterson, "On Guilt, Relativism and Black-White Relations," *American Scholar* 43 (Winter 1973–74): 132.
14. Ibid., p. 125.
15. William Greenbaum, "America in Search of a New Ideal," *Harvard Educational Review* 44 (1974): 436.
16. Patterson, "On Guilt, Relativism and Black-White Relations," pp. 128–129.
17. Ibid., p. 129.
18. See Gordon Allport, *The Nature of Prejudice* (Reading, Mass.: Addison-Wesley, 1954). William A. Newman, *American Pluralism: A Study of Minority Groups and Social Theory* (New York: Harper and Row, 1973).
19. Patterson, "Ethnicity and the Pluralistic Fallacy," p. 11.
20. Thomas Green, "Education and Pluralism: Ideal and Reality" (Syracuse University School of Education, 1966).
21. Andrew Greeley, "On Ethnicity and Cultural Pluralism," *Change*, Summer 1975, p. 41.
22. The teachings of many contemporary religious groups in the United States may be vulnerable here.
23. Contemporary religious training may be threatened here. I consider this problem much more carefully in regard to religious and cultural groups in an analysis of the limitations of choosing an ethnic identity in my paper, "On Choosing an Ethnic Identity." *Philosophy of Education, 1981: Proceedings of the Philosophy of Education Society* (1982) pp. 211–218.
24. *Wisconsin* v. *Yoder*, 406 U.S. 205 (1972). Also see Chapter 4.
25. Newman, *American Pluralism*, pp. 53–63.
26. Pratte, *Pluralism*, p. 72.
27. Ibid.
28. Newman, *American Pluralism*, p. 65.
29. Pratte, *Pluralism*, p. 75.
30. Ibid., p. 76.
31. Ibid., p. 70.
32. Developmental theory in political science takes this position. For a critique see David Apter, "Political Life and Pluralism," in *Pluralism in a Democratic*

Society, ed. Melvin Tumin and Walter Plotch (New York: Praeger, 1977).
33. Newman, *American Pluralism*, p. 68.
34. Seymour Itzkoff, *Cultural Pluralism and American Education* (Scranton, Pa.: International Textbook, 1969), p. 55.
35. Horace Kallen, *Culture and Democracy in the United States* (New York: Boni and Liveright, 1924), p. 124.
36. Spencer J. Maxcy, "Horace Kallen's Two Conceptions of Cultural Pluralism," *Educational Theory* 29, no. 1, (Winter 1979): 36.
37. Ibid., p. 38.
38. James Banks has constructed a model for curriculum development consistent with this approach. See his "Cultural Pluralism: Implications for Curriculum Reform," in Tumin and Plotch, *Pluralism in a Democratic Society*, pp. 226–48.
39. Newman, *American Pluralism*, p. 292.
40. Michael Novak, "Cultural Pluralism for Individuals: A Social Vision," in Tumin and Plotch, *Pluralism in a Democratic Society*, p. 48.
41. Greeley, "On Ethnicity and the Pluralistic Fallacy," p. 10.
42. Ibid.
43. Manuel Ramirez and Alfredo Castaneda, *Cultural Democracy, Bicognitive Development and Education* (New York: Academic Press, 1974), p. 28.
44. As shown in the section "Criticisms of Pluralism" and in Chapter 6, "Cultural Conflict and Cultural Pluralism." There are serious problems with this view.
45. Novak, "Cultural Pluralism for Individuals," p. 42.
46. Thomas Pettigrew, "Racially Separate or Together?" in *Cultural Pluralism*, ed. Edgar Epps (Berkeley, Calif.: McCutcheon, 1974), pp. 1–33.
47. Ibid., p. 16.
48. Ibid., p. 24.
49. Ibid., p. 14.
50. Nathan Glazer, "Cultural Pluralism: The Social Aspect," in Tumin and Plotch, *Pluralism in a Democratic Society*, p. 16.
51. Ibid., p. 23.
52. Ibid., p. 17.
53. Ibid., p. 24.
54. Harold Cruse, *The Crises of the Negro Intellectual* (New York: Morrow, 1967); Stokely Carmichael and C. V. Hamilton, *Black Power* (New York: Random House, 1967); Jesse Jackson, *Chicago Defender*, 8 March 1968, p. 10; Barbara Sizemore, "Separatism: A Reality Approach to Inclusion," in *Racial Crises in American Education*, ed. Robert Green (Chicago: Follet, 1969), pp. 244–79.
55. Harold Cruse as quoted by Sizemore, "Separatism," p. 251.
56. Ron Karenga as quoted by Pettigrew, "Racially Separate or Together?" p. 7.
57. Carmichael and Hamilton, *Black Power*, p. 44.
58. Sizemore, "Separatism," pp. 266–70; Barbara Sizemore, "Shattering the Melting Pot Myth," in *Teaching Ethnic Studies*, ed. James Banks (Washington, D.C.: Council for the Social Studies, 1973), pp. 73–101.
59. Richard Pratte, *The Public School Movement: A Critical Study* (New York: McKay, 1973), pp. 147–56.

4

Cultural Pluralism and the Courts

While there is little doubt that ideologies have shaped the social land-scape of our society and continue to do so, the exigencies of everyday life have perhaps contributed most to our society's form. From the beginning, the cultural diversity of the United States has often led to conflict among different groups, and the need to resolve these conflicts has, over time, given shape to multicultural policy. A review of U.S. history suggests that political ideology does not necessarily characterize the reality established through social intercourse. Thus, if we wish to distinguish *what is* from *what might be*, we need to look at things other than political and social philosophy. To discover the relationship between pluralistic ideals and the functioning of American society, it might be fruitful to describe the principles in terms of how they are applied in the course of human affairs. Perhaps no other institution has been as influential in interpreting these principles as the courts. Balancing conflicting interests, the courts have established precedents that provide substance for our operative ideals. On the premise that the courts have been a primary factor in establishing the meaning of American pluralism, in this chapter we seek to describe cultural pluralism in the United Stattes as established by court precedent.

The First and Fourteenth amendments to the Constitution establish the protection of pluralistic bodies. In part, they read

Congress shall make no law respecting an establishment of religion, or pro-hibiting the free exercise thereof.... No state shall make or enforce any law which shall abridge the privileges of immunities of citizens of the United States; nor shall any state deprive any person of life, liberty, or property without due process of law; nor deny to any person within its jurisdiction the equal protection of the laws.[1]

While establishing the principles supporting pluralism, the amendments have not defined the form of pluralism to be created in the United States. Over the past one hundred years the courts have interpreted and applied these principles to give body to the ideal of cultural pluralism. We review some of the precedent-setting cases and note the direction in which we seem to be moving, further defining the multicultural nature of the United States.

PLURALISM: A RIGHT TO A DIFFERENT WAY OF LIFE

Parents' Right to Choose

Meyer. v. Nebraska[2]— *Parents' Right to Reinforce Ethnicity.*   The first quarter of the twentieth century marked a peak in both American immigration and the nativistic reaction against it. In 1919 Nebraska passed a law limiting the use of and instruction in languages other than English in schools. In part the law stated,

No person, individually or as a teacher shall, in any private, denominational, parochial or public school, teach any subject to any person in any language other than the English language.

Languages, other than the English language, may be taught as languages only after a pupil shall have attained and successfully passed the eighth grade as evidenced by a certificate of graduation issued by the county superintendent of the county in which the child resides.[3]

Robert Meyer, a teacher at Zion Parochial School in Hamilton County, Nebraska, was arrested, tried, and convicted for teaching the subject of reading in the German language to Raymond Parpart. Raymond, age ten, had not attained and successfully passed the eighth grade. Nevertheless, Meyer believed that the law violated his rights guaranteed under the Fourteenth Amendment and appealed to the Nebraska Supreme Court. But the court felt that the state legislature was within its power to regulate education and serve the interest of society and did not rule in Meyer's favor. The court stated,

The salutary purpose of the statute is clear. The legislature has been the baneful effects of permitting foreigners, who had taken residence in this county, to rear and educate their children in the language of their native land. The result of that condition was found to be inimical to our own safety. To allow the children of foreigners, who had emigrated here, to be taught from early childhood the language of the country of their parents was to rear them with that language as their mother tongue. It was to educate them so that they must always think in that language, and, as a consequence, naturally inculcate in them ideas and sentiments foreign to the best interests of this country. The statute, therefore, was intended not only to require that the education of all children be conducted in the English language, but that, until they had grown into that language and until it had become a part of them, they should not in the school be taught any other language. The obvious purpose of this statute was that the English language should become the mother tongue of all children reared in this state.[4]

Despite the unfavorable ruling, Meyer thought he should be protected and so appealed to the U.S. Supreme Court. Here the justices saw things differently. While they did not disagree with the intent of the law, they did disagree with the means by which assimilation would take place. Speaking for the majority, Justice McReynolds made this point clear: "Perhaps it would be highly advantageous if all had ready understanding of our ordinary speech, but this cannot be covered by methods which conflict with the Constitution—a desirable end cannot be promoted by prohibited means."[5]

In the eyes of the Court, the law was overly restrictive. Recognizing that the state has the authority to "do much . . . in order to improve the quality of its citizens, physically, mentally and morally,"[6] the Court also recognized that the individual has certain fundamental rights which must be respected.[7] Among the liberties protected by the Fourteenth Amendment is

the right of the individual to contract, to engage in any of the common occupations of life, to acquire useful knowledge, to marry, establish a home and bring up children, to worship God according to the dictates of his own conscience, and generally to engage those privileges long recognized as common law is essential to the ordinary pursuit of happiness by free men.[8]

In particular, the Court found the right to teach and the right of parents to engage a teacher to instruct their children to be within the liberties of the Fourteenth Amendment.

In order for the state to restrict such liberties, it must be able to show that it is necessary for the protection of a reasonable public interest. In this case, the justices could find no such interest; rather, they concluded "that the statute as applied is arbitrary and without reasonable relation to any end within the competency of the state."[9] Furthermore, the majority found no support for the state's claim that the purpose was to protect the child's health and well-being. They concluded that "the mere knowledge of the German language cannot be regarded as harmful." Hence, the judgment of the Nebraska Supreme Court was reversed.

The *Meyer* case is relevant to the concept of pluralism in several respects. First, the Nebraska law shows that strong assimilationist feelings have played a significant and influential role in our history. This public sentiment has remained with us. Second, the case shows how the Fourteenth Amendment can protect individual liberty and a multicultural way of life from state efforts to eliminate ways different from those of the majority. Third, we can see that a parent has a right to bring up a child and provide instruction for that child in the way the parent deems most fitting unless the state can show some reasonable interest to be at stake. We shall qualify this right in future cases.

Wisconsin v. Yoder[10]—*The Right Not to Attend School*. Jonas Yoder and Wallace Miller were members of the Old Order Amish religion, and Adin Yutzy was a member of the Conservative Amish Mennonite church. They and their families resided in Green County, Wisconsin, and were subject to Wisconsin's compulsory school attendance law that required them to send their children, Frieda Yoder, age fifteen, Barbara Miller, age fifteen, and Vernen Yutzy, age fourteen, to school until age sixteen. The children had all graduated from the eighth grade of public school but had failed to enroll for further schooling when the parents were charged with violation of the law.

At the trial the parents' defense was based on religious belief and the way of life of the Amish community. They believed that compliance with the law was contrary to the Amish religion and that, by sending their children to high school, they would not only expose themselves to the danger of censure by the church community but also endanger their own and their children's salvation. High school (and higher education generally), in the minds of these Amish, is seen as incompatible with their values and way of life. They view secondary education as an impermissible exposure to a "worldly" influence and feel that high school emphasizes intellectual and scientific accomplishments, self-distinction, competitiveness, worldly success, and social life with other students. Amish society, on the other hand, emphasizes informal learning through doing, a life of "goodness" rather than a life of intellect, wisdom rather than competition, and separation from rather than integration with contemporary worldly society.[11] In addition, formal schooling beyond the eighth grade is contrary to Amish belief because it takes children away from their community in the formative adolescent years.

It is important to recognize that the Amish are not altogether opposed to compulsory public education. They agree that elementary education is valuable because their children must have basic skills in the "three Rs" in order to read the Bible, be good farmers and citizens, and be able to deal with non-Amish people when necessary in the course of daily affairs. However, while the Amish accept compulsory elementary education generally, wherever possible, they have established their own elementary schools, which resemble in many respects the small local schools of the past.

In defense of its compulsory education law, Wisconsin argued that states have the power to regulate public education and that such an interest is paramount. Education prepares individuals to be self-reliant members of society, and it is necessary to prepare citizens to participate effectively and intelligently in our open political system. Furthermore, Wisconsin argued that the Amish position would foster ignorance, from which the child must be protected.

The lower Wisconsin court found that the compulsory school attendance law did interfere with the freedom of the Amish to act in accordance with their sincere religious beliefs but also concluded that the requirement of high school attendance was a reasonable exercise of the state's interest. Balancing these interests, the Wisconsin trial court found the Amish parents guilty and fined them $5 each.

Still believing they were right, the Amish appealed the lower court's decision to the U.S. Supreme Court. Upon reviewing the case, the High Court upheld the Amish position. In its decision the Court acknowledged the constitutional power of the state to regulate public education; however, it noted that such power is not unlimited or totally free from a balancing process when it impinges on fundamental rights and interests. In order for Wisconsin to compel school attendance beyond the eighth grade in the face of a claim that such attendance interferes with the practice of a legitimate religious belief, it must appear either that the state does not deny the free exercise of religious beliefs by its requirement or that there is a state interest of sufficient magnitude to override the interest-claiming protection under the free exercise clause of the First Amendment.[12]

The Court's first task was to determine whether the Amish religious faith and mode of life are "inseparable and interdependent." The Court held that "[a] way of life, however virtuous and admirable, may not be interposed as a barrier to reasonable state regulation of education if it is based on purely secular considerations";[13] to have the protection of the religious clauses, the claims must be rooted in religious belief. Although a determination of what is a religious belief or practice entitled to constitutional protection may present a most delicate question, the very concept of ordered liberty precludes allowing everyone to apply personal standards on matters of conduct in which society as a whole has important interests. Thus, if the Amish asserted their claims because of their subjective evaluation and rejection of the contemporary secular values accepted by the majority, their claims would not rest on a religious basis. Philosophical and personal belief rather than religious belief do not meet the requirements of the religion clauses.[14]

After reviewing the evidence, the justices found the conclusion inescapable: Secondary schooling exposes Amish children to worldly influences in terms of attitudes, goals, and values contrary to Amish beliefs. This substantial interference with the Amish child's religious development and integration into the way of life of the Amish community at the crucial adolescent stage of development contravenes the basis religious tenets and practices of the Amish faith for both the parent and the child.[15]

In response to the state's argument that continued secondary education was necessary, the Court found that the evidence in this case was persuasive that an additional one or two years of formal high school for Amish children in place of their long-established program of informal vocational education would do little to serve those interests. In this respect, the value of all education must be assessed in terms of its capacity to prepare the child for life. It is one thing to say that compulsory education for a year or two beyond the eighth grade may be necessary when its goal is the preparation of the child for life in the mainstream of modern society, but it is another if the goal is the preparation of the child for life in the separated agrarian community that is the keystone of the Amish faith.[16]

Chief Justice Berger, speaking for the majority, concluded that the Amish claim "must prevail, largely because 'religious freedom—the freedom to believe and to practice strange and, it may be, foreign creeds—has classically been one of the higher values of our society.'"[17]

In regard to pluralism, the *Yoder*[18] case presented a stronger position than *Meyer*.[19] We can conclude that a way of life that is odd or erratic but that interferes with no right or interests of others will be protected if that way of life is based on religious beliefs. In this case, the Amish were allowed to isolate themselves in order to maintain a different religious subculture. But what practices constitute a threat to the rights and interests of others? We turn now to a clarification of this point.

Qualifications of the Right to Choose: Limitations

Reynolds v. United States[20]—*Polygamy Overruled*. In 1878, George Reynolds, citizen of the territory of Utah, was accused of violating a statute that declared polygamous marriages to be criminal offenses. At the time of his second marriage, he was, and for many years before had been, a member of the Church of Jesus Christ of Latter-Day Saints, commonly called the Mormon church, and a believer in its doctrines. One of the accepted doctrines of the church concerned the duty of male members, circumstances permitting, to practice polygamy. As a member of the church, Reynolds believed that this duty was also enjoined by different books of divine origin including the Bible and that the practice was directly enjoined upon male members by God in a revelation through Joseph Smith, the founder and prophet of the church. Moreover, Reynolds believed that the failure or refusal of male members of the church to practice polygamy when circumstances permitted would be punished, the penalty for such failure and refusal being damnation.[21]

In court, Reynolds established that he had received permission from the recognized authorities in the church, that he was married by an authority of the church, and that the marriage ceremony was performed under and pursuant to the doctrines of the church. He argued that since the marriage was entered pursuant to and in conformity with a religious duty, he was protected by the First Amendment and therefore should be protected from the statute.

In its behalf, the prosecution called expert witnesses who found that objections to polygamy were rooted in early English common law and based on civil (social) moral tenets rather than religious grounds. Testimony was also presented that society would ultimately be harmed by polygamy.

In its decision, the Supreme Court concluded that the statute under consideration was within the legislative power of Congress. The key question, according to the Court, was whether those who make polygamy a part of their religion were excepted from the operation of the statute. Making a distinction between religious belief and religious actions, the Court held that laws are made to govern actions and that while these laws cannot interfere with mere religious belief and opinions, they may do so with practices. It mattered not that Reynolds' belief was part of his religion; to the Court it was still belief and belief only. While Reynolds was free to believe what he wished, he was not free to violate the law established to protect society and the "pure-minded women" and their "innocent children" made victims of such practices.

Prince v. Commonwealth of Massachusetts[22]—*State Protection of Children Upheld*.   Sarah Prince and her nine-year-old niece, Betty, for whom she was the legal guardian, were Jehovah's Witnesses. Engaging in what they believed to be their religious duty, Mrs. Prince and Betty would "engage in the preaching work" by distributing *Watch Tower* and *Consolation*, two religious publications, to passers-by and asking for a five-cent donation per copy.

This practice, in regard to Betty, was in violation of Massachusetts child labor laws, which in part stated that "no boy under twelve and no girl under eighteen shall sell, expose or offer for sale any newspaper, magazines, periodicals or any other articles of merchandise of any description . . . in any street or public place." Mrs. Prince thought this law to be in violation of Betty's "God-given right and her constitutional right to preach the gospel." The state disagreed and held Mrs. Prince responsible, as Betty's legal guardian, for violation of the child labor law.

The Supreme Court saw two main issues at hand. One concerned the rights of the parent and child, namely, the right of the parent to bring up the child in the way the parent saw fit and the right of the child to preach the Gospel by public distribution of *Watch Tower* and *Consolation*. The second issue, to be balanced against the parent's and child's interests, concerned the interests of society to protect the welfare of children so that they are both safeguarded from abuses and given opportunities for growth into free and independent well-developed adults and citizens. In its decision, the Court concluded that "the family itself is not beyond regulation in the public interests, as against a claim of religious liberty."[23] Citing *Reynolds*, the Court argued that neither rights of religion nor rights of parenthood are beyond limitation. Acting to guard the general interests in a youth's well-being, the state may restrict parental control. The state's authority is not nullified merely because a parent bases a claim on religion or conscience.[24] In this particular case, the Court recognized certain potential situations in the defendants' activities that would be difficult for adults to cope with and wholly inappropriate for children to face. Other than the confrontations one experiences when soliciting with religious material, possibilities of harmful emotional excitement and psychological or physical injury existed. Because of these potential outcomes for Betty, the Court concluded that Massachusetts could restrict her religious activities.

The *Reynolds* and *Prince* cases illustrate how and why government might restrict pluralism. Beliefs are always protected, but activities associated with these beliefs may be restricted when the state can show the probability of harmful effects to society or individuals. Other cases support this position. Courts have held that compulsory vaccination is a reasonable exercise of state power,[25] as is the requirement that parents provide competent medical treatment for children whose health is seriously threatened.[26]

Qualifications of the Right to Choose: Support for Pluralism

Pierce v. Society of Sisters[27]—*Private Education Upheld*. The 1923 Oregon Compulsory Education Act required parents and guardians to send their children to a public school. The Society of Sisters was an educational corporation that operated primary schools, high schools, junior colleges, and orphanages. The primary schools taught the sub-jects usually taught in Oregon public schools but also included sys-tematic religious instruction and moral training according to the tenets of the Roman Catholic church. The religious community claimed that the enforcement of the Compulsory Education Act was in violation of the First and Fourteenth amendments on two points: It conflicted with the rights of parents to choose schools where their children would re-ceive appropriate mental and religious training, and it denied the right of schools to engage in a useful business. As in other cases, the Supreme Court recognized

the power of the state reasonably to regulate all schools, to inspect, supervise, and examine them, their teachers and pupils; to require that all children of proper age attend some school, that teachers shall be of good moral character and patriotic disposition, that certain studies plainly essential to good citizenship must be taught, and that nothing be taught which is manifestly inimical to the public welfare.[28]

The Court found nothing in the record to indicate that the Society of Sisters had failed to discharge their obligations to patrons, students, or the state. Under the doctrine of *Meyer*,[29] the Court declared that the Compulsory Education Act unreasonably interfered with the liberty of parents and guardians to direct the upbringing and education of chil-dren under their guidance. In an oft-quoted passage, the Court stated: "The child is not the mere creature of the state; those who nurture him and direct his destiny have the right coupled with the high duty, to recognize and prepare him for additional obligations."[30]

This case supports the findings in *Meyer* and *Yoder*:[31] Parents have the right to control the rearing of their children by choosing the kind of educational experiences they consider most appropriate. But these cases refer to private schools; what of parents' rights to protect their children in public schools? Must parents send their children to private schools to preserve or foster a way of life different from that of the majority? The *Barnette* case addresses this issue.

Barnette v. West Virginia[32]—Mandatory Flag Salute Overruled.

Like many states, West Virginia required children in its public schools to sal-ute the flag as a part of the regular school program. Walter Barnette, however, believed that the pledge violated his religious principles. As a Jehovah's Witness, he based his belief on a passage in Exodus that reads: "Thou shalt not make unto thee any graven image, or any like-ness of anything that is in heaven above, that is in the earth beneath, or that is in the water under the earth; thou shalt not bow down thyself to them nor serve them." Consistent with his faith, he considered the flag an "image" within this command and refused to salute it.

In reviewing the evidence, the Supreme Court concluded that the freedom asserted by Barnette did not conflict with the rights of other individuals, nor did the issue, as the Court saw it, rely heavily on Barnette's religious views. Rather, it recognized that "... many citizens who do not share these religious views hold such a compulsory rite to infringe constitutional liberty of the individual."[33] Rather, "[f]ree public education, if faithful to the ideal of secular instruction and political neutrality, will not be partisan or enemy of any class, party, or faction."[34] This ideal is eloquently stated in the following passage:

... freedom to differ is not limited to things that do not matter much. That would be a mere shadow of freedom. The test of its substance is the right to differ as to things that touch the heart of the existing order.

If there is any fixed star in our constitutional constellation, it is that no official, high or petty, can prescribe what shall be orthodox in politics, nationalism, religion, or other matters of opinion or force citizens to confess by word or act of faith therein. If there are any circumstances which permit an exception, they do not now occur to us.[35]

Public Neutrality Reaffirmed

The Schempp *and* Murray *Cases*[36]—*Prayer Disallowed in Public Schools*. Pennsylvania and Maryland had laws providing for non-denominational religious activities in the public schools. The Pennsylvania statute required that at least ten verses from the Bible be read, without comment, at the opening of each school day; any child was to be excused from the Bible reading upon written request of parents or guardian. The Maryland statute provided for the reading, without comment, of a chapter in the Bible and for the use of the Lord's Prayer. This rule was amended to permit children to be excused from the exercise on their parents' request.

Court actions against these practices were initiated separately in the respective state courts. The U.S. Supreme Court saw the issues of the two cases as substantially the same and, on appeal, handed down one opinion for both. After reviewing past cases, the Court reaffirmed public neutrality and the separation of church and state, declaring that Bible reading and prayers in the schools, whether compulsory or voluntary, were unconstitutional.

The Right to Choose: Conclusions

The cases considered to this point suggest that pluralism might best be understood as one's right to choose and pursue the way of life one deems desirable for self and children. The Constitution generally protects citizens from arbitary or unreasonable control by the government. Thus, *Meyer*,[37] *Yoder*,[38] and *Pierce*[39] illustrate the rights of parents to rear and educate their children as they see fit, even if this life style conflicts with existing social patterns.

Religion played a significant role in several of these cases because the Constitution specifically singles out religious pluralism to be protected; thus, religious claims are among the strongest to receive recognition in support of pluralistic ideals. Based on religious principles, *Yoder* illustrates that a way of life separate and different from that of the mainstream of society can be supported. It also suggests, however, that the same way of life will not be supported on strictly secular grounds.

The courts have also recognized a distinction between pursuing pluralistic goals publicly and privately. In general, the courts advocate government neutrality, particularly with religious pluralism. Thus, *Barnette*[40] and *Schempp*[41] illustrate that public (government) institutions must not support the development of any one religion or, for that matter, religion at all. If an individual or group wishes to protect and ensure the well-being of a given way of life, it must be done through private institutions. *Meyer, Pierce,* and *Yoder* each involved the protection of a group to perpetuate itself through private means. These groups could not have successfully demanded that public institutions support their ways of life. On the other hand, the state does have the power to pursue cultural, philosophical, and political (but not religious) goals through its public institutions; however, barring a compelling interest, it does not have the power to force individuals and groups to participate in these institutions. Thus, the Supreme Court's opinion in *Meyer* questioned the means of reaching assimilationist goals rather than the goals themselves. We pursue this question further in the next section.

EQUAL EDUCATIONAL OPPORTUNITY: INTEGRATION AND ASSIMILATION

The social organization governing the separation or integration of culturally, ethnically, and racially different groups in the United States will have profound implications for pluralism. As we saw in the last chapter, theorists have suggested alternative organizational models ranging from the virtual separation of groups to a completely assimilated and open society. Court precedent also has contributed to the kind and frequency of social interaction among groups.

Early court decisions established a legal base for the separation of racial groups. In 1896, in *Plessy* v. *Ferguson*,[42] the U.S. Supreme Court upheld a Louisiana statute that provided for "equal but separate accommodations for the white and colored races on passenger trains."

The Court applied the test of reasonableness to the legislation that permitted separate accommodations for Blacks and concluded that the state must have broad discretion to decide what was reasonable with reference to the established usages, customs, and traditions of the people and with a view to the promotion of their comfort and the preservation of the public peace and order. Applying this standard, the Court concluded that the law was not unreasonable.

While we recognize the racist intentions and implications of such a law today, the decision provided the support for separate but equal schools.*

Brown v. Board of Education[43]—*School Desegregation*. In 1949, Kansas passed a law permitting the establishment of separate school facilities for Black** and white students. Pursuant to that authority, the Topeka Board of Education elected to establish segregated elementary schools. In a class action suit, Oliver Brown, a student, challenged the constitutionality of segregated schools, claiming that such an arrangement, when conducted by officials pursuant to law, violated the equal protection clause of the Fourteenth Amendment.

The district court found that segregation in public education has a detrimental effect upon Black children, but using *Plessy* as precedent, it denied relief on the grounds that the Black and white schools were substantially equal with respect to buildings, transportation, curricula, and educational qualifications of teachers.[44] Brown appealed to the Supreme Court, where his case was heard along with similar cases from South Carolina, Virginia, and Delaware.

In the decision, the Court addressed itself to this question: "Does segregation of children in public schools solely on the basis of race, even though the physical facilities and other 'tangible' factors may be equal, deprive the children of the minority group of equal educational opportunities?"[45] The Court first viewed the contemporary context of the case and decided that it must be determined on the basis of conditions existing when the Fourteenth Amendment was adopted but in the light of the full development of public education and its present place in American life throughout the nation. The Court held that in the present context: "To separate [minority students] from others of similar age and qualifications solely because of their race generates a

* Though the law was blatantly racist, it provided support for at least one very narrow view of pluralism: the separation of different groups decreases the probability of cultural diffusion and increases the probability of the group maintaining its cultural uniqueness. Thus, in *Yoder*, the Amish sought to separate themselves, as have other groups in the establishing of parochial schools.

** Though the statute referred to the separation of Negroes and white students, we use the more acceptable contemporary label Black students here and elsewhere in this chapter.

feeling of inferiority as to their status in the community that may affect their hearts and minds in a way unlikely ever to be undone."[46]

These findings were based on expert testimony that segregation of white and Black children in public schools has a detrimental effect on the Black children and that the impact is greater when it has legal sanction. The experts believed that the policy of separating races is usually interpreted as denoting the inferiority of the Black group and that this sense of inferiority affects the motivation of a child to learn. Segregation with the sanction of the law, therefore, tends to retard the educational and mental development of Black children and deprive them of some of the benefits they would receive in a racially integrated school system.[47] On the force of these arguments, the Court concluded "that in the field of public education the doctrine of 'separate but equal' has no place. Separate educational facilities are inherently unequal"[48] and violate the equal protection of the laws guaranteed by the Fourteenth Amendment.

The implications of *Brown* were clear: School districts that sanctioned the separation of races must desegregate. Because of the complexities involved and the probable impact of the decision, the Court gave all interested parties a year to study the situation, reconvene, and make proposals on how to proceed. The result was *Brown II.*[49] The first *Brown* case declared the fundamental principle that racial discrimination in public education is unconstitutional. In *Brown II*, the Court said: "All provisions of federal, state, or local law requiring or permitting such discrimination must yield to this principle."[50] Local school authorities would have the primary responsibility for elucidating, assessing, and solving the problems. District courts would be responsible for seeing that public schools complied with all deliberate speed. Moreover, the burden would rest upon the defendants to establish that their actions were in the public interest and were "consistent with good faith compliance at the earliest practicable date."[51]

The immediate impact of *Brown I* and *Brown II* was felt in the South where segregated schools were common and sanctioned by law. The initial reaction of many southern districts, predictably, was resistance; this led to a series of court decisions that clarified and strengthened *Brown.*

Griffin v. County School Board[52]—*The Closing of the Schools*. In 1959, faced with an order to desegregate, the County Board of Supervisors of Prince Edward County, Virginia, refused to appropriate funds for the operation of public schools. In place of the county schools, a private foundation was created that operated schools for white children only. In addition, these children were eligible for county and state tuition grants to help defray the cost of private schools. Public schools continued to operate elsewhere in the state.

After protracted litigation in federal and state courts, the Supreme Court in 1964 struck down as unconstitutional the county's private school strategy to avoid integration. The Court declared that under the circumstances, closing of the Prince Edward County public schools and at the same time giving tuition grants and tax concessions to assist white children in private segregated schools denied petitioners (Black students) the equal protection of the laws guaranteed by the Fourteenth Amendment.[53] In support of this claim, the Court noted that (1) Prince Edward County schoolchildren were treated differently from those of other counties, since they must go to private schools or none at all; and (2) the public schools of Prince Edward County were closed and private schools operated in their place only for constitutionally impermissible reasons of race. In the words of the Court: "Whatever nonracial grounds might support a state's allowing a county to abandon public schools, . . . [the] grounds of race and opposition to desegregation do not qualify as constitutional."[54]

Green v. County School Board[55]—***Freedom of Choice Overruled***.   The *Griffin*[56] case illustrates one blatant attempt to frustrate desegregation, but not all school districts sought openly to avoid the law. Many searched earnestly for an acceptable compromise. One such attempt was a freedom-of-choice plan developed by the school board of New Kent County, Virginia.

At the time of the proposal, New Kent County was a rural county in eastern Virginia, with about half of its population Black. There was no residential segregation; persons of both races resided throughout the county. The school system had only two schools, the New Kent School on the east side of the county and the George Watkins School on the west side. New Kent School was a combined elementary and high school serving the white population, while Watkins served the combined elementary and high school Black population. There were no attendance zones. Each school served the entire county, with twenty-one buses transporting students to their respective schools. It is important to note that the segregated system was initially established and maintained under the compulsion of Virginia constitutional and statutory provisions mandating racial segregation in public education.

In 1965, in order to remain eligible for federal financial aid under the Civil Rights Act of 1964, the school board adopted a "freedom of choice" plan for desegregating the schools. Under the plan, each pupil, except those entering the first and eighth grades, would annually choose between the New Kent and Watkins schools. Pupils not making a choice would be assigned to the school previously attended, but first and eighth graders were required to make an affirmative decision. The school district argued that such a plan completely satisfied the requirements of the *Brown* decision because every student, regardless of race, could freely choose which school to attend and that the plan could be held unconstitutional only if the Fourteenth Amendment were read as universally requiring compulsory integration. Nevertheless, Charles Green and other students thought the plan was unconstitutional and filed suit against the school board. In their suit, they argued that despite the freedom of choice, the extent to which the schools remained segregated reflected the district's lack of compliance.

The Court ruled in favor of Green. Rejecting the school board's reasoning, the Court held:

[The] transition to unitary and non-racial system of public education was and is the ultimate end to be brought about.[57] . . . School boards such as the respondent operating state-compelled dual systems at the time of *Brown II* were clearly charged with the affirmative duty to take whatever steps might be necessary to convert to a unitary system in which racial discrimination would be eliminated root and branch.[58]*

The significance of *Green* to pluralism resides in the clearly stated affirmative stance to integration. *Brown* ruled against the intentional segregation of schools. *Green* ruled that not only is intentional segregation unconstitutional but that segregated school systems must be dismantled "root and branch." The criterion for compliance, then, is evidence of integration. This principle was further developed and clarified in *Swann* v. *Charlotte-Mecklenburg Board of Education*.

Swann v. Charlotte-Mecklenburg Board of Education[59]—*Clarifying Desegregation Guidelines*. In reviewing a North Carolina case in 1970, fifteen years and numerous cases after *Brown*, the Supreme Court recognized a need to "try [to] amplify guidelines . . . for the assistance of school authorities and courts" dealing with further desegregation cases. As an illustration of this necessity, the Court pointed to the Fifth Circuit, where 166 school desegregation cases had been appealed between December 1969 and September 1970. The case chosen for Su-

---

* The inadequacy of the freedom-of-choice plan should not be interpreted as an overruling of all such plans. In the Court's words: "All we decide today is that in desegregating a dual school system a plan utilizing freedom-of-choice is not an end in itself." The Court's key consideration in the ruling was the development of "a plan that promises realistically to work, and promises realistically to work now." As we shall see in *Swann*, the Court supported a modified freedom-of-choice plan that allowed students to transfer from a school where they were in the racial majority to a school where they would be in the racial minority. We shall also see that in such plans the school district must provide the transferring student free transportation and available space in the school to which the move is to be made.

preme Court consideration involved a school system in Charlotte, North Carolina, and was typical in that the segregation of the district's schools was the result of earlier policies sanctioned by law. Efforts to dismantle the dual systems had been ineffective. Of 84,000 students attending 107 schools, approximately 29 percent (24,000) were Black; about 14,000 of these Black students attended 21 schools that were at least 99 percent Black. Relying on *Green*, which required school boards to "come forward with a plan that promises realistically to work . . . now" petitioner Swann sought further relief.

The Court addressed four areas:[60]

1. To what extent racial balance or racial quotas may be used as an implement in a remedial order to correct a previously segregated system
2. Whether every all-[B]lack and all-white school must be eliminated as an indispensable part of a remedial process of desegregation
3. What the limits are, if any, on the rearrangement of school districts and attendance zones, as a remedial measure
4. What the limits are, if any, on the use of transportation facilities to correct state-enforced racial school segregation.

In response to each question, the Court held:

1. *Racial quotas*: The constitutional command to desegregate schools does not mean that every school in every community must always reflect the racial composition of the system as a whole . . . the very limited use made of [racial] ratios—[not] as an inflexible requirement, but as a starting point in shaping a remedy—[is acceptable].[61]
2. *One-race schools*: [While] the existence of some small number of one-race, or virtually one-race, schools within a district [does] not in and of itself [denote] a system that still practices segregation by law. . . . The courts should scrutinize such schools, and . . . [require] the school authorities . . . to satisfy the court that their racial composition is not the result of present or past discriminatory action on their part.[62]
3. *Attendance zones*: [A student] assignment plan is not acceptable simply because it appears to be neutral. [For] such plans may fail to counteract the continuing effects of past school segregation . . . no rigid rules can be laid down to govern [conditions in different localities].[63]
4. *Transportation*: [T]he remedial techniques [of requiring bus

transportation as a tool of school desegregation is] within that court's power to provide equitable relief. . . . An objection to transportation of students may have validity when the time or distance of travel is so great as to risk the health of the children or significantly impinge on the educational process.[64]

The Court also held that neither school authorities nor district courts are constitutionally required to make year-by-year adjustments of the racial composition of student bodies once a unitary system has been achieved.[65]

The findings of *Green*[66] and *Swann* indicate that dual educational systems must be dismantled and integration of races must take place in schools evidencing segregation caused by government action. Nevertheless, it does not follow that schools must have a fixed racial balance or that no one-race schools may exist. In cases where one-race schools exist, the school district must show that the racial composition is not a result of discriminatory action. In pursuit of desegregation, courts may manipulate attendance zones and require busing. Once a dual system has been dismantled, local authorities must see to it that future school construction is not used to reestablish such a system.[67]

Johnson *and* Lee *Cases—Voluntary Ethnic Separation Denied*. The effects and applications of *Brown, Green*, and *Swann* were not confined to the South. In *Johnson* v. *San Francisco*,[68] a suit was filed against the San Francisco Unified School District to achieve racial integration of the public schools. Despite San Francisco's claim that, unlike southern school districts, the racial separation in the schools was a result of residential de facto segregation, the district court found San Francisco to be in violation. The court based its decision on the view that any action, rule, or regulation "by school authorities which creates or continues or heightens racial segregation of school children is 'de jure.'"[69] If a school board draws attendance lines that provide for reasonable racial balance and if solely by virtue of population mobility the racial balance of the school becomes lopsided, that segregation is de facto. If school officials were aware of the population shift and drew attendance lines year after year, "knowing that the lines maintain or heighten racial imbalance, the resulting segregation is de jure."[70] Because San Francisco's schools were segregated and because no evidence was presented to show that the school authorities had ever changed any attendance boundaries for the purpose of eliminating racial imbalance, the court found de jure segregation. The court further stated that school board members, though acting in innocence, could be culpable. . . . if their official action "creates or continues or increases substantial racial imbalance in the schools, [the action is de jure]."[71]

The court, in a detailed plan, directed the school district to desegregate.

The San Francisco plan to desegregate was far-reaching and affected many ethnic groups. One aspect of the plan was the reassignment of pupils of Chinese ancestry to elementary schools away from their neighborhoods. Prior to the implementation of the plan, the neighborhood elementary schools attended by the Chinese Americans were predominantly Chinese—of 482 students in one school, 456 were Chinese; in a second school, 230 of the 289 students were Chinese; and in the third school, 1,074 out of 1,111 students were Chinese. Chinese American parents objected to the reassignment of their children and filed suit on their behalf. In *Guey Heung Lee* v. *Johnson*,[72] they requested that the school district and the courts continue the pattern of neighborhood schools to allow children of Chinese ancestry to attend school together. The parents argued that important cultural values could not be preserved and passed on to future generations if the children were dispersed throughout the city. In addition to the Chinese cultural heritage, the parents believed the very survival of their language might be in jeopardy if their children could not remain together.

In reviewing the request, Justice Douglas, speaking for the Supreme Court, found that until 1947 the California Education Code provided for the governing board of any school district to "establish separate schools for Indian children . . . and for children of Chinese, Japanese or Mongolian parentage."[73] Based on this fact and on the finding of the *Johnson* case, Douglas employed the principles established in *Brown*[74] and *Swann*.[75] Because there was no evidence to show that the San Francisco authorities have effectively eliminated all vestiges of earlier state-imposed segregation, the Chinese request for segregation was denied. In language supportive of the ideal of integration, Douglas approvingly quoted the lower district court:

The Judgement and Decree now to be entered is of less consequence than the spirit of community response. In the end, that response may well be decisive in determining whether San Francisco is to be divided into hostile racial camps, breeding greater violence in the streets, or is to become a more unified city demonstrating its historic capacity for diversity without disunity.

The school children of San Francisco can be counted upon to lead the way to unity. In this and in their capacity to accept change without anger, they deserve no less than the whole-hearted support of all their elders.[76]*

The language in *Lee*[77] clearly emphasizes a brand of pluralism incorporating integration. This decision might be contrasted with the

---

* In deference to the Court, it should be pointed out that while the integration plan was upheld, the Court did recognize the interests and concerns of the Chinese parents, noting that the plan made possible bilingual classes as well as courses that taught the "cultural background and heritages of various racial and ethnic groups."

Yoder[78] decision discussed earlier. *Yoder* allowed the Amish to separate themselves, while *Lee* required the Chinese to integrate. In terms of pluralistic ideology, the two cases may seem inconsistent, but there are some important differences between them. First, both argued that certain cultural qualities were at stake: The Amish sought relief on religious grounds, while the Chinese based their arguments on strictly ethnic variables. Second, the Amish were attempting to withdraw from the public schools and to rely on their own informal private institutions to further religious and cultural security. The Chinese, on the other hand, sought to use the public schools for cultural support. It is quite probable that the Chinese could establish private schools that would support their cultural ideals much as religious groups have established parochial schools (see *Meyer*[79] and *Pierce*[80]).

In protecting groups from unreasonable government intervention, the First and Fourteenth amendments provide for groups to perpetuate and reinforce their cultural life styles as private undertakings. It seems clear that while government must enforce neutrality in public institutions in regard to religious ideology, cultural and social ideology is another matter. Government institutions, schools in particular, may reinforce those doctrines, values, and life styles that it deems valuable. In this respect, compulsory integration might be characterized as reinforcing an assimilationist ideology.

BILINGUALISM, INTEGRATION, AND ASSIMILATION

Initially, the *Brown*[81] decision was seen as affecting primarily the relationships between whites and Blacks, but as court cases moved north and west, it became evident that other ethnic groups would be affected as well. Several cases in Texas (*Hernandez* v. *Texas*;[82] *Cisneros* v. *Corpus Christi*[83]) identified Hispanics as an identifiable class, and as we have seen, *Johnson*[84] so identified the Chinese. Cases involving these groups were complicated by the fact that students often came to school with a dominant language other than English. Integrating the schools, then, sometimes resulted in mixing non-English-speaking children with children and teachers who spoke only English. Increasingly, courts have taken these variables into consideration.

United States v. Texas[85]—*Bilingualism for Integration.*   In a desegregation suit, the San Felipe Del Rio Consolidated Independent School District was found in violation of the Fourteenth Amendment as set forth in *Brown*[86] on the basis of its discrimination against Mexican American students. In a move to dismantle the dual system "root and branch," the court adopted a plan that included extensive bilingual/bicultural components. The school district questioned the legitimacy of these programs.

In its decision, the appeals court acknowledged Mexican Americans to be an identifiable minority "subject to protection under Title 6 of the Civil Rights Act of 1964 and the Fourteenth Amendment, as applied to racial and ethnic discrimination in public schools."[87] Moving to the question of the necessity of bilingual/bicultural components in the schools, the court was particularly impressed by expert testimony describing problems commonly faced by Mexican American students. The evidence showed that

... Mexican-American students exhibit numerous characteristics which have a causal connection with their general inability to benefit from an educational program designed primarily to meet the needs of so-called Anglo-Americans. These characteristics include "cultural incompatibilities" and English language deficiencies—two traits which immediately and effectively identify those students sharing them as members of a definite group whose performance norm habitually will fall below that of Anglo-American students who do not exhibit these traits.[88]

Next, the court raised the question of the relationship between these characteristics and the establishment of a unitary school system. Ruling in support of the bilingual programs, the court concluded that

... [L]ittle could be more clear ... than the need in the newly consolidated school district created as a result of this Court's earlier order for special educational consideration to be given to the Mexican-American students in assisting them in adjusting to those parts of their new school environment which present a cultural and linguistic shock. . . . [T]he Anglo-American students too must be called upon to adjust to their Mexican-American classmates, and to learn to understand and appreciate their different linguistic and cultural attributes. The process ... will not only constitute an educational enrichment but, also, will bring the school system as a whole closer to that goal or state-of-being referred to by the Supreme Court as a unitary system.[89]

Thus the court upheld bilingual/bicultural programs as a vehicle for the attainment of a unitary school system with "true integration as opposed to mere desegregation," and ruled that programs were to be not only for minority students but for Anglo students as well, to facilitate integration and interaction among the two groups. The programs, then, are a means to facilitate this transition. For some, however, the value of bilingualism has not been in its assimilation function but in its ability to provide equal educational opportunity for non-English-speaking students.

Lau v. Nichols[90]—*Bilingualism and Equal Educational Opportunity.*
The requirement of bilingual education to achieve equal educational opportunity rests on the premise that students who do not understand English are effectively foreclosed from any meaningful education when English is the sole language of instruction. Such was the claim in *Lau* v. *Nichols.* Following the desegregation of the San Francisco school sys-

tem in 1971, there were 2,856 students of Chinese ancestry in the school system who did not speak English. Of these, about 1,000 received supplemental courses in the English language. The remaining 1,800 did not receive supplemental or bilingual instruction.

The class action suit was brought by 13 non-English-speaking Chinese American students who alleged that they were being effectively denied an education because they could not comprehend the language in which they were being taught.* They argued that the failure either to teach them bilingually or to teach them English should be prohibited on the grounds that (1) failure to do so was a violation of equal protection under the Fourteenth Amendment, and (2) it was a violation of the Civil Rights Act of 1964.

The facts clearly supported the claims that the non-English-speaking Chinese were not benefiting from their educational experience. Indeed, the school district noted the frustration and poor per⁻ formance created by the students' inability to understand the regular work. Predictions were made that substantial numbers would "drop out and [become] another unemployable [person] in the ghetto."[91] The district argued, however, that discrimination was not being practiced because the students were being taught in the same facilities, by the same teachers, and at the same time as everyone else.

The district court and the circuit court of appeals both ruled in favor of the school district. The arguments in support of this ruling focused primarily on the fact that the alleged violation was not based on prior segregation. "More importantly," the appeals court stated, "there is no showing that appellants' lingual deficiencies are at all related to any such past discrimination."[92] The court suggested, then, that the students' failure was of their own making, not state-related, and thus of little consequence when school resources were limited. The court further observed:

Every student brings to the starting line of his educational career different advantages and disadvantages, caused in part by social, economic and cultural background, created and continued completely apart from any contribution by the school system. That some of these may be impediments which can be overcome does not amount to a "denial" by the [school district] of educational opportunities . . . should the [district] fail to give them special attention. . . .[93]

On appeal to the Supreme Court, the lower court's decision was reversed. The High Court's opinion supported the arguments presented at trial by the Chinese-speaking students:

* Interestingly, what was sought was not specifically bilingual education but only that the board of education apply its expertise to the problem and rectify the situation. Teaching English to the students would be one choice; giving instruction to them in Chinese would be another.

[B]asic English skills are at the very core of what these public schools teach. Imposition of a requirement that before a child can effectively participate in the educational program he must already have acquired these basic skills is to make a mockery of public education. We know that those who do not understand English are certain to find their classroom experiences wholly incomprehensible and in no way meaningful.[94]

While the Court laid to rest the argument that equal access to facilities provides equal treatment and equal educational opportunity, it did not base its decision on a constitutional requirement; rather, support was found in the Civil Rights Act of 1964. The act forbids discrimination on the grounds of race, color, or national origin by any agency receiving federal financial assistance. Because the support for the ruling came from the Civil Rights Act, there is still not a constitutional right to a bilingual education or even an education from which one can benefit. Thus, a district that does not receive federal funds would not be compelled to offer non-English-speaking students bilingual education. The constitutional issue has been raised elsewhere, however, with some support.

Serna v. Portales Municipal Schools[95]—*A Constitutional Test*. The *Serna* case is remarkably similar to *Lau* and was working its way through the courts at approximately the same time. The city of Portales, New Mexico, is residentially segregated; Mexican Americans inhabit the north side of the city and Anglos the south side. The elementary schools are located in residential areas and therefore reflect the ethnic composition of their respective neighborhoods. The focal point of the action was the education offered in one of the Mexican American elementary schools. Plaintiffs asserted that educational discrimination existed throughout the Portales school system as a result of an educational program tailored to the middle-class child from an English-speaking family, without regard for the educational needs of the child from an environment in which Spanish is the predominant language spoken. Such a program, it was claimed, denies equal educational opportunity to Spanish-speaking children.

As in *Lau*, the plaintiffs presented evidence that the Spanish-speaking children's achievement was consistently lower than that of the children at the other schools. They did not claim that this difference was caused by differential treatment in regard to facilities, teachers, or program; to the contrary, they argued that lower achievement resulted because school programs were substantially the same. Furthermore, they did not argue that the present system was in any way the result of state action. The Portales School District basically defended its position in the same manner as did San Francisco: Because the needs of the non-English-speaking students did not result from state action and because the district did not create these problems through any classification or racially motivated discrimination, they were under no legal obligation to provide compensatory programs.

The district court that tried the case, unlike the trial court in *Lau*, was not interested in the fact that the situation of these Mexican American students did not result from state action. Placing its decision squarely on the constitutional issue, the court concluded that when children are placed in a school atmosphere that does not adequately reflect the educational needs of the minority, the conclusion is inevitable that the children do not, in fact, have equal educational opportunity and that a violation of their constitutional right to equal protection exists. Unfortunately, this line of reasoning was not tested in higher courts. While *Serna* was on appeal to the circuit court, the Supreme Court handed down the *Lau* decision, and in the light of this decision the appeals court refused to rule on the constitutional issue of equal protection, upholding the ruling as a violation of the Civil Rights Act.

While the constitutional right to bilingual education would serve as a stronger base to support programs, the Civil Rights Act and the Constitution have basically the same implications for pluralism. In no court case was bilingualism/biculturalism supported on the grounds that it contributed to the development or preservation of a group's cultural heritage. On the contrary, where bilingual programs have been mandated by the courts, the purpose has been to enhance assimilation. Thus, in *United States* v. *Texas*[96] a "unitary" integrated system was created that went beyond the "mere mixing of races." In *Lau* the intent of the Court was to establish programs to teach non-English-speaking Chinese students English so that they could benefit from the English-oriented program. While *Serna* probably provides the strongest support for bilingualism under the ruling that "a student who does not understand the English language and is not provided with bilingual instruction is therefore effectively precluded from any meaningful education,"[97] the objective remains the same; bilingualism is seen in the eyes of the court simply as a vehicle to integration.

Two other observations on integration might be made before leaving the discussion of bilingualism. First, in the *Lau* decision, Justice Blackmun qualified his support for such programs by pointing to numbers: "When, in another case, we are concerned with a very few youngsters ... I would not regard today's decision ... as conclusive upon the issue. . . . For me, numbers are at the heart of this case. . . ."[98] This qualification was echoed by the appeals court in *Serna*.

Second, and on a positive note, in *Keyes* v. *School District No. 1*,[99] a school desegregation case involving Mexican Americans, a federal judge allowed several elementary schools to remain segregated upon the request of parents. In support of this move, the judge stated, "Some representatives of the Mexican-American community... have expressed a desire not to desegregate... during the period that the [desegregation] program is developing. The court can see advantages in this and therefore holds that desegregation is not in its best interests."[100] In the same decision, the judge continued: "... [I]n some of the schools which have a preponderant Chicano population it has seemed to the court more desirable to pursue bilingual and bicultural programs than to change the numbers."[101]

On the surface, the separation allowed by *Keyes* seems inconsistent with the *Lee* decision,[102] in which Chinese Americans were forced to integrate. However, we need to recall the guidelines set down in *Swann*,[103] wherein the Supreme Court recognized that in some instances certain schools could remain one-race schools. Inaccessibility was one such instance and served as one of the justifications in *Keyes*.

NATIVE AMERICANS: A SPECIAL CASE OF PLURALISM[104]

In several respects, Native Americans are unique when compared to other ethnic groups in the United States. Because of this, many of the legal principles discussed in regard to other ethnic groups are not applicable. Perhaps the most significant difference has to do with their position in relation to the federal government and the states. In the leading case of *Worchester* v. *Georgia*,[105] the Supreme Court said that Native American tribes held the unique status of being nations within the United States. The Court described these Native American nations as distinct, independent, political communities where "nation" was interpreted to mean "a people distinct from others" in the traditional sense implied by nations of the world. The result of the decision was that Georgia could not regulate the internal affairs of the Cherokee nation. In 1959, this principle was upheld in a ruling in a dispute between Arizona and the Navajo.[106] But if these tribes are to be considered nations, they are a special kind of nation in the eyes of the federal government. In the earlier decision, the Court described them as "domestic dependent nations" whose relation to the federal government "resembles that of a ward to his guardian."

The status of Native American tribes as nations has several consequences relevant to our discussion. One is that it removes the tribes from state control and regulation and places them under the control of the U.S. government. In regard to Native Americans, Congress has assumed the power that states typically hold over other ethnic groups. This power encompasses determining the manner in which education is to be provided. With this unique relationship in mind, then, we turn to issues of pluralism for Native Americans.

Are Racially Identifiable Schools Permissible?

We have seen in *Brown*[107] and its progeny that public school segregation on the basis of race and ethnicity is unconstitutional. The constitutional propriety of federal schools for Native Americans presents an entirely different issue because Native Americans are distinct, independent, political communities. Through exercise of the constitutional power to make treaties, wage war, and regulate commerce with Native American tribes, the federal government has set aside geographically and politically separate areas to be occupied by Native Americans. Although assistance has been provided over the years to those Native Americans who wish to relocate in urban areas, federal policy has been directed primarily toward support and protection of the integrity of tribal self-government on reservations. Federal schools typically serve those Native Americans who have maintained a geographic and social separation from the mainstream of society. It is important to note that this is not designed to promote racial segregation but is the result of geographic and political separation of Native American nations. One evidence of this can be seen in the fact that white children have been eligible for enrollment in "Native American" day and boarding schools upon payment of tuition.

Geographic isolation aside, there are some grounds for maintaining or creating Native American schools when it can be shown with some uncertainty that the maintenance of an identifiable racial school confers a benefit on Native American children. For example, the government may discharge its trust responsibilities by operating schools designed to provide specialized training for gifted Native American artists from rural areas (e.g., The Institute of American Indian Arts in Santa Fe, New Mexico) or by providing a higher quality vocational program than would otherwise be available to Native Americans living on reservations (e.g., The South-Western Indian Polytechnic Institute in Albuquerque, New Mexico).

May the Government Support Native American Community-Controlled Schools?

Federal and state governments have been prohibited from supporting religious education, and state funds cannot be used to support racially segregated private schools (*Griffin*).[108] There is a precedent, however, for federally funded Native American schools. Indeed, this funding has been an obligation of the government in its guardian position. The government may operate its own schools (e.g., Bureau of Indian Affairs) or may contract that responsibility to another party (e.g., Native American tribes). It does not follow that Native American community schools can discriminate against students who are not Native

Americans. If an Native American community school is supported to a significant extent by programs not designed specifically for Native Americans (compare Johnson-O'Mally funds with Title I funds), then the school probably could not give preference to Native Americans in admission, nor could it in any other way discriminate on the basis of race.

A separate issue concerns the exclusion of persons who are not Native Americans from the school board of a federally funded Native American school. Where educational programs on the reservations are administered by Native American tribes or by tribally chartered corporations, the constitutional policy of tribal sovereignty should prevail.

State-Created Native American Schools

May a state deliberately create a racially imbalanced school district at the request of Native Americans? Ordinarily, such state action would not be consistent with applicable constitutional standards. Because of the unique position Native Americans have under the Fourteenth Amendment, however, there are circumstances that will justify a departure from the general rule.

In many instances, geography provides the compelling explanation for the creation of racially imbalanced Native American school districts. Nevertheless, when the effect of redrawing school district boundaries creates an increase in racial separation, equal protection problems are normally raised (*Brown*).[109] At present it is not clear if this obstacle can be overcome. The basis for overcoming "equal protection" would lie in (1) the tradition of sovereignty enjoyed by Native American nations; and (2) the supremacy clause of the Constitution, which makes state authority subordinate to federal authority. The sovereignty argument, simply stated, is that since Native American nations are sovereign, they should be able to establish their own school districts. The supremacy argument is based on federal policy having led to the creation of Native American reservations and calling for their perpetuation. Thus the policy is one of autonomy and separation. Since state action is subordinate to federal policy, states should allow this separation to continue.

The conflict lies in the fact that the Fourteenth Amendment is also supreme law. If the separation of Native American districts could be shown to be discriminatory, it could be ruled unconstitutional. One author believes this obstacle could be overcome in most cases, particularly if no prior de jure segregation was involved and if the separation were at the request of the Native American group.[110]

Although this discussion of Native American policy is extremely brief, it should be clear that Native Americans are in a unique position in respect to legal issues supporting pluralism. Unlike other ethnic and cultural groups, Native Americans may maintain cultural separation if they choose, and this separation can often be supported by public funds. It should also be noted that while Native Americans may separate themselves, states may not discriminate against them. Thus, Native American children have a right to attend integrated public schools where it is geographically feasible and have the right to an education from which they can benefit.

SUMMARY

The literature of the past two decades has generally been supportive of an ideal of cultural pluralism for the United States, but it does not provide the framework for the legal interpretation of pluralism as practised in the United States. The legal realities of American pluralism, as established by court decisions, at best portray pluralism as a passive or neutral position of government toward culturally different groups. In this sense, pluralism exists to the extent that government may not interfere with a group's efforts to pursue goals different from those of the majority as long as these efforts are private, receive no public financial support, and do not pose a threat to society.

It is questionable whether "pluralism" is the proper label for what is happening in the public domain. In decisions supporting equal opportunity, the courts have rendered ethnicity, like religion, irrelevant to secondary levels of interaction. If it is fruitful to distinguish between such ideologies as cultural pluralism, assimilation, and the open society, these court decisions suggest that the operative ideal in the United States is one of the latter two. Thus, if our goal is to replace judgment on ascribed status with judgment on achieved status, our goal is an open society but not necessarily a culturally diverse society. If we wish cultural pluralism to become the operative ideal in American society, we must recognize that our current legal framework, with the possible exception of decisions concerning Native Americans, does not support it, and no support for it can clearly rest on constitutional grounds. If legal grounds for support of this ideal are desirable, they must be constructed by federal or state legislatures.

NOTES

1. U.S. Constitution, Amend. I and XIV.
2. *Meyer* v. *Nebraska*, 43 S. Ct. 625 (1923).
3. Ibid., p. 626.
4. Ibid.

5. Ibid., p. 617.
6. Ibid., p. 626.
7. Ibid.
8. U.S. Constitution, Amend. XIV.
9. *Meyer* v. *Nebraska.*
10. *Wisconsin* v. *Yoder,* 406 U.S. 205 (1972).
11. Ibid., p. 211.
12. Ibid., p. 214.
13. Ibid., p. 215.
14. Ibid., pp. 215–16.
15. Ibid., p. 218.
16. Ibid., p. 222.
17. Ibid., p. 238.
18. *Wisconsin* v. *Yoder.*
19. *Meyer* v. *Nebraska.*
20. *Reynolds* v. *United States,* 98 U.S. 244 (1878).
21. Ibid., p. 261.
22. *Prince* v. *Commonwealth of Massachusetts,* 64 S. Ct. 438 (1944).
23. Ibid.
24. Ibid., p. 442.
25. *Jacobson* v. *Massachusetts,* 25 S. Ct. 358 (1904).
26. *People* v. *Pierson,* 68 N.E. 243 (1903).
27. *Pierce* v. *Society of Sisters,* 268 U.S. 510 (1924).
28. Ibid., p. 534.
29. *Meyer* v. *Nebraska.*
30. *Pierce* v. *Society of Sisters,* 45 S. Ct. at 573 (1924).
31. *Wisconsin* v. *Yoder.*
32. *Barnette* v. *West Virginia,* 319 U.S. 624 (1943).
33. Ibid., pp. 634–35.
34. Ibid., p. 637.
35. Ibid., p. 642.
36. *Abington School District* v. *Schempp,* 374 U.S. 203 (1963).
37. *Meyer* v. *Nebraska.*
38. *Wisconsin* v. *Yoder.*
39. *Pierce* v. *Society of Sisters.* 268 U.S. 510 (1924).
40. *Barnette* v. *West Virginia.*
41. *Abington School District* v. *Schempp.*
42. *Plessy* v. *Ferguson,* 163 U.S. 537 (1896).
43. *Brown* v. *Board of Education of Topeka,* 347 U.S. 483 (1954). *Brown I.*
44. Ibid., p. 486.
45. Ibid., p. 493.
46. Ibid., p. 494.
47. Ibid.
48. Ibid., p. 495.
49. *Brown* v. *Board of Education,* 349 U.S. 294 (1954). *Brown II.*
50. Ibid., p. 298.
51. Ibid., p. 300.
52. *Griffin* v. *County School Board of Prince Edward County,* 377 U.S. 218 (1964).

53. Ibid., pp. 229–30.
54. Ibid., p. 231.
55. *Green* v. *County School Board of New Kent Co.*, 88 S. Ct. 1689 (1968).
56. *Griffin* v. *County School Board of Prince Edward County.*
57. Ibid., p. 1693.
58. Ibid., p. 1694.
59. *Swann* v. *Charlotte-Mecklenburg Board of Education*, 402 U.S. 1 (1970).
60. Ibid., p. 22.
61. Ibid., pp. 22–25.
62. Ibid., pp. 25–26.
63. Ibid., pp. 27–29.
64. Ibid., pp. 29–31.
65. Ibid., pp. 31–32.
66. *Green* v. *County School Board of New Kent Co.*
67. *Swann* v. *Charlotte-Mecklenburg Board of Education.*
68. *Johnson* v. *San Francisco Unified School District*, 339 F. Supp. 1315 (ND Calif. 1971).
69. Ibid., p. 1316.
70. Ibid., p. 1318.
71. Ibid., p. 1319.
72. *Guey Heung Lee* v. *David Johnson*, 404 U.S. 1215 (1971).
73. Cal Educ. Code S 8003 (West's, 1975).
74. *Brown* v. *Board of Education of Topeka.*
75. *Swann* v. *Charlotte-Mecklenburg Board of Education.*
76. *Johnson* v. *San Francisco Unified School District*, at 1323.
77. *Guey Heung Lee* v. *David Johnson.*
78. *Winsconsin* v. *Yoder.*
79. *Meyer* v. *Nebraska.*
80. *Pierce* v. *Society of Sisters*, 268 U.S. 510 (1924).
81. *Brown* v. *Board of Education of Topeka.*
82. *Hernandez* v. *Texas*, 347 U.S. 475 (1954).
83. *Cisneros* v. *Corpus Christi Independent School District*, 467 F. 2d. 142 (1972).
84. *Johnson* v. *San Francisco Unified School District.*
85. *United States* v. *State of Texas*, 342 F. Supp. 24 (1971).
86. *Brown* v. *Board of Education of Topeka.*
87. *United States* v. *State of Texas.*
88. Ibid., p. 26.
89. Ibid., p. 28.
90. *Lau* v. *Nichols*, 94 S. Ct. 786 (1974).
91. Ibid.
92. *Lau* v. *Nichols*, 483 F. 2d. at 797 (1973).
93. Ibid.
94. *Lau* v. *Nichols*, 94 S. Ct. at 788 (1974).
95. *Serna* v. *Portales Municipal Schools*, 351 F. Supp. 1279 (1972).
96. *United States* v. *States of Texas.*
97. *Serna* v. *Portales Municipal Schools*, at 1279.
98. *Lau* v. *Nichols*, 94 S. Ct. at 790 (1974).
99. *Keyes* v. *School District No. 1*, 380 F. Supp. 673 (Colo. 1974).

100. Ibid., p. 692.
101. Ibid., p. 687.
102. *Guey Heung Lee* v. *David Johnson.*
103. *Swann* v. *Charlotte-Mecklenburg Board of Education.*
104. The substance for this section is taken from Daniel M. Rosenfelt, "Indian Schools and Community Control," *Stanford Law Review* 25, no. 4 (April 1973): 489–550.
105. *Worchester* v. *Georgia*, 31 U.S. 16 Pet. 214 (1832).
106. *Williams* v. *Lee*, 358 R.S. 217 (1957).
107. *Brown* v. *Board of Education of Topeka.*
108. *Griffin* v. *County School Board of Prince Edward County.*
109. *Brown* v. *Board of Education of Topeka.*
110. Rosenfelt, "Indian Schools and Community Control," pp. 489–550.

5

The Ideal of Cultural Pluralism and the United States

THE UNITED STATES AS A PLURALISTIC SOCIETY

We have accumulated a wide assortment of information on the nature of cultural pluralism: theoretical models attempting to account for the dynamics of cultural diversity in the United States, several ideological alternatives each presented as the ideal that is to define the pluralistic nature of the United States in the future and guide social and educational policy, and a sketch of the operative ideal that has evolved out of court precedent and currently defines the boundaries of American pluralism. This chapter attempts to define further a policy of cultural pluralism capable of guiding future actions, particularly those within the realm of public education. But first let us take another look at the United States as an example of a pluralistic society.

We said in Chapter 2 that in the ordinary language sense, cultural pluralism conceptually requires that four conditions be met: (1) cultural diversity must be present within the society, (2) membership in a common politic and some minimal interaction must exist between and among groups, (3) coexisting groups must share approximately equal political, economic, and educational opportunity, and (4) the society must value cultural diversity and hold cultural pluralism as an ideal. We may now ask, To what extent does the United States satisfy these four conditions?

The first two conditions are easily met. The United States, as a country, is a political body with a diversity of groups that interact in a variety of ways. With particular regard to diversity we can make a strong case if we use "culture" in its broadest sense to include racial, religious, national origin, behaviorally different, and political groups. Indeed, in Chapter 2 we suggested that there are not only many different groups but many different kinds of groups; for examples we distinguished between race, religion, national origin, behavior, and special-interest groups. Under the contemporary construct of "'race'"* we typically include Black, white (also called Causasian), Asian, Native American, and sometimes Hispanic. Religious diversity is most often understood as consisting of three general groups—Catholics, Protestants, and Jews—[1] but we also recognize that there are subgroups within these groups and that other smaller religious groups exist as well. Listings of national origin groups usually include "white ethnics" (e.g., Polish, Italian, Greek, Slavic, and Irish), Hispanics (e.g., Cubans, Puerto Ricans, and Mexicans), and Asians (e.g., Chinese and Japanese). Behaviorally different groups are subcultures that depart from the core American life style. The Amish and Hutterites are notable examples, but other less cohesive groups, such as Appalachians, may also be classified here. Finally, we may wish to acknowledge political groups such as the handicapped, homosexuals, and women and other contracultural groups such as communists.

To add to and complicate American diversity, these different categories are by no means pure. There is a significant overlapping of groups among categories, and no clear pattern is obvious. Thus, Blacks are considered primarily a "racial" group, also a political minority, and only in a minor sense a behaviorally different group. Another "racial" group (such as some Asians) may in significant ways constitute a behaviorally different group but, because of greater economic autonomy, be less of a political minority—consider, for example, the Chinese. Thus, the United States has a variety of different kinds of groups, with each kind boasting further diversity.

Equal opportunity, the third condition of cultural pluralism, is a more difficult requirement to meet. Some groups, particularly religious groups, enjoy relative equality within society, and a number of ethnic groups have achieved relative success in society (e.g., "white ethnics" and Asian Americans). Nevertheless, equal opportunity for many of these groups was achieved only after considerable struggle and sustained effort. A number of groups, particularly Blacks, Hispanics, and Native Americans, have been involuntarily segregated from the main-

---

* It is important to note that "race" is not used here to denote any physiologically or biologically fixed subspecies of human beings but is seen as a social construct rooted in social ideology. See William Newman, *American Pluralism*, Chap. 6, for a discussion of the sociology of race.

stream of society and are denied equal access to social rewards and resources. Though political, economic, and educational institutions are in principle open to members of these groups, it is clear that they do not function so as to afford equal opportunities. Thus, the existing state of affairs in America is mixed, with some groups clearly enjoying equal opportunity while others are the subject of discrimination, though the last twenty-five years have marked an effort to alleviate the disadvantaged position of these groups. During this time we have seen the proliferation of civil rights legislation, attempts to desegregate schools and achieve equal educational opportunities, the advent of federally funded programs aimed at helping minority students, bilingual education, affirmative action, and an effort to enforce fair housing and employment practices. Many of these efforts have not realized their objectives, but they stand as evidence to the commitment to achieving equal political, economic, and educational opportunity for all. Thus, while the total evidence for meeting our third condition remains mixed, at the present time the scale would seem to tip in favor of accepting it.

The fourth condition is the most challenging. To the extent that groups wish to withdraw from the Union and establish independent states, they contradict the ideal of pluralism, but the threat to the pluralistic ideal from this camp is probably relatively slight. The Black separatist movement of the 1960s provides one basis for questioning our commitment to cultural pluralism, but even at its height, the movement was relatively small and confined mostly to extremists. Most representatives of the Black community in the United States seem committed to altering the social system to provide Blacks with equal political, economic, and educational opportunity; and those who see separation as desirable view it as a means to inclusion in the power matrix of society and thus only as a temporary condition.

A far more serious threat to cultural diversity and the ideal of cultural pluralism comes from the majority segment of society. Historically, the evidence is clear: The dominant majority has taken one of two positions in the treatment of culturally different populations, either exclusion and exploitation or assimilation. Thus, some groups, notably Blacks, Hispanics, and Native Americans, were segregated from the mainstream of society and denied access to the advantages of social institutions. When these groups and the majority of other non-Anglo-Saxon Protestants have been included, it has been with the understanding that "foreign" ways be abandoned and replaced by "American" (i.e., Anglo-Saxon) ways, as evidenced by the strong nativistic feelings, legislation, and policies that developed during the first quarter of the twentieth century. These very sentiments forced the development of case law revealed in our analysis of the courts and cultural pluralism. Indeed, while the legal precedents that grew out of these cases support equal opportunity, by enforcing assimilationist policies they often contradict the requirement of valuing cultural diversity.

The American commitment to cultural pluralism cannot be judged on historical grounds alone, though there seems to be a historical commitment to protect religious pluralism and tolerate cultural diversity in the private segments of society as long as no threat is posed to the general social welfare. Perhaps more important is the current support for cultural pluralism. While past commitment in the United States to the pluralistic ideal is suspect, it is within the realm of possibility that, as a society, we are now willing to reconsider the ideal. The resurgence of ethnic consciousness, the tendency of government to recognize ethnic claims and demands, and the advent of social programs supporting pluralism such as the funding of ethnic heritage studies and multicultural and bilingual education all stand in support of this. In the future, we may look back only to see these efforts as a sporadic fluctuation in a long stream supporting cultural homogeneity. If we move to ward embracing pluralism in a more positive way or if the opportunity to move in this direction exists at present, we may yet fully meet the conditions of a culturally pluralistic society. Only time will tell.

THE PLURALISTIC IDEAL FOR THE UNITED STATES

Assuming we value cultural pluralism as a social ideal and are willing to commit ourselves to attaining it, we are faced with identifying which of the alternatives presented in Chapter 3 are worth working for. Presumably we can eliminate the nonpluralistic ideologies of assimilation, amalgamation, and the open society from consideration, though the individual autonomy of the open society may have considerable appeal to many. In fact, it is probable that in advocating cultural pluralism, some simply desire to eliminate prejudice and discrimination on the basis of race, religion, and ethnicity from social situations and do not implicitly or explicitly support cultural diversity. Be this as it may, our concern is with those ideological alternatives that meet our four stated conditions. Our problem arises when we realize that a number of alternatives fall within this category and are quite different from one another in respect to specific goals, social organization, the role of government, and educational program. In an attempt to shed some light on the question before us, it may be useful to assess each alternative for its social fit or applicability to the contemporary American situation.

Classical Cultural Pluralism

The emphasis in classical cultural pluralism is on maintaining the integrity and viability of the cultural group as a relatively autonomous, intact, social collective. A high degree of separation and cultural uniqueness will be present. Government will recognize the legitimacy of the group as both a cultural and political entity. Education will for the most part be under the control of each group and will be designed for the socialization and enculturation of children, thus ensuring the transmission of the culture from one generation to the next and the survival of the group. Two forms of social organization are considered with this model: segregated pluralism, in which each group exists more or less within its own geographic region; and integrated pluralism, in which, even though residential segregation may exist, members of different groups can be found living in ethnic communities that repeat themselves across a wide geographic area.

The main advantage of classical cultural pluralism is in the ability of groups to protect and perpetuate themselves. This is particularly true for segregated pluralism, where both primary and secondary relationships will remain almost exclusively within the cultural group, thereby keeping cultural diffusion at a minimum as well as reducing cultural attrition due to intermarriage and the surge of other cultural ways. Even with integrated pluralism, primary relationships will remain within the group, and only a minimum degree of cross-cultural interaction at the secondary levels will be tolerated, with group cohesiveness being reinforced through the development of a strong sense of identity and a network of social sanctions.

The security of diverse cultural groups in society is not achieved without cost. Critics of classical cultural pluralism argue that it is pluralistic for groups only and that the opportunities and freedom of individuals are sacrificed. That is, because of the closed nature of groups, individuals are restricted from mobility outside the group both by constraints imposed by the group and by the unaccepting attitudes of other groups. This seems clearly to contradict the stated goals of many ethnic groups within the United States. In particular, many white ethnics, even while maintaining ethnic communities, clubs, and churches, enjoy a high degree of social mobility and cross-cultural interaction and see no advantage in what they perceive to be a step backward. Thus, individuals from Polish, Greek, Italian, Irish, and Slavic backgrounds can enjoy the advantages of their ethnic heritage but do not wish to be trapped or confined by it. The same case is made by some spokesmen for ethnic minority groups. For example, while as a group Blacks have not achieved the level of acceptance and mobility that white ethnics have, this is generally the expressed goal—even those arguing for separation see inclusion as the ultimate outcome. For Hispanics and Native Americans, goal agreement is less clear. Some spokesmen for these groups seem to argue for greater inclusion, while others emphasize the protection of the culture and the viability of the cultural community. Regardless of the emphasis, most will agree that the individual should have some choice in the matter, and this is precisely the weak point of classical cultural pluralism.

From the foregoing discussion it may seem apparent that classical cultural pluralism is not acceptable as the model around which to build American pluralism, but we should not be too quick to draw this conclusion. There are groups within the United States and its trust territories for whom the model might be appropriate. Consider the Amish. They came to the United States in the 1700s seeking relief from religious persecution. Since that time, Old Order Amish have maintained agricultural religious communities largely separate from the American mainstream. They use horsedrawn carriages; speak in the Pennsylvania German dialect; have a distinctive plain and simple dress for both men and women; and have taboos against electricity, telephones, automobiles, and tractors with pneumatic tires. Further, no formal education beyond the elementary grades is a rule of life, and high school or college diplomas are forbidden.[2] The primary function of the Amish school is not education in the narrow sense of instruction but the creation of a learning environment coterminous with Amish culture. The Amish school atmosphere supports the values and attitudes of the separated community, and individuals are socialized to develop their skills and personalities within the small community. There is sharp discontinuity for the Amish child who is removed from the Amish community and put into the consolidated school in the larger society.[3] Given the separatist goals and the successful nature of the culture, then, is not classical cultural pluralism based on segregated pluralism an appropriate model for the Old Older Amish?

Critics may still argue that, as simple and romantic as the Amish way of life appears, the fact remains that Amish children, because of the parochial nature of their education and the limited nature of outside experiences, lack the individual freedom and opportunity to choose beyond the Amish culture. Thus, their potential as human beings is limited—their destiny is chosen by their parents.

This argument has a certain amount of appeal and logic behind it. Its flaw is its failure to recognize that choice is not absolute but always exists in some limiting cultural context. That is, choices are always confined to a limited set of alternatives contained within a particular sociocultural complex. Given one complex with a particular set of norms, values, expectations, and alternatives, one set of choices will exist; given another complex with a different set of norms, values, expectations, and alternatives, a different set of choices will exist. One cannot be said to be better than the other; they are simply different. Thus, freedom, choice, and opportunity can be assessed and evaluated only from within the normative structure of the particular culture in question. One cannot legitimately evaluate and criticize the opportunities within one cultural system on the basis of the norms of another system or model.*

In application to our example of the Amish, we must realize that both the Amish culture and the dominant mainstream culture are self-contained systems, each with its own ontological and axiological perspectives. For the Amish, life is to be simple and directed toward salvation. For the dominant mainstream, individualism, self-reliance, and materialism are stressed. Alternatives and choices exist within each system. Amish children, just like children growing up in a middle-class suburb, are free to determine their destinies within the bounds defined by their culture. In this sense, cultural directives can be likened to a road map: Once the destination is known, by providing direction they free rather than restrict the individual. It is important to note that our particular preoccupation with freedom and choice is itself a manifestation of a cultural value. Thus, when we claim that the opportunities of Amish children are limited, we are speaking from the limited perspective of Protestant tradition and from a particular conception of freedom in which individual autonomy is important.

If classical cultural pluralism is an applicable model for the Amish, are there other groups for whom it would be appropriate? The three characteristics that make the Amish suitable for the model are (1) their relative isolation as a group, (2) the viability of the culture as a separate and autonomous community, and (3) the desire of the group to voluntarily segregate itself and maintain its separation. Are there other groups with these characteristics? While the Amish are perhaps the leading example, there are other candidates.

One possible group is the Hopi. Occupying the same geographic area for centuries, the Hopi lay claim to the distinction of maintaining the oldest continuously inhabited community in the United States. Now to avoid any initial misunderstanding, it should be made clear that the Hopi, as well as other groups we will consider, do not all maintain the same traditional life style. Individuals range along the entire continuum from relatively "culture pure" to assimilated. A number of individuals, for example, hold professional positions and/or live in metropolitan areas and visit the mesa villages only occasionally. Similarly, the Hopi villages vary in their degree of commitment to traditional ways, some rejecting the white man's world almost entirely and others borrowing from it freely. Nevertheless, a number of viable and

---

* This is not to say that some cultures are not more restrictive or confining than others, especially toward different people within their boundaries, or that we endorse a complete sense of cultural relativism. These are separate issues. Rather, the point is that different cultural systems must be seen as parallel to one other if we are to avoid comparing apples and oranges.

voluntarily separated Hopi communities flourish in the high deserts of northeastern Arizona. The life style is distinctly Hopi, as is the primary spoken language, and both primary and secondary relationships are almost entirely culture bound. While the press of the white and technological world is felt, there appears to be no immediate threat to the stability of the Hopi culture and identity. Thus, the argument that a Hopi education would prepare children for a disappearing way of life and its corollary that we should educate Hopi youth to assume positions outside the reservation are weak. This, of course, does not mean that we should in any way enforce the maintenance of the Hopi way of life or restrict the mobility of individuals, but that our purpose, consistent with the model of classical cultural pluralism, should be to recognize the legitimacy, viability, and independence of Hopi culture as an alternative way of life in the United States.

Native American groups such as the Navajo, the Pueblo Indians of New Mexico, and the Indians and Eskimos of Alaska also seem to fit the pattern. If we extend our analysis outside the fifty United States to our trust territories, such as Puerto Rico, Guam, and the Mariana Islands, where we maintain educational institutions and highly influence general educational policy, we have another set of candidates. Because the individual circumstances of these cultures varies, each must be considered independently. To the extent that they remain removed from the mainstream of American culture and wish to continue this relationship, however, a model of classical cultural pluralism with segregated pluralism may be the ideological model most appropriate to guide educational policy and program development. Other ideological models that emphasize a high degree of interaction among groups, integration, and a need to develop and share a significant common culture may not be consistent with the sociocultural realities of these groups, their goals, or the concept of cultural pluralism.

There may yet be another kind of group besides those characterized by segregated pluralism to consider under the ideal of classical cultural pluralism. Following the desegregation of San Francisco schools, a group of Chinese Americans requested of the courts that they be allowed to maintain their segregated schools in order to protect the Chinese American culture, identity, and language from outside influences. This effort to remain segregated and rely on their own institutions was also made by a group of Mexican Americans following the desegregation of Denver schools. These events suggest that even within a state of integrated pluralism (but where residential segregation exists), a model of classical cultural pluralism may be considered.

In the case of San Francisco, the Chinese, by means of voluntary segregation, have created and long maintained their own 'Chinatown," which they consider to be a viable cultural community. Indeed, it is possible to spend one's entire life in Chinatown, speak only Chinese, and still have one's economic, social, and personal needs met in a satisfactory manner. For many individuals of Chinese ancestry, both primary and secondary relationships remain exclusively within the culture. For others, even while secondary relationships include interaction with individuals from outside the community, their loyalties clearly remain within the cultural community. Thus, in the course of work, say as a shop or restaurant owner or employee, an individual may deal with the general public on a daily basis but never leave Chinatown, or individuals may leave the community to take advantage of the wide offerings of a large city but, upon completing their business, return again. Of course, many individuals in and from San Francisco's Chinatown extend both primary and secondary levels of interaction far beyond the cultural community. Given the social context in which we are considering the ideal, this mobility is perfectly consistent with classical cultural pluralism. It must be remembered that we are not considering adopting the ideal as a guide for the society in general but for specific cultural groups. In the case of San Francisco's Chinatown and perhaps other viable cultural communities, such as some Mexican American communities, the issue is whether the culture should be allowed to voluntarily maintain a high degree of separation and autonomy if it so desires or whether some other, more "liberal" conception of cultural pluralism *requiring* a greater degree of integration should prevail. If we should opt for the ideal of classical cultural pluralism, viable cultural communities that pose no threat to the general welfare of society would be allowed to maintain a high degree of autonomy and separation and to transmit their culture from one generation to the next without interference from the greater society. Individuals who found the cultural community too limiting or were unable to meet their needs within its boundaries would be free to venture out to the degree they found necessary. In order to make this possible, individuals within the culture would have to learn basic skills for coping in the larger society (e.g., the English language), but the cultural community would not be *forced* to socialize its children to assume positions outside the community.

To summarize, we have seen that as *the* ideal to guide social policy, classical cultural pluralism is unacceptable. Many cultural, racial, ethnic, and religious groups in the United States currently maintain a life style inconsistent with it and desire a social organization with greater intergroup mobility and interaction than is possible within the ideal. There are also subcultures for whom the ideal seems quite appropriate, in particular groups that are voluntarily segregated and wish to remain so in order to maintain and perpetuate a life style different from that of the mainstream culture. Thus, for groups with no desire and no need to prepare their members to assume positions in the mainstream culture, the ideal of classical cultural pluralism may be appropriate.

Modified Cultural Pluralism

The ideal of modified cultural pluralism places a much greater emphasis on a common culture held among the diverse groups in society and on interaction between members of different groups than does classical cultural pluralism. Groups maintain a certain degree of distinctiveness but also see themselves as belonging and contributing to the larger American culture and society in a significant way. In the political-social-economic arena, individuals are represented and lobby as group members, each group getting its fair share of social rewards. Education is designed to develop tolerance of, respect for, and understanding of cultural diversity but also to develop a unique common American culture.

The advantages of modified cultural pluralism as a social ideal are in the balance between group identity and security on the one hand and individual mobility and opportunity on the other. Because cultural diversity is officially recognized and accepted, groups need not fear for their well-being. In fact, as groups lobby for special interests, there will be a tendency for group identity and solidarity to increase. On the other hand, an individual's cultural identity will be largely irrelevant in secondary relationships. Thus, an individual's opportunities for employment, housing, education, and the like will be based on achievement and not on cultural attributes. But the consequences of the constant interplay and exchange among different groups will be the constant modification of the group. This is not to say that the group's political identity is in any way threatened but to acknowledge that the cultural behaviors, beliefs, values, and attitudes of the group will change and adapt in response to social demands and influences. This may not be any great problem for groups in society not concerned with perpetuating a specific traditional culture, but for groups that do have such a concern, this consequence may be seen as a distinct disadvantage.

The ideal of modified cultural pluralism appears to complement the positions of several cultural groups within society. White ethnic groups have undergone substantial changes toward the development of a common American culture since the first immigrants arrived in the United States, but they have not disappeared or lost their distinctiveness. Particularly in the large urban areas of the Midwest and East, Greek, Italian, Polish, Jewish, and Irish neighborhoods are evident. Even in the nation's suburbs and the West, where ethnic neighborhoods are not as common, churches, clubs, and social organizations serve as the nucleus for ethnic associations. For the most part the cultural characteristics of these ethnic groups no longer resemble those from which they originated, but the groups remain significantly different and tend to identify themselves ethnically and act as political entities. Politicians and pollsters have long recognized the political significance of these groups. The recent resurgence of ethnic consciousness and demands that they be included as groups in educational and cultural programs is further evidence that ethnic identity is still important. In terms of the goals of white ethnics, there seems to be no desire to move toward the greater autonomy or separation characterized by classical cultural pluralism. In fact, the resurgence of ethnic identity among these groups is in part a result of efforts to protect the relatively advantaged hard-won positions in the mainstream culture from inroads being made by minority groups and an uncertain economy. White ethnics, then, see themselves as part of a larger American social, economic, political, and cultural system that is worth defending and participating in. Further, ethnic identity remains important for many individuals personally and for the groups as a means to engage the social system.

Modified cultural pluralism also appears to be appropriate for many Blacks. Because slavery so disrupted the African cultures Black people brought with them, contemporary Black culture heavily reflects the Black experience in the United States. As would be expected under these circumstances, while Blacks have developed a unique identifiable and rich culture enabling them to adapt to a hostile social environment, with a few notable exceptions, as a group most accept the advantages of the mainstream culture. What has frustrated many contemporary Blacks has not been attempts of the dominant majority to integrate them but a refusal to allow them to participate in society as equals. Thus, the continued evolution of culture in response to the social circumstances characteristic of modified pluralism presents no problem for Blacks. On the other hand, there is no danger of Black identity and solidarity being weakened in the near future. Blacks pioneered the current resurgence of ethnic identity in the United States and have been the main force propelling the ideal of cultural pluralism directly before us. Further, Blacks have demonstrated time and time again their willingness and ability to function as a political interest group.

Other groups for which the ideal of modified cultural pluralism may be acceptable but for which it does not apply as completely are Hispanics and Native Americans. It is important to note that both groups are themselves heterogenous: "Hispanic" is a broad category that includes Mexican Americans, Latinos (Spanish-speaking people from Central and South America), Cubans and Puerto Ricans; and the category "Native American" includes all the different American Indian tribes. If we emphasize here the more inclusive generic labels "Hispanic" and "Native American," not particularly concerning ourselves with cultural qualities or issues, and concentrate on treating each collective as a single special-interest group—a political collective—the ideal of modified cultural pluralism works best. There are advantages to be gained by these groups' seeking recognition as single cohesive units; as unified political collectives, rather than individual subgroups, they command more power and thus will be more effective in their competition with other groups for social rewards and representation. The difficulty with this arrangement lies in the heterogeneity of the groups that form each of these collectives. While as political interest groups they share many of the same traits and goals, in some important ways they are quite different.

Some Native American tribes have their native culture intact, while others are highly assimilated; some inhabit remote areas, while others are adjacent to large white populations; and some have a relatively secure economic base, while others are almost totally dependent on government aid. Similar differences can be found among Hispanics. Mainland Puerto Ricans as a group are a culturally different, economically deprived people living in a state of residentially segregated integrated pluralism in close proximity to other cultural and ethnic groups. Mexican Americans, on the other hand, are concentrated in the Southwest, and within this concentration further diversity can be found. Some Mexican American communities are in urban areas; others are largely rural; still others are migrant in nature. There are also class, cultural, political, and social differences. For some communities, the central concern may be preservation of the culture and a desire for greater autonomy; for others, culture may be of secondary importance, with economic considerations taking priority; and still others may see political issues as most salient. Cubans who immigrated in the 1950s and 60s, for the most part, have secured economic and political security and have managed to develop and maintain an advantaged life style. However, the most recent immigrants are of a lower social class and have not established themselves on the mainland.

There are, then, both advantages and disadvantages in adopting the ideal of modified cultural pluralism for Hispanics and Native Americans. For some members of these groups it seems to fit nicely; for others, another ideal might be more appropriate. Though it would be most efficient to treat Hispanics and Native Americans as single unitary political collectives, it might well be advantageous to adopt a flexible approach with these groups that would allow them to be recognized as single political collectives for some purposes (e.g. affirmative action) but treated individually for others (e.g., ethnic studies programs).

Some groups seem not to fit the ideal of modified cultural pluralism at all. A number of groups (e.g., the Amish) require greater autonomy and segregation than the modified ideal can offer, and others
would find it too confining. Members of some groups, for example,
tend to avoid representing themselves or lobbying as a special-interest
group, preferring a low profile, and either compete in the marketplace
as individuals or find support among themselves. The ethnic group
popularly known as WASPs, or Anglos, seems to be one such group.
One characteristic of this group, in fact, is that its members tend to
define other people as "ethnic," but they refrain from applying the
label to themselves. They prefer to think of themselves as individuals
and define their identity on the basis of class and status variables such
as occupation, education, and income and on the basis of personal
achievements and concerns. With this frame of reference, WASPs view
the tendency of other ethnic groups to act as political interest groups as
illegitimate and troublesome. From the WASP point of view, cultural
heritage should be strictly a personal and private matter, and individuals entering the sociopolitical arena should do so as members of
special-interest groups formed around social issues, not on the basis of
ethnic heritage. Thus, though WASPs in many ways act as an ethnic
group, if they supported pluralism at all, they would be more inclined
to dynamic pluralism than modified cultural pluralism.

Yet another class of individuals challenges the application of the
ideal of modified cultural pluralism. Milton Gordon suggests that certain people form special communities where identity is developed
around ties other than ethnic ties.[4] Intellectuals and artists tend to be
this way, each group made up of individuals from various cultural
backgrounds, but these backgrounds are seen as irrelevant to group
membership and identity. Identity is formed around some other set of
presumed common characteristics. For the art community, it may be a
commitment to aesthetic expression and the assumed life style that develops around it. For intellectuals, it may be inquisitiveness or the pursuit of knowledge. Regardless of the actual characteristics of these
groups, the important point is that their members come from different
cultural backgrounds but tend to identify and define themselves on the
basis of some set of qualities that does not include ethnic heritage. Because of this, a social ideal that acknowledged people in terms of some
cultural affiliation would be inappropriate.

What, then, is our judgment of modified cultural pluralism? Like
classical cultural pluralism, it seems to fit some groups better than
others. Many individuals in the United States, such as white ethnics,
already function within the scope of the ideal's social arrangements;
and members of some other groups, such as Blacks and some segments
of the Hispanic and Native American communities, aspire to be more

fully included within its operative boundaries. But groups exist for whom the ideal does not apply, some seeing it as a threat to cultural survival and others seeing it as too restrictive and confining because of the imposition of ethnic affiliation. To accommodate the different kinds of groups within our social structure and their differing goals, perhaps a greater emphasis on choice would provide the working ideal we are seeking.

Cultural Pluralism as Voluntary Ethnic Choice

Freedom and autonomy, popular themes within the political ideology of the United States, are emphasized in the "new" pluralism. With these emphases, cultural pluralism per se is not a means either to protect the cultural integrity of groups or to distribute political power and social rewards equitably among different ethnic groups. While these may result, the key thrust is to guarantee individuals the right and opportunity to make of their cultural heritage and identity whatever they desire. Within this ideal, an individual can choose to be associated with the interests of a cultural or ethnic group, choose not to be associated at all, or choose some position in between. Individuals, then, learn to tolerate diversity but also to respect the individual's wishes for group association. In school, students learn of group differences, the contributions of the different groups to society, and the importance of ethnic affiliation to many people. They also learn the danger of stereotyping and of responding to an individual as a member of a group before learning about that individual as a person. Students further acquire the skills and information to allow them to understand and define their own ethnicity and to choose what role it will play in their relationship with society.

On first appearance, the ideal of cultural pluralism as free ethnic choice meets the diversity of multicultural needs of the United States perfectly. Individuals who desire to voluntarily segregate themselves and maintain alternative subcultures can do so, and those not as concerned with the preservation of traditional culture can associate for political and social advantage or can for purposes of identity choose to disassociate themselves from their ethnic heritage altogether. Individuals can also associate themselves in different ways in different contexts and at different points in time. Thus, one may choose in professional contexts to minimize one's ethnic heritage but in social affairs to rely on it heavily. Or at specific points in their life individuals may desire either to emphasize or to minimize the importance of their ethnic heritages.

The opportunity and ability to choose the meaning of one's ethnic heritage and the role it will play in one's life, as appealing as it may be, is not without its difficulties. These difficulties arise out of the potential conflict between the interests of the individual and those of the group. A more careful look at what choice entails suggests that when individuals are able to exercise free ethnic choice, a threat to the stability of ethnic and cultural groups exists from two different sources; conversely, when groups' interests are allowed to prevail, the autonomy of the individual is threatened.

When we think of free choice existing for some individual in a particular context, we normally assume that there are no external restraints blocking the individual from exercising options or forcing the adoption of one position over another. Thus, if an otherwise qualified individual is forced to attend certain schools, is channeled into certain occupations, is treated socially in a particular manner because of ethnic background, or is denied by the dominant group the opportunity to practice the ways of his or her native culture, we are justified in claiming that free choice has been denied in these matters. Recognizing this, those advocating the ideal of free ethnic choice have demanded a relaxing of the social barriers that have traditionally restricted the mobility of individuals in society on the basis of ethnic criteria or that have made mobility contingent upon assimilation. Applying the same principle, advocates of the ideal have also recognized the danger for the individual of restrictions emanating from that person's own cultural group, and here we find the first source of potential conflict. In order to become a more effective political lobby, a group may apply pressure on its individual members to conform. This limits the individual's autonomy and is illegitimate from the standpoint of the ideal of free ethnic choice.

But the freedom gained by the individual is made at the expense of the group: Groups can function as political lobbies only when they can present themselves as a united front; if disagreements exist within the group or it appears that because of a lack of solidarity the group cannot make good its threats or promises, the power structure with which it is negotiating need not take it seriously. Thus, though the ideal first appears to protect the interests of both individuals who choose to collectively assert their ethnic identities and those who choose to minimize their ethnicity, to the extent that the latter exercise their choice the collective is weakened, and to the extent that the former exercise their choice individual autonomy is weakened. It will be recalled from our earlier discussion that this was the basis of one criticism of pluralism.

The second conflict between the individual's free choice and the stability of the group is rooted in the actual process of making a choice. Besides the absence of possibly limiting external restraints, choice involves the ability of the individual to recognize and consider different alternatives. Thus, an individual raised in a restrictive and sheltered environment and unaware of any other options life may have to offer will be unable to choose an alternative life style. Similarly, an individual brought up to dogmatically hold certain beliefs and values and adhere to a particular way of life because of indoctrination, conditioning, or manipulation may find alternatives beyond choice. In recognizing that for choice to be able to occur an individual must be intellectually able to consider various alternatives, we see that individuals must become aware of their own ethnicity, of the values, beliefs, feelings, and behaviors that they grow up with and take for granted, because only through such an awareness and understanding does an individual become capable of deciding the meaning these are to assume in his or her life. This requires, within this ideal, an educational curriculum that exposes individuals to a wide variety of experiences, to a questioning and reevaluation of values and beliefs, and to the development of the skills necessary to function successfully in a variety of situations.

But if this kind of curriculum leads to greater autonomy for individuals, it also threatens the stability of traditional cultures. The survival of many groups depends upon the ability to transmit the culture— beliefs, values, feelings, and customs—from one generation to the next; to encourage children to question these traditions and experience alternatives is to invite disaster. Both the Amish and Chinese Americans recognized this in their respective court actions designed to retain a limited educational environment. Thus, to adopt an ideal of free ethnic choice for individuals is almost certainly to deny pluralism for some groups. If groups are to have the choice to determine their own destinies, they must be able to ensure a commitment on the part of each successive generation to the group's ways. This will entail an enculturation that relies in part on indoctrination, conditioning, and manipulation. Such is the way of cultural transmission.

To summarize, free ethnic choice as the ideal of cultural pluralism has both advantages and limitations. Its greatest advantages can be found in extending the democratic ideal of individual choice and autonomy to the domain of ethnicity. Many individuals already find themselves in this favored position, and many others who currently find themselves restricted by either the dominant culture or their own cultural group would benefit from its further application. But to impose the ideal indiscriminately to all cultural ethnic groups without regard to their special circumstances would almost certainly do damage to the groups. For while autonomy for the individual is preserved in a most satisfactory manner, pluralism for groups, particularly those groups that wish to voluntarily segregate themselves in order to maintain a traditional culture significantly different from the mainstream, is threatened.

Cultural Pluralism as Integration

Integration as a social policy grew out of the social conditions that generated the contemporary interest in cultural pluralism. As a policy, it sought to provide better opportunities for disenfranchized racial groups to benefit from the advantages of mainstream society. As an ideology of cultural pluralism, integration retains this focus and is based on the belief that this state of affairs can be reached and maintained only if the diverse groups in society are perceived and experienced as interrelated components of the same society existing in an organic relationship. That is, while each group retains its distinctive identity, the identity of each is incomplete until understood as a complement to the whole of society. Within this framework, the institutionalized mixing of diverse groups is desirable, and cross-racial friendship and racial interdependency are expected to develop. The expected result will not be a complete obliteration of ethnic and racial distinctiveness but the expansion of opportunities for members of both minority groups and the dominant majority. The decision to live in ethnic and social neighborhoods, for example, will become the choice of the individual and will no longer result from exploitation and discrimination. Schools will be racially integrated at all levels whenever possible; interaction between members of diverse groups will be encouraged; and differences will be downplayed and commonalities and interdependency emphasized. Within the curriculum, historical and contemporary strife and competition between groups will be of less importance than the development of and commitment to a common culture. Schools will remain neutral in the development of a specific cultural identity, leaving such tasks to the community and the home.

When applied to contemporary society, the ideal of cultural pluralism as integration fits best those groups that are behaviorally similar to the dominant culture but because of racial prejudice have been involuntarily segregated and disallowed full participation in society. In particular, it applies to Black Americans but also extends to members of other ethnic minorities who, against their wishes, have been relegated to marginal positions in society. The key advantage to this ideology is that it will loosen the hold racism has on our culture and thereby extend equal opportunity to all members of society, regardless of race or ethnicity. No one can argue that such an achievement is not sorely needed or long overdue. In this sense, the ideal unquestionably is justified in playing some role in the pluralistic nature of our society.

But to say that the ideal is compelling for some segment of society is not to say that it should be adopted as the overall guiding ideology. As *the* ideal it is inadequate for at least two reasons. First, a number of sociocultural groups in society are already well integrated into the social fabric and have other agendas. For example, Novak suggests that white ethnics tend to be concerned with being recognized as contributing ethnic groups to society and with developing cultural self-awareness.[5] Similarly, social minority groups such as women, homosexuals, the handicapped, and other contracultural groups are well integrated into society but nevertheless suffer discrimination. Members of these groups would profit from a broad interpretation of the ideal of cultural pluralism that would include the protection and tolerance of a wide variety of life styles and belief systems. Their agenda focuses not on integration or even self-awareness but on acceptance and equal treatment. Of course, the goals of both kinds of groups are not incompatible with those of integration. We might argue that inasmuch as the groups are integrated and share in the benefits of society, they approximate the ideal; and to the extent that they are deprived of the rewards of society, the ideal has not yet been fully met. The point remains that for groups that are already integrated, the ideal of cultural pluralism as integration ignores their ideological concerns.

Another and more important limitation of cultural pluralism as integration is that it fails to consider groups that wish to remain voluntarily segregated from mainstream society or to participate in society only marginally. The adoption of forced integration would violate the spirit of pluralism for these groups. Thus, as we have seen, people like the Amish, some Native Americans, and perhaps some segments of the Asian and Hispanic populations of the United States wish to maintain a high degree of separation and distinctiveness and therefore fall outside the province of integration. The ideal also fails to adequately guide policy governing people under the trust of the United States for whom, because of their geographical separation and the stability of their own cultures, the prospects of integration into our mainstream society remain slight. It is even conceivable that segments of the Black population, for whom integration seems most appropriate, might choose to develop highly autonomous communities where cross-cultural interaction is confined primarily to secondary relationships. The question becomes, should we adopt a policy that mitigates against this possibility or allow the decision to rest with individual communities? The ideal of cultural pluralism as integration has drawbacks.

Cultural Pluralism as Separation

In its strongest form the ideology of separation is not within the boundaries of pluralism. It will be recalled that diversity within society is a necessary condition of cultural pluralism. To the extent that groups wish to withdraw from society and establish an independent polity of their own, they violate this condition. This need not concern us here, for there seem to be no viable groups within our present society that seriously take this position. Perhaps the closest we come to finding this extremist view is in a small but vocal radical element in Puerto Rican politics.

The more moderate ideological form of separatism rejects the permanent and complete separation of racial minorities from the rest of society but also rejects integration as a means of extending equal opportunity. Not until minority groups have developed a position of power based on group solidarity and political and economic strength will they be able to participate in society on an equal basis. Integration prior to their attaining a position of strength, according to this view, will result in the continued domination and exploitation of minorities by the dominant majority. Prior to full participation in society, then, minority groups must separate themselves from the racist and exploitive majority and develop parallel institutions. During the separation a strong sense of identity and cohesiveness will develop, as will a relative degree of self-reliance. Once able to bargain from a position of strength, minority groups will move toward a more full integration into society. The ultimate goal is full and equal participation in society based on a sharing of power. Group distinctiveness and identity will remain and will support the group's function as a political lobby and interest group. Education is very important at the separation stage. Schools will have the dual role of developing a strong sense of group identity and commitment and of preparing individuals to assume productive and supporting roles that contribute to the overall strength of the group. Schools will be locally controlled and will incorporate a strong ethnic studies program.

It is interesting that the ideology of cultural pluralism as separation is designed to benefit the same groups as the ideology of integration. It is a means to secure a greater degree of opportunity for involuntarily segregated and exploited minority groups that share a high degree of cultural similarity with the dominant majority. In this sense it is especially appropriate for Blacks and the more behaviorally assimilated members of other minorities, such as Hispanics and Native Americans. The key difference between the ideologies of integration and separation is the means to achieve the desired end. If we were to modify the ultimate goal of separatism away from power inclusion and toward a position more skeptical of the benefits of joining the dominant majority, however, its appropriateness as a model might extend to other groups. For example, if we were to emphasize separation for the purpose of developing and maintaining a life style and institutions parallel to the dominant society, the ideology would assume the characteristics of classical cultural pluralism and apply to groups such as the Amish and in varying degrees to some Native American, Asian, and Hispanic communities. Within this modified formulation, groups would remain separate; develop a strong sense of ethnic identity and cohesion; and develop parallel social, economic, political, and cultural institutions capable of neutralizing attempts by the dominant majority to discriminate and exploit. They would not ultimately integrate into mainstream society but would maintain alternative life styles.

As a primary ideology of cultural pluralism for the United States, separatism shares with other models the problems of being too limited in its application. Groups already integrated and participating in the power structures of society will not find the model appropriate. Similarly, if power inclusion and ultimate integration are retained as desired goals, groups wishing to maintain voluntary segregation will not accept it. And if the ideal is modified toward classical cultural pluralism to include groups wishing to maintain voluntary segregation, it loses its impact for involuntarily segregated groups that desire full and equal participation in society. Thus, the ideal of separation remains as a possibly useful strategy on which to base a model of cultural pluralism for some groups, but as the one best ideal it is insufficient.

Dynamic Pluralism

Dynamic pluralism begins with the judgment that cultural pluralism, to the extent that it emphasizes diversity based upon cultural, ethnic, and racial variables, is too narrowly conceived. As an ideal, dynamic pluralism recognizes cultural heritage and ethnic identity as the foundations for the values and commitments that serve as the basis for the formation of other special-interest groups. While individuals must be raised in some cultural community, their commitments must finally lie with the best interest of the larger community. Based on the method of intelligence, "communities" of interest will form, being composed of people who perceive social problems in a common way. The life span of the "communities" may be relatively short or may endure over time, depending on the nature of the problem and the interests of the members. In any case, the special-interest groups through which individuals address social problems and participate in policy are constantly in a dynamic state; they rise and fall with changing social conditions. An education tailored to support dynamic pluralism would impart a value for a diversity of ideas, values, and ways of confronting the problems of life. The ultimate value taught, however, would be a commitment to the method of intelligence for solving social problems.

The appropriateness of dynamic pluralism as the ideology of cultural pluralism for the United States must be appraised in a slightly different manner than the other ideological models considered to this point. It is not offered as an answer to the extant needs of American social groups; rather, it recasts these problems in the context of the ideological theory of democracy. Ethnicity and its attendant problems comprise an important variable in the complex of modern societies, but ethnicity does not comprise the whole; in the final analysis it may take a back seat to other variables. Thus, by this formulation, cultural pluralism involves more than just the special interests of cultural, racial, and ethnic groups in society. It involves questions of moral principles, questions involving the organization and structure of society, and, at bottom, questions about the goals of society; these are questions in which we all have a stake.

Many social problems go far beyond the boundaries drawn on the basis of ethnic group interests. But it must also be realized that dynamic pluralism is founded in a particular ideology of democratic literalism that assumes a highly integrated society and the establishment of a fairly broad common culture. It further assumes a particular way of conceptualizing and solving social problems, a process based in the scientific and democratic traditions of the West. In the light of the dominant cultural traditions of the United States, all this can probably be considered appropriate. But again, the ideology assumes that what is appropriate for the dominant mainstream society is appropriate for all. It fails to allow for different life styles based on what may amount to be radically different perceptions of the world. If all groups are expected to fall within the boundaries of dynamic pluralism and if the individual members of these groups are prepared to participate in such a society, the potential for substantively different life styles will be highly limited. It is for this reason that it is inappropriate as an overarching ideal for all of society.

There are two other grounds on which dynamic pluralism might be questioned, though these are by no means certain. First, by characterizing ethnic groups as primarily political interest groups the ideal may be underestimating the strength and importance of ethnicity in the modern world. While most students of ethnicity are not ready to believe that the phenomenon is rooted in some primordial condition of humankind, they also no longer believe that it is simply a primitive form of political organization that will give way to modernization. (Refer to Chapter 2.) Ethnicity, in spite of modernization, continues to be an important force throughout the world. In the United States, no less than in other countries, many people continue to define themselves, their interests, and their associations in accordance with ethnic criteria. To require people to place the interests of the larger and necessarily more impersonal community ahead of one's ethnic or personal interests and to rely on the objective and rational processes of science rather than the subjective, emotional, and nonrational side of humans so often associated with group loyalty and commitment may be asking more than is humanly possible. We may be overestimating the discursive (i.e., rational and scientific), side of humans. In view of our sociocultural history—the force of ethnicity/nationality, the endurance of religion, and our fascination with the arts and other nonrational modes of expression—there is every reason to believe that the nondiscursive nature of humans is at least as compelling. Thus, even if we desire the social arrangements entailed by dynamic pluralism, it may well be that the best we will attain is a modest approximation.

The final objection to dynamic pluralism is that with its emphasis on the dynamic nature of groups and on concern for the problems of the larger community, the commitment and resources needed to address racism and other problems confronting minority groups may be diminished. The reasoning underlying this fear is that at any given time there is some limited quantity of social resources and human energy available to address social needs; the greater the number of groups seen as legitimate contenders for these resources, the greater the likelihood that they will be distributed across a broad base rather than concentrated on minority problems. Further, there is the fear that because the best interests of the larger social community take precedence over the interests of any particular group and because minority groups are only weakly represented in the power base of the larger community, there will be a tendency to address the interests of the dominant majority at the expense of those of the minorities.

The practical effects of dynamic pluralism that this criticism describes are well within the realm of possibility. This is not, however, a true criticism of the ideal but rather of the commitment of society as a whole to address the problems of minority groups. In principle, discrimination and racism could be considered a threat to the best interests of society and thus their elimination could become a national priority. The fact that this has not occurred is evidence that other communities of interest perceive other problems as of equal or greater importance. Of course it is this balancing of interests within a pluralistic society that is offered as one of the strengths of cultural pluralism. As we have pointed out, however, neither "best interest" or balance is always subjected to the method of intelligence featured in dynamic pluralism. In the end, it will make little difference to minority groups whether a faillure to address their needs results from a lack of national commitment or an inadequacy of the ideal.

In sum, dynamic pluralism as the ideal of cultural pluralism fails to adequately address the pluralistic nature of the United States. Though it offers a broad and useful way to conceptualize how pluralism might function in the politics of the mainstream society, it does not provide for different life styles outside this mainstream. Further, there is the danger that it underestimates the force of ethnicity and overemphasizes the power of rationality and the scientific method.

A Model for American Pluralism

Our brief analysis of the appropriateness of each of the alternative ideological models of cultural pluralism for American society seems to leave us in a problematic position. Each alternative seems reasonable when viewed in a particular context and applied to a limited set of groups, but no one model seems able to accommodate the requirements of all groups. We hinted at the reasons for this earlier in the chapter when assessing the diversity of American society. Not only is there a diversity of cultural groups, but there is a diversity of kinds of groups. That is, while groups can be identified and distinguished on the basis of national origin, they can also be identified and distinguished on the basis of their behavioral (cultural) and structural assimilation, geographical segregation and integration, residential segregation and integration, social class (i.e., those groups that share in the economic and political rewards of society as opposed to those groups that are effectively excluded from these rewards), social and cultural goals, or some combination of these qualities. Since ideologies are in part designed to meet the perceived needs of some particular group in some particular sociocultural context, these differences contribute to the development of alternative ideologies that have limited application. Just as the general ideological appeal for cultural pluralism has relevance only for societies with culturally diverse populations, specific ideological species of cultural pluralism will have relevance only for those groups they are designed to serve. Thus, the conclusion that no one model of cultural pluralism best suits the needs of all groups should come as no great surprise.

How problematic is this result? It will be recalled that the search for a clearly articulated statement of the ideal of cultural pluralism that outlined specific goals and policy guidelines was undertaken initially because as an ambiguous slogan statement cultural pluralism was unable to guide the development and evaluation of social policy. Thus, while appeals for the adoption of the ideal of cultural pluralism could make us aware that something was the matter and could generate an emotional commitment and sense of common purpose, the systematically ambiguous slogan could not provide the blueprint for social change or for the construction of more desirable social arrangements. This could be achieved only by delimiting the slogan by means of associating it with certain values, beliefs, and practices. Since those rallying behind the adoption of cultural pluralism clearly desired some transformation in society (as opposed to, say, simply increasing group cohesiveness), this delimitation was seen as vital. But now as we survey the ideological landscape of cultural pluralism, we see that the efforts to add specificity to the ideal have been successful—in fact, they appear to have been too successful, for we have not one ideological statement capable of guiding social policy but several that depart from one another in significant ways. While we are no longer faced with the problems associated with ambiguity, we now seem to be faced with the equally difficult decision of selecting among alternatives each of which have strengths and weaknesses in their application to American society.

Potentially there are some real dangers resulting from the existence of competing ideological expressions of cultural pluralism. Granted that at the slogan stage efforts at social change were hampered by ambiguity, considerable strength was achieved through a strong sense of common purpose and united effort. Now the potential exists for the movement to be weakened by a struggle of the various alternative positions among themselves to achieve prominence. If such a struggle endures, some material and personal resources that would otherwise go to the support of cultural pluralism are likely to be diverted for the struggle and thus weaken the overall movement. Similarly, the divisions that may result from an internal struggle may render any one position incapable of mustering enough strength to make itself felt in social policy. Thus, "divide and conquer" may weaken the ideal of cultural pluralism. Finally, when there is internal dissension, it is generally easier for those hostile to the ideal to avoid considering it seriously. Citing the confusion within, opponents may claim that advocates themselves do not know what they want and thus the issue is not worthy of serious consideration.

While the potential for internal conflict is real, it is by no means inevitable. Indeed, if the existence of alternative ideological positions has a dysfunctional potential, the potential also exists to convert these into real assets. Several points support this possibility. First, as was initially sought, we now have clearly articulated ideological statements capable of guiding social policy. Second, unity within the movement for cultural pluralism need not rely on a specific ideological statement but can be based on the acceptance of the four general conditions established in the use of the concept in ordinary language. Third, there may be considerable utility in recognizing the legitimacy of several specific alternative positions.

The first point has already been discussed. Simply, if an ideal is to guide social policy, it must be specific enough that a set of criteria can be derived and applied in the construction and evaluation of social policy in particular situations. Several such positions have been developed.

The second and third points are related. Earlier in our analysis of the meaning of "cultural pluralism" we found that the use of the concept in ordinary language assumes general agreement on four necessary conditions. We now argue that the spirit of pluralism for the United States might be best served by putting our faith in these broadly stated conditions and allowing a plurality of specific models to exist, the application of each being reserved for the social context in which it is most appropriate. That is, in order for the ideal of cultural pluralism to be of greatest benefit to society, it may well be that we do not need and should not seek one specific ideological model. Each of the alternative positions being considered, though they differ in regard to specifics, is consistent with the general ideal and thus has a common basis of agreement. By recognizing that each specific alternative may be appropriate to some social contexts and set of groups, but not to all, we can avoid viewing the alternatives as competitors and hence can preserve their common bond and mutual commitment. By proceeding in this manner we can avoid the potential dangers of internal strife while retaining the benefits of having specific ideological statements. Further, by allowing for a plurality of ideological models we are able to avoid the limitations inherent in adopting any one particular position. Thus, we are theoretically able to acknowledge and respond to the needs and wishes of different groups in society. By so doing we create a much richer form of pluralism than would otherwise be possible. In effect, we have a two-tier pluralism—a pluralism of pluralism, if you will—a plurality of models of pluralism each legitimate in its own right and potentially appropriate to some group or set of groups in society.

Theoretically this two-tier pluralism we are arguing for is sound. The question remains, Can such a model be applied in practice? The central challenge will be in determining which specific models should be applied to which specific groups or kinds of groups and under what conditions.

Consistent with the nature of ideological positions, it will be likely that some advocates within various positions will argue that their model should be universally applied. Undoubtedly the enthusiasm of these persons will be grounded in the genuine belief that their position is in the best interests of society and all the individuals it will affect. We might also expect that some individuals will be willing to allow for a plurality of models to operate but will wish to specify that only one model is appropriate to a particular group or kind of group. That is, an individual may be willing to concede that groups like the Amish and Hutterites should be allowed to adopt a policy of classical cultural pluralism but believe that the model to govern policy relating to all ethnic minorities—Hispanics, Blacks, and Asians in particular—should be pluralism as integration. Thus, despite the contrary wishes of some parents or local communities, because the advocate believes it is in the best interests of society, this model will be imposed on all members of the relevant group. In the same fashion, some may wish to impose separatism for all Blacks or modified cultural pluralism for all Hispanics. The tendency to move in this direction may in part result from the recognition that if a group is to function effectively as a political interest group, it must maintain a high degree of cohesiveness; to allow different segments of an ethnic community to go their separate ways is to weaken the power base of the whole.

All the positions taken above have one common flaw: They all violate the spirit of pluralism. If pluralism as a general ideal is good for society as a whole, it would be reasonable to believe that it would also be good for the individual groups in society and, thus, should be retained in the application of its more specific ideological alternatives. It will not do to replace one dogmatism or authoritarian system for another, no matter how laudatory its principles sound. To adopt one species of pluralism and impose it on all groups or one particular group or set of groups is inconsistent with the condition of pluralism that requires that a diversity of positions be valued. This condition would also seem to imply that the individuals affected should have considerable say in the decision, since the ideal of pluralism presupposes that the diversity within society is a result of the wishes of the constituent groups. In other words, to value diversity in society is to value the freedom that allows diverse groups to define the nature of their own being.

Our position, then, is that each group or subgroup (e.g., community) should be the primary determinant of which ideological model of pluralism best suits its goals and social situation. The adoption of this approach would reinforce both democracy and pluralism, the two core values this country currently claims to espouse. Within this model, our approach to different groups will most likely vary from situation to situation. Social policies regarding the native peoples living in areas geographically isolated from highly integrated postindustrial cosmopolitan areas will probably differ from those regarding groups more closely tied to the "mainstream" society. Similarly, policies regarding members of one ethnic group in a particular community may vary from the policies regarding members of the same ethnic group in another community. It will be impossible beforehand to predict the mosaic that will eventually develop, assuming of course that one is allowed to develop.

While self-determination will play an important role in the development of social policy, it must be clear that this will not be the only operative variable. Obviously, we live in an interdependent society where the actions of one group affect the well-being of many others. Such a society cannot exist if the possible range of alternative actions of any particular group is not limited to those that will not cause serious harm to society or undermine the principles on which it is founded. The determination, then, of the ideological model to govern the social policies toward some particular group must be evaluated in the light of the larger social context in which the group exists. Though the desires of the group demand considerable respect, ultimately the decision must rest on some higher authority, and the principles on which the higher authority will base its judgment will be those found in the social ideals of democracy and cultural pluralism.

We might take this opportunity to respond again to critics of cultural pluralism who fear that the adoption of the ideal will lead to unbridled ethnicity and the intensification of conflict between ethnic groups. Suppose, to use an extreme example presented by Orlando Patterson, an ethnic subculture believed in human sacrifice as one of their religious practices. Would this practice be allowed by the larger society under a policy of cultural pluralism? Clearly the answer would be no. They would undoubtedly be forced to conform to the society's universal prohibition against murder. For a less extreme but more controversial example, consider the issue of abortion: Is this murder or not? Here we have a conflict over whether a value should be universal or particularistic, and unlike the first example, the answer is not at all clear. Pluralistic societies will be faced with many such questions and must decide them based on some theory of justice that weighs the rights of individuals and groups against the best interests of society as a whole. As we suggested, in the form of pluralism for which we are now arguing, universal and particularistic values would be dialectically balanced against each other, the universal values of equality, freedom and democracy, as well as the particularistic values associated with the maintenance of cultural diversity.[6]

This said, we must realize that while there is a danger in allowing too much autonomy for individual groups, a greater danger probably exists in overzealous efforts to protect society by dominating and repressing culturally different groups. Certainly this has been the case historically.

Perhaps it is appropriate to make a few comments pertaining to the development of educational programs within the model we are advocating. Because specifics will vary from context to context with the adoption of particular ideological models of pluralism and because the specifics for each ideological model have already been suggested elsewhere, these comments must remain general.

Obviously the educational program within any pluralistic ideology must impart a value for the general principle of pluralism. Of special importance is developing a tolerance for groups culturally different from one's own and a disposition to allow other groups to define for themselves the life style they wish to pursue. It is important for the members of each group to realize that, as distinct and isolated as they may or may not be, they are still members of a larger society and ultimately must consider the effects of their practices on other members of the society.

In regard to educational programs, some groups will assume the total responsibility for educating their youth and/or remain segregated from other groups in society. Some groups will participate in public educational institutions and maintain a high degree of interaction with the members of other groups. In the latter case, multicultural and bilingual programs will be appropriate for many settings. Perhaps the first step in designing such programs will be to assess the relevant contextual variables of the situation. These include cultural, social, and educational variables; demographic data; local legal requirements; and the like. These factors determine the thrust of any project and will necessarily lead to a diversity among programs. For example, it should be evident that the contextual variables for Puerto Rico differ radically from those for San Francisco, that those for Native Americans near or in a metropolitan area differ from those for Native Americans in isolated areas, and that those for urban Blacks differ from those for rural Mexican Americans. If there is an underlying theme to govern multicultural education in particular or education in a multicultural society in general, it is this: Currently there is a search for the "real" meaning of pluralism or at least for a model capable of resolving conflict and debate within the movement. If the spirit of pluralism is to be followed, we should expect to develop not one national model but a number of regional and local models that meet the needs of various groups.

SUMMARY

The United States is a complex society. Its pluralism is defined not only by a diversity of cultural groups but also by a diversity of kinds of groups. When the degree to which the nation fulfills the conditions of a culturally pluralistic society is evaluated, ratings are mixed. With respect to some groups, the nation does well; but with others, a commitment to equality and diversity appears to be missing.

The complexity in the kinds of groups existing in society creates other problems. Assuming we desire to pursue the ideal of cultural pluralism, we are faced with determining just what the ideal entails for different groups. At least six conceptual models for pluralism have been suggested, each in some way different from the others in social organization, goals, and values advocated. Each model seems particularly appropriate for some group or set of groups but not for others. Thus, the adoption of any one particular model would have limited application.

The negative consequences of selecting a particular ideological model of pluralism can be avoided by relying on the broadly stated principles of the ideal as a foundation and acknowledging the appropriateness of each of the more specific models for application in the contexts each serves best. Thus, by adopting a pluralistic approach to the establishment of an ideal of cultural pluralism we can attain a much richer form of pluralism than would otherwise be possible. The interests of the larger social community will be recognized as relevant, but the main determinant of which ideological model will govern policy development for a particular group will be the desire of that group itself. The final result will be a society with a diversity of groups and social and educational policies.

NOTES

1. Will Herberg, *Protestant-Catholic-Jew* (New York: Doubleday, 1955).
2. John A. Hostetler and Gertrude Enders Huntington, *Children in Amish Society, Socialization and Community Education* (New York: Holt, Rinehart and Winston, 1971), p. 4.
3. Ibid., p. 9.
4. Milton Gordon, "Toward a General Theory of Racial and Ethnic Group Relations," in *Ethnicity: Theory and Experience*, ed. Nathan Glazer and Daniel Moynihan (Cambridge, Mass.: Harvard University Press, 1975), p. 85.
5. Michael Novak, "Cultural Pluralism for Individuals," in Tumin and Plotch, *Pluralism in a Democratic Society*.
6. Bob Suzuki, "An Asian-American Perspective on Multicultural Education: Implications for Practice and Research," ERIC ED 205633, November 1980, p. 12.

6

Cultural Conflict and Cultural Pluralism

In 1967, following four summers of unprecedented racial disorder in American cities, President Lyndon B. Johnson established the National Advisory Commission on Civil Disorders, to be known as the Kerner Commission. The group's task was to explain the outbreak of urban violence. In 1968, after eight months of extensive research, interviews, and hearings across the country, the commission concluded that "white racism is essentially responsible for the explosive mixture which has been accumulating in our cities since the end of World War II."[1]

The report seemed to establish quite clearly that in the United States cultural conflict, particularly violent conflict, has at least in part grown out of the struggle of oppressed and dominated people to free themselves. It has been a struggle of individuals relegated to a position of second-class citizenship and humanity on the basis of ethnic criteria, with the goal of simple recognition and acceptance as human beings of equal status.

The Kerner Commission offered a series of recommendations as essential steps if society was finally to assume the responsibility to form a more just social order. Though the task seemed monumental, the hope remained that significant headway could be made through a reordering of national priorities, particularly in housing, employment, and education. In particular, education could supply additional support for such ideals as equal educational opportunity and cultural pluralism. Racial integration, supported mainly by the courts, was viewed both as a means of creating greater educational opportunities for minority students and as a step toward the creation of a more unified society. Multicultural education in the school curriculum could validate and accommodate cultural differences: America's youth would learn to understand, respect, and value the cultural diversity from which it was formed and of which America continues to boast; enrichment and compensatory education programs at the preschool, primary, and secondary levels could strengthen the intellectual underpinnings of academic achievement as well as encourage students to continue in school; and teachers and administrators would be taught about the cultural backgrounds of their students and about constructing more responsive learning environments for culturally diverse students.

Cultural conflict is often a result of some imbalance or dysfunction in society, and the indictment of white society handed down by the Kerner Commission was undoubtedly correct with respect to reason and discrimination. But as a general explanation of cultural conflict, this view may be exaggerated. Indeed, serious social problems must be addressed, but there is also growing evidence that the successful treatment of these problems will not eliminate cultural conflict. We explore this thesis in greater detail in this chapter. In our inquiry we seek to understand the nature of cultural conflict in a pluralistic society: What is it? How prominent will it be? What are its causes? What forms will it take?

THE NATURE OF SOCIAL CONFLICT

What It Is

Social conflict can be defined as a "form of group relationship (or interaction) involving a struggle over the rewards or resources of a society or over social values, in which the conflicting parties attempt to neutralize or injure each other."[2] It should be apparent that in our definition of social conflict, no mention has been made of violence or disruption. Although these tend to leave the greatest lasting impression of conflict, they are not an inherent or inevitable quality of social conflict; they are but one possible outcome. This view is discussed in greater detail as we explore the functional aspects of social conflict.

In order to better understand the struggle over social rewards and resources, societies can be viewed as distribution systems. In other words, the benefits a society has to offer are distributed to its members through various social institutions and according to the rules and norms that govern such institutions. Three basic kinds of rewards exist: material rewards, such as material goods, wealth, and property; status rewards, such as honor, privilege, and prestige; and power, that is, the ability to determine one's own actions and the actions of others, regardless of the desires of those others. Social conflicts arise as groups try to secure a favorable position and an advantage over other groups in the allocation process. Groups struggle to gain and maintain material rewards, status, and the positions of power normally considered vital to securing the first two. Conflict over rewards tends to be heightened by the generally accepted view that these rewards exist in fixed or limited quantities and that what one group gains is lost by the other.

Conflicts may also arise over social values. We have long recognized that there is no one best way of life, one best way of assessing truth, or one absolute way of determining moral standards. These tend to be subjective in nature and cannot be determined by science, logic, or authority. Thus, the many life styles, values, and moral standards reflected in our society are all in principle equally legitimate. Conflicts occur as these alternative views and practices come into contact, and there are clashes over visibility, prominence, and support. For example, this may result when one group views the beliefs and practices of another group as a threat to the general welfare of the public. This frequently occurs when moral issues are at stake, as in controversies over abortion, polygamy, capital punishment, and sexual practices. It may also occur as groups compete for the necessary resources to protect, perpetuate, or broaden their life styles and value preferences. Thus, various special-interest groups lobby and struggle for the adoption of norms and rules, legislation, and financial assistance that support their value preferences and ways of life. Political, social, and educational issues are frequently of this type.

Cultural conflict can be considered as one form of social conflict. In this sense, cultural conflict can be said to occur when social conflict takes place between different cultural groups; when culturally, ethnically, or racially identifiable groups clash over material rewards, status, power, or values. The important condition of this definition of cultural conflict is that the conflict is based on the cultural, ethnic, or racial distinctiveness of the contending parties. Thus, if an elite (primarily Protestant) social club refuses to accept a Jewish applicant as a member because the applicant's educational and occupational credentials do not meet the expectations of the group, no cultural conflict exists. If the would-be member meets the educational and occupational qualifications and is denied membership on religious or ethnic grounds, however, cultural conflict exists. The roots of cultural conflict are found in cultural differences or identity.

Theories of Social Conflict

Consensus Theory.   There are two general schools of thought concerning the nature of society. Although they are variously labeled, they tend to juxtapose the natural state of societies.[3]

One school of thought tends to treat cultural conflict as a social disease. Modern, complex societies are characterized as groups that develop a consensus of social values, an inherent stability and order of social institutions, and a gradual integration of social groups; conflict, nonconformity, and deviation are seen as results of the inadequate socialization of groups and individuals. Social scientists accepting this theory hypothesize that eventually order and stability will result from group interaction in society;[4] that is, human social relationships naturally tend toward the development of consensus, cooperation, and interdependence. At times something may interrupt or interfere with this natural state, resulting in temporary instability and social conflict, but as the interfering variables are resolved, order and stability will return. We shall term this school of thought "consensus theory."

Consensus theory is reflected in many policies concerning the treatment of minorities in the United States. It is assumed that cultural conflict results from the unwillingness of the dominant white majority to allow minorities equal status in society and, therefore, that white racism is the interfering variable that blocks the natural trend toward consensus and stability. Thus, many policies are clearly directed toward the inclusion of minorities into the mainstream of society on an equal basis. If this theory is correct, we can expect that to the degree we are successful with this undertaking, cultural conflict will decline.

The consensus view of society can be seen in many of the cultural diversity theories reviewed in Chapter 2. Assimilation and amalgamation both depict cultural conflict resulting from the instability brought about by immigration. Assimilation predicts that as the "foreign" populations adjust to and adopt the values and life style of the majority culture, order and stability will return. Similarly, amalgamation predicts stability and order after a period of adjustment, only this time the adjustment will occur as a result of the melting pot and the creation of a new American culture.

Even theories of cultural pluralism are based on a consensus view. Classical cultural pluralism hypothesizes that the various ethnic groups will live side by side in a state of mutual respect and toleration—that is, in peaceful coexistence. Although conflict may be present initially, the theory contends that after some period of instability, the groups will live in a relatively harmonious state. Modified cultural pluralism differs from classical cultural pluralism in that it predicts a higher level of interaction and interdependence. The eventual result of stability and order are the same, however. In fact, metaphors used to describe the resulting balance of diversity suggest a state of affairs far richer than a homogeneous society. For example, society is likened to an orchestra, where each instrument (ethnic group) maintains its integrity but also complements the contributions of the others and lends balance and "flavor" to a harmonious creation far beyond the possibilities of any individual effort. Thus in a pluralistic society conflict is viewed as a temporary phase in group relations that exists until a state of "unity through diversity" develops. Each group comes to view cultural diversity as positive and complementary to its own well-being.

To a certain extent, consensus theories are still fashionable. They are influential in the development of policy concerning the interaction among different cultural groups. Unfortunately, adherents of such theories seem to be pursuing a blind alley. We have good reason to believe that social conflict will be a permanent, and perhaps at times functional, feature of society.

Conflict Theory.   The second general school of thought concerning the nature of society sees change, rather than order, as the ubiquitous feature of modern societies. Called conflict theory, this view rejects the position that deviation and group conflict are dysfunctional; instead, it interprets them as important sources of social change. Accepting this thesis, many contemporary students of social conflict, recognizing conflict as a salient feature in society, have come to view society as dynamic and incorporating both change and order, both conflict and consensus.[5] This dialectical perspective, as William Newman points out, "grants that *both* change and order are ubiquitous and explains the ways in which these two aspects of society are essentially interrelated."[6] This is to say that social conflict is to be viewed *not* as an anomaly or dysfunction in society but as a natural part of an ongoing process, complementary to order and stability. Thus, both change and order, both conflict and consensus, are thought to be elements that characterize all societies and group relationships in societies.

According to this viewpoint, different cultural and ethnic groups may establish patterns of association with one another, but it is unrealistic to expect conflict among the groups to diminish. Social relationships are characterized by a complement of conflict and consensus with both being enduring features of normal modern societies. Any adequate theory of group relationships in the United States, then, would have to incorporate both aspects. This is precisely where consensus theories went wrong. By emphasizing the consensus-order nature of group relationships, they were unable to account for the continued and recurring eruption of cultural conflict. One must not conclude that the rejection of consensus theory as an accurate description of modern societies entails the abandonment of ideals like cultural pluralism and social justice. Nothing could be farther from the case. It does mean, however, that we realistically contemplate and plan for the social dynamics inherent in such a society. It is important to recognize that social conflict will not go away. The most we can hope for is to manage it and to maximize its functional value.

CONFLICT AND THE MULTICULTURAL SOCIETY

Social Conflict in the United States

The American culture is, like any modern culture, complex and dynamic. It is a network of interrelated, overlapping, and even contradictory social patterns, mythologies, and norms that change with time. Adding to the complexity affecting the overall character of American culture are the many diverse cultural influences due to the pluralistic nature of the country. Nevertheless, an American character seems to be reflected in us all in one way or another and to endure over time. We are not alike in our manifestation of this character, nor do we adopt it equally, yet in a certain sense we are Americans.

One of the qualities of this character is what anthropologist Francis Hsu calls the American core value of self-reliance.[7] According to Hsu, Americans put great value on self-reliance. This can be seen in our praise of the individual who overcomes great odds to accomplish some task or in our respect for the individual who follows a personal goal; in our reluctance to accept socialism as a political label when describing the United States and in our efforts to characterize ourselves as a country with a free-enterprise system; and in the way we view people who are dependent on others, whether economically, socially or spiritually. In school we urge students to achieve independently; psychologically speaking, we look down on the person with a "dependent personality"; and we associate public assistance (welfare) with failure and lack of worth.

Hsu underscores our commitment to self-reliance when comparing parents in traditional China, where self-reliance was not an ideal, with parents in the United States. If the Chinese parents were economically unsuccessful but their children were able to provide for them generously in their old age, they would be most happy and content and would be likely to brag to others about it. In contrast, American parents who had not been economically successful might derive some benefit from the prosperity of their children but certainly would not want anybody to know about it. In fact, they would resent any reference to such assistance, and at the first opportunity to become independent of their children, they would try to do so.

It should be obvious that because humans are social beings, no individual can be totally self-reliant. As humans, we depend on other people intellectually and technologically, socially and emotionally. Hsu argues that this dependence, combined with the basic American value of self-reliance, creates problems for the individual, the most notable of which is insecurity.

Insecurity, together with the need to demonstrate one's self-reliance, fuels competition between individuals and groups and leads to preoccupation with status-giving groups and discrimination. Here's how it happens: The value of self-reliance has its origin in commitment to the social and political ideals of equal opportunity and social mobility, in other words, belief that an individual's success is restricted only by the personal limits of ability. (For example, we insist that everyone has an equal chance to be President.) Individuals, then, constantly look for opportunities to secure a better position in life. More successful individuals prove to be more self-reliant. It is equally accurate to state this the other way around: More self-reliant individuals are more successful.

But individuals cannot manage alone. We depend on others to meet our needs. The social relationships we cultivate become very important, and some are likely to be more beneficial than others. Astute individuals constantly look for social groups that will carry them the farthest. By the same token, members of existing groups will want to maximize the strength and effectiveness of their groups by admitting only individuals who will contribute to the group in some way. Group membership thus becomes a very important commodity. It is important for individuals to belong to the right groups, while the groups must be very selective of their members. This can readily be seen in our preoccupation with group status in the United States. We are constantly making judgments about which groups are better and more prestigious, and we go out of our way to place individuals we meet for the first time in a context of group association; we want to know the person's occupation, place of residence, social circle, and so on.

This tendency to use others as a means of social mobility leads to a sense of insecurity for individuals. While constantly looking for an opportunity to move up to more effective groups with higher status, one must also constantly guard against being displaced by others from below. This also happens to groups. Groups are very conscious of their status and power with respect to other, competing groups. Groups endeavor to move ahead of other groups, as well as to guard against those farther back.

One result of this dynamic interplay among individuals and groups is that individuals tend to demonstrate their self-reliance by virtue of the groups they belong to. The person who is able to move to high-status groups demonstrates power and independence. Similarly, the group that can manipulate and define the status position of other groups demonstrates its power and the ability to provide for itself. Another result is discrimination. As both individuals and groups jockey for position, discrimination is used as a weapon to preserve status. Groups discriminate against "undesirable" individuals (i.e., individuals with lower status who might wish to join the group) and against other groups to protect themselves from encroachment from below. Individuals are careful not to associate with or give advantage to others who might endanger their security as members of existing groups. The opportunity to move to more desirable groups is also protected in this way.

The net effect of our preoccupation with self-reliance is a very group-conscious society. We are constantly defining and identifying individuals by virtue of group association. When group distinctions are not apparent, we form new ones. Further, we are constantly preoccupied with passing judgment and assigning value to these groups and their members. These status assignments play a prominent role in the way we treat people. We discriminate against, exclude, and manipulate members of groups assigned lower status. And we are constantly trying to relegate groups to a relatively low status because this has the effect of elevating our own relative status.

All of this sounds very much like what is happening in the United States. Hsu describes it as resulting from the core value of self-reliance accentuated by a fear of dependency. Whether the value of self-reliance is the determining factor or not, social relationships in the United States can be characterized as highly competitive, stratified, and status oriented.[8] Competition and achievement, both at the interpersonal and intergroup levels, are prescribed norms in our society. We view this way of life positively for the most part, motivating us to do the best we can. We also believe that it supports the democratic ideal of achievement through ability. But if the social norms of competition and achievement provide the opportunity, at least in principle, for social mobility and equality, they also contribute to the frequency of social conflict. William Newman,[9] reviewing the literature on social conflict, presents this relationship in the form of two sociological propositions.

Proposition 1: The frequency of integroup conflict in societies is directly proportionate to the degree to which different social groups view each other as competitive threats to their social resources, to resources that they wish to obtain, or to their basic social values.

Proposition 2: The degree to which different social groups view each other as competitive threats, and therefore the frequency of social conflict between them, is directly proportionate to the degree to which competition and achievement are prescribed norms in society.

Proposition 1 says that we should expect conflict to occur when two or more groups are competing for the rewards that society has to offer. These may be material rewards (e.g., money, jobs, or housing), or they may be social rewards of power or status. Proposition 1 also tells us that conflict is likely to occur over value differences. Proposition 2, which assesses the likelihood that different groups will view one another as competitors, says that if competition and achievement are emphasized in society, groups are much more likely to believe that other groups are competing against them. As a result, each group will attempt to get a competitive edge and outdo the other; and social conflict will increase.

Again we can see that social relationships in the United States fit this pattern perfectly. We are a pluralistic nation, a nation with a great number of cultural, political, religious, racial, and other special-interest groups. For whatever reason, as a society we have embraced competition and achievement as social norms. Predictably, various groups view one another as competitors in a struggle over resources, power, and status.

The competition is even more serious because these rewards are perceived as finite. To use everyday terms, this is a "fixed pie" perspective. There is only so much pie to go around, and the bigger piece of pie one person or group gets, the smaller the other pieces. That is, what the winner gains is what the loser has lost. This is what some social theorists call a negative-sum game,[10] in contrast to a positive-sum game where it is possible for each competing party to reap a net gain in overall position. Because in the United States the general view is that individuals and groups are competing for limited amounts of material rewards, status, and power and that one group's gain will be another's loss, social conflict is intensified.

To summarize, the social structure in the United States seems to be set up in such a way as to generate social conflict: We are very group conscious; we are highly stratified, with some groups on top and others on the bottom; we view the stratification system and competition over placement in it as desirable and legitimate. Thus, we can expect group conflict to be a continuing feature of our society. The question, then, becomes not the existence of social conflict but the nature of the conflict. While group conflict is likely to endure in our social relationships, will conflict continue among racial, ethnic, and cultural groups? And if so, what direction will it take?

Cultural Conflict in the United States

Without significant social change in the competitive ethic, our stratification system and the resulting group conflict will be enduring features of our society. Even those who support the value of equal opportunity do not deny this. However, they hope that certain qualities beyond the control of the individual will cease to be factors in competition. That is, such qualities as sex, race, ethnicity, or physical handicap should be irrelevant and illegitimate in the stratification system. One's relative position in society should be based solely on achievement (what one can do) and not on ascribed characteristics (what one is). Occupation, effectiveness, and skill should be the determining factors in the distribution of social rewards and position, assuming, of course, that each functions independently of ascribed qualities. While there would still be winners and losers, we would expect a proportional distribution of minority individuals at all levels.

In principle, this goal may be within the realm of possibility, but it does not appear likely. We have seen that social groups compete and will continue to compete and thus conflict with one another, and we have seen that ethnicity is likely to continue to play a significant role in group identity. It is highly unlikely that we will ignore such distinctions in our social competition. It is not reasonable to expect that we can view these groups as important in one setting but not another. This is particularly true when we are inclined to continually reevaluate each group in respect to placement in our stratification system. If we expect cultural, ethnic, and racial aspects of social conflict to decrease, we should also expect the importance of these qualities to decrease in society at large. That is, ethnic, cultural, and racial identity would need to be increasingly irrelevant in human affairs. This is unlikely to happen, in view of our earlier discussion of ethnicity; equally important, it seems to contradict the positions of many advocates of cultural pluralism who wish to maintain cultural distinctiveness and cultural identity. The point is, as long as we are a competitive society and as long as cultural, ethnic, and racial differences are important, these differences will contribute to group identity, group competition, and group conflict.

One other factor points to the probability of continued cultural conflict. As we have seen, not all social conflict is over social rewards and resources or status positions; groups also engage in social conflict over the goals and ideals they choose to value. This is particularly true in a society that supports the ideal of cultural pluralism. If cultural pluralism is understood to mean toleration and support of meaningful cultural differences in society, we should expect that life styles, goals, values, interests, and world perceptions will vary among groups and that at times these differences will clash with one another. This will be especially true in a society like the United States that has traditionally encouraged the integration of groups at secondary levels of interaction. Thus, while value conflicts may arise from insensitivity, prejudice, or one group trying to dominate or control another, these need not be the only sources. Conflicts may arise from significant and legitimate differences of opinion, life style, beliefs, and preferences that affect the well-being of society as a whole. Consider, for example, the value differences in issues such as abortion, religious education, sex education, the purposes of schooling, and choices of goals toward which limited resources should be applied. Similarly, conflicts resulting from life-style differences may center around hygiene habits, time orientation, privacy, or styles of interaction. Value conflicts can be seen not as an anomaly but as one component of a dynamic society where cultural differences play a meaningful and significant role in the lives of the people.

Areas of Expected Cultural Conflict

Material Rewards and Resources.   Cultural conflict is the form of so-cial conflict that has received the greatest attention in the United States in recent times. Minorities have found themselves, as a group, effec-tively excluded from the rewards and benefits of society. Historically, they have received a disproportionately small share of material re-wards, been relegated to the lowest status positions, been denied access to social institutions and other traditional channels necessary to compete effectively, and been denied the power positions necessary to alter the existing state of affairs. Finding themselves in such a position, minority groups, spearheaded primarily by the Black civil rights move-ment, have pushed for change. But change does not come easily. Socially dominant groups, correctly perceiving the challenge as a threat to their favorable position and the social norms that maintain it, gener-ally will not give up their position voluntarily.[11] The result is cultural conflict.

At times the struggle has been violent, and at times it has pro-ceeded through institutional channels such as the courts and legislative bodies. Some of the conflict has centered on making existing norms and institutions more responsive to minority-group demands, and much of the work in the courts, at the polls, and in modifying certain aspects of the educational system reflects this. Other efforts concen-trated on altering the norms and rules of institutions. The Civil Rights Act of 1964, for example, modified some previously accepted rules con-trolling access to the distribution system; consider bilingual education and affirmative action as cases in point.

One effect of the conflict initiated by the Black civil rights move-ment has been to heighten the ethnic consciousness of other groups and broaden and differentiate cultural conflict over social rewards. Fol-lowing the Black precedent, Hispanics, Asians, and Native Americans have sought greater social parity. The combined efforts of these minority groups in turn served as a catalyst to raise ethnic consciousness among white ethnic groups who perceived themselves as being the most vulnerable in the reallocation of political power and economic power. In the stratification system, the newly entrenched white ethnics would be the first to be displaced. This threat to white ethnics has led to greater solidarity within their groups, stronger white ethnic identity and pride, and demands that social institutions be responsive to their ethnic needs as well. It has also led to an increase in negative feelings and attitudes among various groups, often referred to as cultural backlash.

Public schools are one social institution that continues to be an arena for cultural conflict over social rewards. Schools, long considered to be vehicles for upward mobility, have traditionally provided the skills, knowledge and credentials necessary for entrance into the distribution system of material rewards, status, and power; individuals screened out early in school or designated undesirable are effectively eliminated from favorable positions in the larger social system. It is no wonder that schools were one of the first institutions to come under attack for their lack of responsiveness to minority needs.

The main thrust for redress in the public schools began in 1954 with the landmark case of *Brown* v. *Board of Education*. The case demonstrated that Blacks were not receiving the opportunity for an education equal to that of the more advantaged white majority. In the years of conflict that followed, courts have insisted that minorities receive an equitable share of educational resources including material goods, physical facilities, qualified teachers, social services, and access to instructional services. The most evident and controversial means to this end has been the desegregation of schools. Support for equal educational opportunity has also been found in affirmative action programs that attempt to facilitate the entrance of minorities into more strategic positions and into institutions of higher education. Even bilingual education, perceived by some as a means to protect cultural values and heritage, can be interpreted in this manner. As was established in Chapter 4, the main thrust of the law on bilingual education has clearly been the integration of non-English-speaking students into the mainstream of education.

Bilingual education is also a good example of the continued battle over limited resources to fund educational projects. In a shrinking economy, there is increasing competition for resources needed to fund education. Since the funding of one plan means the exclusion of another, conflict along cultural lines is sure to develop. Bilingual education, ethnic studies and multicultural education, and remedial academic programs for struggling minority students must compete with one another and with other programs for funding. The conflict is especially exacerbated when federal funding expires and school systems are asked to support the compensatory programs themselves.

Values. Social conflict over values provides another setting for cultural conflict. While a struggle over the resources required to fund institutions and programs that support a given value system or life style are one manifestation of value conflicts, struggles over values are much more inclusive and often do not involve material resources. If the concept of cultural pluralism is to be meaningful in any strong sense, we must assume that important cultural differences will exist (i.e., different life styles and values will coexist in society). We must further expect that some of these differences will be incompatible with others and that at times they will clash to produce cultural conflict, not just between two identifiably different cultural (i.e., ethnic or racial) groups but between the ways of life of the groups.

The case of the Amish provides a contemporary and salient example. As we saw, the Amish migrated to the United States two centuries ago in search of religious freedom, established religious communities, and in many ways segregated themselves from mainstream society. Today, living much the way they have in the past, they refuse to send their children to school beyond the elementary grades because schooling violates their religious teachings and threatens the viability of the Amish community. It has been argued that because of their limited formal education, Amish children are deprived of the opportunity to grow intellectually and academically and thus participate in the mainstream of society should they wish to do so. On these grounds, Wisconsin argued that Amish parents should be found guilty of violating the Wisconsin compulsory education law. A clear conflict developed between the values of the Amish community and what the state perceived to be an overriding social interest. The conflict did not involve social resources—indeed, the Amish wished to forfeit their "opportunity" to use public resources and chose to rely totally on their own.

Other examples abound. Also in the area of religious beliefs, we have seen conflict arise over the medical treatment of children, particularly over compulsory immunization in order to attend public schools; over prayer in public schools; over the funding of parochial schools; and over participation in various public school activities such as physical education, sex education, and flag salutes. Examples of cultural conflict based on differences other than religious differences are also common. The Native American concept of the proper use of land has been in conflict with the views of some other groups. School desegregation orders have conflicted with both Chinese and Chicano desires to maintain voluntarily segregated cultural communities. The moral standards of local communities have at times been in conflict with the selection of "appropriate" teaching material and textbooks by some schools. Even the goals of education may be in conflict with a cultural community's perception of the "good life." In particular, this is possible when the state and federal governments establish educational goals and schools for cultural groups traditionally isolated or segregated (or both) from modern "developed" society. This has occurred in the West and South Pacific, in Alaska, and in certain culturally or geographically isolated areas within the forty-eight contiguous states.

As the above examples suggest, the public schools have been particularly vulnerable to cultural value conflict because they are of necessity the traditional meeting ground of diverse cultural groups. In addition, the public schools have typically been established and operated by individuals representing the interests of the larger social community (i.e., the district, state, or nation). It is difficult for one institution, particularly an institution originating outside the community, to try to define and meet the needs and expectations of culturally diverse groups. Unless public schools move toward greater decentralization and community control, these conflicts will continue.

Interaction Styles.   Cultural conflict as we have been discussing it so far involves confrontation. Thus, our mental image is of two or more individuals or groups battling over material rewards, status, power, or values. But we can also talk about two ideas or positions being in conflict with one another *without* suggesting a battle. We simply mean they are incompatible or irreconcilable. In this sense, it is possible for two ideas, positions, beliefs, or life styles to be in conflict without the outward manifestation of social conflict implied in the "struggle" sense of the term. Such might be the case if the contenders had no need to interact or compete with one another or if they were unaware of each other, and the resulting social arrangement might be described as peaceful coexistence.

Peaceful coexistence is one way multicultural theorists have characterized a functional, culturally plural society. Though diverse views will often be incompatible, social conflict will be avoided because each group will respect or tolerate alternative positions. The Amish way of life, for example, may be in conflict with that of postindustrial society. No social conflict need develop, however, as long as the larger social community is content to let the Amish be. In the same manner, many potential clashes between conflicting values, life styles, and perceptions can be avoided.

Difficulty arises as interaction between and among conflicting positions increases. Incompatibilities once tolerated or respected because they had no impact on alternative views may suddenly become troublesome. Language differences, styles of interaction, and different ways of perceiving the world become increasingly relevant. This sort of conflict often occurs for cross-cultural travelers and in such cases is called "culture shock."

One need not travel to experience conflict and culture shock. Increased interaction of different groups results from urbanization, integration, and the fuller participation of culturally different groups at secondary levels of interaction (e.g., the marketplace) and increases the potential for cultural conflict. Anthropologist Edward Hall describes one such conflict, a result of differences in culturally influenced "action chains," arising between an Anglo rancher and a rancher of Spanish heritage in New Mexico.[12] So it was when the Anglo rancher, apparently by mistake, put a fence across his Spanish neighbor's property. The first the Anglo rancher knew of the problem was when he found the fence ripped out of the ground and cut to pieces. For the Spanish rancher this was but the first step (lowest level) in the action chain. For the Anglo, however, this was the last and most serious in a chain of events. He was ready to fight!

"Action chains" are the normal sequences of events (or behaviors) that make up more complex behaviors. For example, when an Anglo has some problem, the normal sequence (action chain) is to inform the other party (probably informally at first) that a grievance exists. Should this fail, the conflict progresses to a more formal level, for example, an attorney may be hired to serve notice about the grievance. The conflict may proceed to court. Direct physical (violent) confrontation with the contending party is only a last resort. The action chain of the Spanish is quite different. Spanish culture typically relies on a greater sensitivity and awareness in its members. (Anthropologists call this high-context culture.) When a grievance arises, the person with the problem is likely to complain to friends and family members about the problem but not to confront the contending party directly. The offender is simply expected to know that something is the matter. When the first person's frustration reaches its limits, this individual party acts outwardly and directly against the second person. This is the first direct act. Should this fail, the conflict escalates to a more formal level, and courts and attorneys are typically the last step.

In *Ribbin', Jivin', and Playin' the Dozens*,[13] Herbert Foster offers numerous examples of how differences in culturally acceptable behavior collide as white middle-class teachers enter predominantly Black inner-city schools. The rules of appropriate and expected social behavior held by students are often different from those to which the teacher is accustomed. One example Foster offers deals with the testing of individuals to determine their inner strength. Picture yourself as a new teacher walking down the hall during passing period in an inner-city high school. As you approach a group of three Black male students, one sticks his arm out and blocks your way. Do you stop, walk around the students, duck under the arm, say "excuse me," or push the student out of your way? If you are uninitiated to inner-city "games," you may perceive the action as a direct confrontation and a physical threat. In fact, as Foster describes the school in which he worked, the students wish to see if you can be intimidated, and no physical threat is intended. But it should be clear that cultural differences may result in the misperception of cues, the misunderstanding of behavior, feelings of anxiety, and the like. Communication, teaching, and learning can be seriously hampered because neither the teacher nor the student understands the other's behavior.

Schools are a particularly likely spot for this form of cultural conflict to occur because they are frequently established and operated by one cultural group for another. While teachers may find that they are unable to cope effectively, often the situation is reversed, and the student is the one left in an unfamiliar and unresponsive environment. Some incompatibilities are straightforward and easily perceived but often misunderstood. For example, a middle-class Anglo teacher may interpret "aggressive" physical behavior as a physical threat rather than a normal style of interaction or a form of testing. Similarly, the quiet "withdrawn" behavior attributed to traditional Chicano and Native American students may be perceived as a lack of interest, low motivation, or more seriously, limited intellectual ability. In the same way, the cooperative tendencies of some cultural groups may be in conflict with the teacher's valuing of independence, self-sufficiency, or competition.

Cognitive Styles.   Culturally influenced styles of behavior have been discussed in multicultural literature now for a number of years. Anglo teachers have been admonished not to force Chicano or Native American students to look them in the eye. Differences have been suggested in orientation to time, competition, authority figures, use of language, personal space, and the appropriate "wait time" a teacher should exercise when expecting a student response, to mention only a few. But a less obvious and potentially more important area of cultural difference exists that has only begun to be researched. Cognitive styles and ways of perceiving the world are highly influenced by culture as well. Furthermore, these areas remain largely invisible to the casual classroom observer.

In very simple terms, cognitive style is the manner in which one encounters, orders, and thinks about the world. It is a pattern or style of internal response to environment. While mental activity itself is an inherent part of our physiological nature, much of the way it is directed toward the outer environment is culturally determined. From birth forward, the world is mediated by cultural variables. Even sensory data are modified by cultural variables. At the babbling state of language development, for example, the young child is capable of hearing all human sounds. Evidence suggests that as children mature, this wide range of ability is lost, and youngsters become fixed on those verbal sounds reinforced by the language of their culture. Visual perception is no less influenced by culture. It remains as "a blooming, buzzing, confusion" until defined by a cultural frame of reference. Thus, Australian bushmen of one tribe do not perceive the shape of a circle, and Eskimos do not develop the snow blindness visitors from other cultures experience. Even more striking, one study reviewed by anthropologists Kluckholm and Strodtbeck revealed that even when sight was restored to blind persons, those who had been deprived of visual experience since infancy still were unable to "see."[14]

Culture, then, plays a prominent role in what one "sees," both literally and figuratively. It provides the constructs necessary for one to organize and categorize the world. Indeed, it provides the structure from which the world is created for the individual. Culture also influences the way the mind works and the way one comes to know the world. It seems to influence, for example, whether one encounters the world in wholes or parts, analytically or intuitively, deductively or inductively. The research of Ramirez and Castaneda supports this view by showing that traditional Mexican Americans tend to be field-dependent, that is, to rely on the surrounding field or environment for cues in perceiving or interpreting stimuli or data; Anglos tend to be field-independent, for example, to focus on specific stimuli or data without regard to the surrounding field (environment).[15] There even seems to be a correlation between cerebral hemispheric dominance and culture. In two separate studies, Navajos and Hopis both demonstrated a significantly greater proclivity to right-brain dominance than did Anglos.[16]

The significance of the above findings is not yet clearly established, but unquestionably their potential relevance is great. When students and teachers are from different cultures, a student may sit in a classroom and not be able to see, hear, conceptualize, or mentally process the information presented by the teacher. The student's cognitive style may be in conflict with the style on which teaching and learning are based in the classroom. Moreover, these cultural determinants and differences will remain hidden from view: The student and the teacher may speak what appears to be the same language, and the conflict will be apparent only by the child's inability to learn.

Learning Styles.   Closely associated with cognitive styles are learning styles. Cognitive style encompasses the way one perceives and thinks about the world and includes thinking, perceiving, remembering, and problem solving. Learning style means the method by which one comes to know or understand the world, the accustomed pattern used in the acquisition of information, concepts, and skills. Obviously, cognitive styles and learning styles are closely related. They may even be considered two different facets of the same thing. But from a pedagogical point of view, it is advantageous to distinguish between them. It is necessary to understand that people not only perceive the world in different ways but also come to learn about the world in different ways and under different conditions.

Rita and Kenneth Dunn have identified eighteen different elements in four major categories of learning style.[17] The first category is environmental elements. For example, some individuals require absolute silence when they are concentrating, others can "block out" sound, and still others actually require background "noise" when they are trying to learn. Other environmental variables that affect learning are temperature, light, and the physical environment (i.e., design, carpeting, and chairs).

The second category consists of emotional elements: motivation, persistence, responsibility, and a need for structure. Responsible, persistent, and motivated students need to be taught differently from those who lack one or more of these qualities. Moreover, it is quite apparent that different kinds of stimulation motivate different students in different ways. Students also respond differently to structure. Some require specific directions, sequential tasks, frequent feedback, and continuing support; others learn better when presented with a number of choices and a flexible structure they can mold themselves.

The third category is sociological elements, factors making the social environment most conducive to a child's learning. Some individuals learn best when alone, others with peers, some with adults, and still others in some combination of these social environments.

The final category identified by the Dunns consists of physical elements: perceptual strengths, intake, time of day, and need for mobility. For example, some children show a preference for auditory stimuli, some for visual stimuli, some for tactile/kinesthetic, some for visual-tactile, and some for a combination of stimuli of these four major senses. A need to eat, drink, or nibble when studying, concentrating, or trying to internalize is also part of how some people learn, as is the time of day when one's energy is at a peak. So, too, is the ability to remain stationary for longer or shorter periods of time.

As with cognitive styles, much remains to be done in exploring the relationship between learning style preferences and cultural groups. There is evidence, however, that there is some connection and that cul-

turally influenced styles may conflict with one another. An ethnographic study of the Yaqui Indians in Guadalupe, Arizona, for example,
revealed several very important differences between Yaqui learning
style and that in the typical public school classroom.*[18] One difference
is that Yaqui children tend to avoid unfamiliar ground where trial and
error or an inquiry method of reasoning is required. This behavior can
be understood when one recognizes that Yaqui children tend to come
to school believing that a respectful attitude toward any task includes
doing the task well. A task done well is a task done according to recommended or correct form. For Yaquis, the activity itself is as important as the purpose or goal of the activity. If it cannot be done well,
there is little reason to engage in the activity at all. Teachers must carefully prepare children for such activities and avoid asking them to per-
form or recite before they have mastered the task. Often, however,
teachers ask students to first try on their own or to use inquiry
methods, or they urge students to "be creative." Another characteristic
of Yaqui learning is heavy reliance on watching and modeling desired
behavior. Oral instruction and direction is minimal by Anglo middle-
class standards. In the Yaqui community, learning the correct way to
do a task by watching it being performed repeatedly by others is highly
reinforced. In contrast, both the middle-class non-Yaqui home and the
school rely predominantly on oral instruction and the manipulation of
language to organize and make sense out of the world. The tendency
of teachers to introduce almost all new concepts and give all instruc-
tions verbally will conflict with the traditional cultural patterns reinforced in the Yaqui community.

Ramirez and Castaneda have found learning styles of traditional
Chicano students conflict with those often reinforced in the public
school classroom.[19] Traditional Mexican American students tend to be
motivated when the subject matter is related to personal and family experiences and concerns but less motivated by abstract, objective, and
unemotional presentation of information. Similarly, traditional Mexican
American students tend to be very sensitive to the social environment,
preferring personal, informal relationships with authority figures.
Some teachers may find that this interferes with their objectivity and
their ability to maintain an efficient classroom. The sensitivity of traditional Mexican Americans to the social environment also suggests that
these students have a high need for guidance, direction, and support
from authority figures; they are particularly sensitive to both praise and

---

* There is a great danger here of overgeneralizing and stereotyping students on the basis
of culture or race. It should be recognized that when anthropologists and sociologists
draw conclusions, they are referring to general population patterns that, while true for
the group as a whole, may not be true for any particular individual. Thus a teacher must
be alert to differences but must not assume they are there simply on the basis of outward
appearance. This is also true for the conclusion that Ramirez and Castaneda reach about
Mexican Americans, to be discussed shortly.

criticism from the teacher. Finally, traditional Mexican American students are often accustomed to a more cooperative style of interaction than allowed in many classrooms and tend to do poorly in situations that demand individual competition.

We can see that different life styles, perceptions, cognitive styles, and learning styles will exist in a society that is truly culturally plural. At times, these differences will conflict with one another, but this cultural conflict need not develop into social conflict or work to the disadvantage of any particular group as long as the cultures remain isolated or do not compete with one another. As interaction among different groups increases, the opportunity for potential damage can be reduced by allowing for alternative styles, particularly cognitive and learning styles. Through concern, research, and sensitivity, school environments and teaching styles can be adjusted to accommodate those of the student body. Nevertheless, some differences are not likely to be accommodated even when there is a desire for cultural pluralism because some styles of interaction and patterns of behavior are likely to threaten, confuse, or irritate others even when they are understood.

Personal Conflicts within a Multicultural Society

Our exploration of cultural conflict has concentrated on conflict between groups or individuals. While this has been the most pressing concern for those investigating cultural conflict, cultural diversity may contribute to an increased frequency of personal, inner conflict as well.

Internal conflict has primarily been the subject of study by psychologists. It occurs when a person is motivated to engage in two or more mutually exclusive activities or when incompatible or mutually exclusive values present themselves in the form of an actual or potential choice or decision. Psychologists see inner conflict as part of the natural psychological growth of the individual and, in varying levels of intensity, part of everyday life. It is often associated with anxiety or frustration. At times inner conflict and the accompanying frustration and anxiety will arise from cultural differences in society.

Internalized Responses and Feelings.   In discussing the impact of culture on cognitive styles and learning styles, we saw that culture has a profound effect on the development of an individual's internalized patterns. During enculturation, individuals develop needs, preferences, and styles of interaction often associated or paired with certain emotional, psychological, or physiological responses. Thus, the same stimulus may elicit a feeling of joy (or fear) in the members of one group, while it leaves those of another cold and unmoved; people from one culture may need privacy as a regular part of their lives, while members of another may come to depend on a high level of social commitment and interaction; and members of one group may develop a loud and "aggressive" interaction style that individuals from a different culture may find threatening.

Much cultural conflict has resulted from misunderstandings or from an inability to communicate effectively because of ignorance of the meaning of certain cultural behaviors. Through a sensitive cultural awareness program it would be possible to develop a greater knowledge about different cultures and thus facilitate communication and interaction. While such efforts will go a long way toward bettering intercultural relations in a multicultural society, problems will remain. Even though individuals may come to understand and appreciate the cultural patterns of a different ethnic group, these patterns may continue to elicit an adverse physiological, emotional, or psychological reaction. Though cognitive awareness may dispel misconceptions and threats on the intellectual level, subconscious conditioned affective responses may remain. Thus, while knowing why the situation is the way it is, an individual may not be able to avoid feeling uncomfortable.

In a simple but illustrative example of this phenomenon, anthropologist Clyde Kluckholm[20] tells of a trader's wife a number of years ago in Arizona who would serve guests a mild-tasting white meat similar to both chicken and fish yet quite distinct in its own right. Questioned as to the ingredients of the dish, she would refrain from answering until all had eaten their fill—whereupon she would explain that it was freshly killed rattlesnake. Some guests reacted with involuntary vomiting. Similar stories are told about American military personnel in Southeast Asia who were served dog.

The consumption of food, of course, is largely within the individual's control, but many other variables exist that have the potential to elicit adverse reactions. Violations of personal space, privacy, time structures, orderliness, hygiene, noise, population density, display of emotions, and communication styles are but a few. Feelings of frustration, anxiety, irritation, anger, fear, and annoyance may all arise involuntarily when one is placed in a situation in conflict with enculturation patterns. Even when one fully understands the circumstances surrounding the stimulus and is aware that the source of the response is rooted in early personal experiences, the response may persist, creating inner conflict.

An individual can escape from inner conflict caused by unpleasant involuntary reactions or avoid the reactions altogether by avoiding contact with the triggering stimulus, but this means limiting the interaction of culturally different groups. Conflict may then arise when the individual is forced to choose between being exposed to adverse stimuli for the benefits to be gained by interaction and avoiding the negative stimuli but forfeiting the advantages of interaction. Consider, for example, a researcher attracted to an environment for its rich research

potential who also perceives the environment as extremely threatening, or a teacher who understands the cultural basis of loud and
"aggressive" actions of the students but is nevertheless incapacitated
by it, or an individual with a liberal intellectual view of homosexuality
and public displays of affection who feels strongly repulsed by the sight
of two men affectionately embracing.

At times one can avoid adverse physiological, psychological, and
emotional responses while continuing to interrelate with the source of
the negative stimulus. Such is the case when one can control or extin-
guish the triggering stimuli. Thus, a teacher who becomes tense in the
face of an active, noisy classroom can "lay down the law" and maintain
a tightly controlled classroom. Similarly, a teacher uncomfortable with
close affective personal relationships with students can remain at arm's
length and behave in a businesslike manner. But while this tactic may
relieve one form of conflict, it should be apparent that it is likely to create others. A teacher's personal conflict may center on the decision
whether or not to be effective instead of having to decide whether or
not to interact with students. That is, the teacher may have to decide
either to ignore the cultural learning and cognitive styles of the students and preserve personal mental health or to be more effective in
the classroom but experience considerable discomfort. Beyond personal
conflict, it is also possible that if the teacher fails to acknowledge the
cultural needs of the students or represses culturally appropriate behaviors, the personal conflict will become a form of social conflict.

Role Conflict.   A second source of inner conflict likely to be accentuated by multiculturalism is the gap between the different roles one is
expected to play and those one wishes to assume. We all take on a variety of social roles in our everyday life. One can be a mother, wife, professor, voter, Democrat, and runner all at once. Some of these roles are
very specific and matter only during certain times. Being a good professor is very important during work hours, but the professor drops this
role in order to be a good wife and mother once the workday has
ended. Other role identities are relevant most of the time. For example,
the facts of one's age, race, and sex are not easily changed; in any case,
these more permanent roles serve as an identity kit that we constantly
use to define who we are. They become the backdrop against which
more specific roles are acted out. At times there may be conflict, but
most of us have for the most part successfully integrated our various
roles or at least learned to alternate from one to another without
difficulty.

A pluralistic society tends to create problems in role identity. Different cultural groups may project a different meaning and set of expected behaviors onto the same identity role. Thus, to be Black may
mean something quite different to the Black community than it does to

the white community. Similarly, appropriate student behavior as defined by a youngster's peer group may conflict sharply with the expectations of the teacher. In such cases, either the individual must create enough role distance between the competing positions to avoid conflict or a choice must be made between the two. Inner conflict results when the former is not possible and the individual finds value in both roles. For example, a high school student may recognize the advantages of studying and doing well in school but may also value the social acceptance of his peer group, which views school strictly as a social event. Another example is the role conflict sometimes experienced by professional Black women. Although Black women may find themselves in a position to move upward occupationally, it has generally been thought inappropriate for them to compete against Black men for a position. Because of the historically poor social position of Black men in our society, it is considered a greater advantage to Blacks as a group for men to assume positions of status and power.

In the first example, conflict arises from two culturally different perceptions of appropriate role behavior. The second problem illustrates how role conflict might develop within a single cultural group. Here, the conflict arises between individual aspirations and group expectations.

Personal as well as social conflict, then, will occur in the culturally plural society. Despite increased cultural awareness and toleration, individuals are likely to experience adverse physiological, psychological, and emotional reactions when exposed to certain cultural stimuli. They are also likely to experience increased role conflict as interaction between culturally different populations increases.

A TYPOLOGY OF CONFLICT

There are many different ways to distinguish among various kinds of conflict.[21] We have described conflict over social rewards (e.g., material rewards, resources, status, and power), conflict resulting from differences in values and life-style preferences, personal inner conflict, and role conflict. These distinctions tend to emphasize the situations in which conflict is likely to develop. Each kind of conflict has a distinct basis, but in many cases the outward manifestations of conflict are not identical with the actual point of conflict.

Realistic and Nonrealistic Conflict

On the basis of the earlier work of sociologist George Simmel, Lewis Coser differentiates between *realistic* and *nonrealistic* conflict.[22] Realistic conflicts arise from the frustration of specific demands within a relationship and from estimates of gains by the participants, are directed at the presumed frustrating object, and are thus seen as a means toward a specific end. In *realistic* conflicts, one party wishes to right a wrong or to protect or further its own interests. In *nonrealistic* conflicts, however, the conflict arises exclusively from aggressive impulses that seek expression regardless of the object. Here the conflict is an end in itself, and the object of contention is purely accidental or arbitrary. While both kinds of conflict involve the interaction of contending parties and outward manifestations of conflict, nonrealistic conflict is occasioned not by the rival goals of the antagonists but by the need for at least one of them to release tension.

So that there is no misunderstanding, it should be pointed out that there is actual social conflict between two or more parties in both realistic and nonrealistic conflicts. In the ordinary use of the term, both conflicts are experienced as *real* conflict by those involved. However, Coser uses the term "real" in a technical way in order to differentiate the sources of conflict. Conflicts arising out of the objective circumstances of the situation are realistic (real) in that there is an actual point of contention. Nonrealistic conflicts arise from the emotional or psychological states of one or both parties. What *appears* to be the object of contention is in the final analysis irrelevant.

Perhaps a couple of examples will make this point clearer. Consider workers who go on strike to force the exclusion of Black fellow workers from the shop in order to maintain higher wage rates. If indeed this is an accurate account of the situation, the conflict, as defined by Coser, is realistic. We would expect the conflict and discrimination to decrease once the workers have secured the desired wage rates, even if the wage rates can be secured through means other than exclusion of Black workers. But should the workers maintain the discriminatory practice when more effective means to the same end are available, according to Coser it is probable that nonrealistic elements such as prejudice are at the root of the conflict.[23] Anti-semitism can be analyzed in the same way. When discrimination is caused by conflict of interests or values between Jewish and other groups or individuals, it is realistic. However, insofar as the conflict is primarily a response to frustrations, and Jews merely appear suitable objects for a release of aggression, it is nonrealistic. Actually, in the latter case it matters little whether the object of discrimination is Jews, Blacks, Chicanos, homosexuals, or some other group.

Distinguishing these kinds of conflict should help in identifying conflict management strategies. Realistic conflict should cease if the participants can find equally satisfying alternative ways to achieve their ends.[24] That is, in realistic conflict, some means of resolving the issue is always potentially available to the participants. Nonrealistic conflicts leave few alternatives or means of directly resolving the conflict. Because the conflict is an end in itself, the only choice to be made is the object toward which the aggression will be directed, and management of the conflict will ultimately involve removing the causes of the underlying aggression or tension. Frequently, aggression and tension arise from deprivations and frustrations stemming from the socialization process; other related sources may be adult obligations and conflicts, and the projection of originally realistic antagonisms that for various reasons could not be expressed or directed at their proper object (transference).[25]

Displaced Conflict, Misattributed Conflict, and False Conflict

Mortin Deutsch offers another set of categories for distinguishing among different kinds of conflicts.[26] Though his typology consists of six different conflicts, three of his distinctions complement the distinctions we have already made and will aid in understanding conflict in a culturally plural society.

At times during realistic conflict, the description of the problem given by one or more of the participants does not capture its true nature. One such problem, which Deutsch calls *displaced conflict*, occurs when the parties in conflict are arguing about the wrong thing. In displaced conflict, an objective basis of the conflict exists, yet the conflict being experienced—the manifest conflict—is not the true point of contention. Rather, an underlying stress exists, giving rise to tension or irritability and leading each side to be unduly sensitive to slights, argumentative, and the like. Often the manifest conflict is a symbolic or symptomatic form of the underlying conflict. Consider these illustrations:

A school board may be struggling with a teachers' union over the transfer of a teacher. The underlying conflict may really center on power, on which group has the right to make certain decisions.

A racial dispute may involve alleged police brutality in dealing with Black citizens. The underlying cause may be the unequal distribution of power and resources rather than the occasion in question.

A teacher may punish a student for failing to follow established classroom procedures when the real problem can be found in the teacher's feelings of insecurity in the face of cultural disparity.

The tendency in the management of displaced conflict is to treat the manifest symptoms. Frequently, this results only in temporary resolutions. Unless the underlying problem is dealt with, or unless the manifest conflict can be separated from the underlying issues and treated in isolation, the conflict simply reemerges.

A second kind of conflict that fails to characterize the true nature of the problem is what Deutsch calls *misattributed conflict*.[27] Here the conflict is between the wrong parties and, as a consequence, usually over the wrong issues. For example, when there is a shortage of good jobs, antagonism rather than cooperation between white and Black workers may reflect a faulty attribution; personal difficulties may be thought to result from competition from the other racial group, while the real culprit may be the industrial system or the government. Frequently, divide-and-conquer tactics are evident in such struggles. Instead of directing their energy toward the true culprit in a conflict situation, individuals and groups fight among themselves. The resolution of conflicts involving misattribution, like that of displaced conflict, involves seeing beyond the apparent conflict to its true sources.

The final kind of conflict with which we shall be concerned is *false conflict*. "This is the occurrence of conflict when there is no objective basis for it."[28] That is, while the contending parties find themselves in the midst of conflict, the conflict is based on misconception or misunderstanding and not on any real point of contention. Thus the meaningful interaction of two groups or individuals may be prevented by differences in customs, manners, and perceptions not because they are incompatible but because they are not adequately understood. For example, in a school setting, members of one group may interpret the casual undisciplined manner of another group as laziness and lack of motivation; an individual may interpret the "aggressive" behavior of another as a physical threat; a teacher may unwittingly use competitive games to try to motivate students from a noncompetitive culture; or an individual may misinterpret the shy, retiring behavior of another as disinterest or dislike.

It should be apparent that the resolution of false conflicts will ultimately be based on greater understanding and communication between contending parties. We must also avoid the tendency to believe that because they are not reflections of true conflicts (i.e., realistic conflicts), we need not be as concerned about them. False conflicts always have the potential to turn into true conflicts, particularly in a competitive, suspicious atmosphere. If misunderstanding and miscommunication persist, it is likely that the needs of some groups will not be met. Moreover, false conflicts have the potential to needlessly fuel the tensions and frustrations on which nonrealistic conflicts are based.

THE FUNCTIONAL ASPECTS OF SOCIAL CONFLICT

Social conflict is often identified with its most visible manifestations, namely, individual and collective violence and disruption. Most people therefore tend to view conflict as a threat to the existence of civilization and its individual members. According to psychoanalytic theory, all conflict between human beings is viewed as irrational and something to be eliminated. Antipathy to others is often viewed as displacement of hostility initially felt toward one's parents, or displacement of unexpressed anger originally directed toward someone else. As we have seen, much of contemporary sociological theory also has regarded social conflict as an abnormal condition that is disruptive of social order and should be eliminated. Talcott Parsons, perhaps one of the most influential contemporary students of sociology, saw conflict as having primarily disruptive, dissociating, and dysfunctional consequences. Conflict appeared to him as a partly avoidable and partly inevitable and "endemic" form of sickness in the social body.[29]

It is understandable that we generally view conflict as undesirable. It has brought much pain and suffering to the world, and has caused much inconvenience by disrupting our social institutions and daily affairs. Indeed, the uncertainty and insecurity generated when the normal order of things is called into question may well produce the greatest anxiety over conflict. Yet it must be recognized that in every social structure there are occasions for conflict because individuals and subgroups are likely to make, on occasion, rival claims to limited resources, status, power, or values, particularly in a pluralistic society. But this need not be violent or disruptive. Whether conflict promises to play a functional role in society or threatens to tear it apart depends in part on the social structure within which it occurs. Conflict tends to be dysfunctional when there is insufficient toleration and institutionalization to accommodate it. What threatens the equilibrium of a social structure is not conflict but the rigidity of the structure, which permits hostilities to accumulate and become focused on one major issue.[30] In societies with flexible structure, where social institutions provide for and tolerate conflict, frequent small encounters will occur whenever a resolution of tension seems to be indicated and will remain focused primarily on the conditions that led to their outbreak.

Lewis Coser, in *The Functions of Social Conflict*, has perhaps described most extensively and systematically the functional aspects of conflict in society. Basing his work on the earlier writings of George Simmel, Coser carefully establishes that social conflict can serve to benefit society as a whole as well as smaller social units.

Identity and the Group-Binding Functions of Conflict

Conflict contributes to the development and maintenance of both personal and group identity. Psychoanalytic theory has emphasized that through opposition to wishes of their parents, children acquire a sense of their own identity. It is believed necessary for children to oppose parental authority particularly during the preschool period, and during adolescence as well, in order to begin to view themselves as persons with distinct wishes, talents, and self-worth different from those of others.[31] A similar process operates at the group level. Sociologists generally accept that the distinction between ourselves, our own group, and everybody else is established in and through conflict. Group boundaries are defined and maintained in reference to other groups viewed in some way to be different or in opposition to the goals of one's own "in" group. Thus, conflict with other groups contributes to the establishment and reaffirmation of the identity of the group and maintains the group's boundaries against the surrounding social world. Conflicts concerning nationality, ethnic group, culture, and politics provide widespread examples of this phenomenon.

Consider ethnicity: In one sense, ethnic groups are arbitrary. In their native lands, for example, Eastern and Southern Europeans generally did not identify themselves on the basis of some national ethnic criterion but usually by affiliation with a particular village, family, or geographic region. It was their arrival in the United States and the strong nativistic reaction they received that gave form to the modern ethnic distinctions of Italian, Greek, Slavic, Polish, and so on. Thus the dominant majority, in an attempt to preserve the status quo, gave birth to white ethnic distinctiveness in the United States. A similar process can be seen with the Native American movement. The American Indian traditionally identified with a particular tribe. It was the whites who saw them as Indians or belonging to tribal nations, and only recently have Native Americans begun to define themselves as one common people.

The role that conflict has to play in the process can be illustrated by considering how often we think of ourselves as Earthlings. We don't— except in modern cinematography. But should we be invaded by *alien* beings, as portrayed by Hollywood, the distinction would suddenly become important. A new ethnic group of Earthlings would suddenly be created.

Group identity can in turn serve as part of an individual's personal identity. Conflict contributes to personal identity inasmuch as it results in a person becoming aware of personal social and economic interests, values, beliefs, and social behavior patterns. That is, one becomes aware of, defines, or chooses a self in opposition to competing alternatives. Faced with conflict situations, an individual is often forced to make a commitment and take a stand and to clarify who he or she is. Thus, to be Black, Chicano (or some other ethnic minority), or, for that matter, man or woman, in our society can be more than a biological fact. To define oneself socially in these terms entails identifying with certain social and political attitudes; it engenders a sense of belonging.

Interestingly, the identity achieved through conflict does not necessarily result in one group or person viewing another negatively, though this is often the case. An out-group can, at times, become a positive reference for the in-group or individual. Thus, conflict may help create role models as one comes to aspire to or be motivated toward some of the competitor's qualities. This often occurs in a stratified social system like the United States where competition and upward mobility are prescribed norms. Members of groups that have been frustrated in their attempt to secure a relatively favorable position in the stratification hierarchy, and the accompanying rewards, may view more successful groups with envy. For example, though they continue to compete, the less advantaged group may view some of the more successful group's qualities, such as hard work, thrift, solidarity, and the like, along with their social position and accompanying life style, as desirable.

Conflict, then, serves to establish and maintain the identities and boundary lines of societies and groups. Conflict with other groups contributes to the establishment and reaffirmation of the identity of the group and maintains its boundaries against the surrounding social world.[32]

In a brief digression, we should note that public education often seems designed to eliminate open conflict between differences in ideas and ways of life. As a matter of policy, elimination of conflict is often sought by inducing conformity and by exposing students only to noncontroversial ideas. If confrontation with disparate points of view contributes to the formation of an individual's identity, the tendency of public education to stay away from controversy may be doing students a disservice. It would be unfortunate if harmony was achieved at the expense of students' sense of personal identity.

Development and Maintenance of Relationships

Intergroup Relationships. Another function of social conflict is to establish a starting point for interaction. It seems to be one way of acquiring knowledge of, or making contact with, a previously unknown person, and it may well "break the ice" for subsequent friendly relations.[33] The very act of entering into conflict with another person establishes a relationship where perhaps none existed before and thus offers the opportunity for the struggling parties eventually to become associated. An example is two small children, strangers prior to combat over a toy, who feel acquainted because of the encounter and proceed to become friends and to play with the toy cooperatively. Adult behavior offers similar examples.

Similarly, conflict creates rules for the interaction of contending parties. The beginning is likely to be the recognition that the opponents already have common interests and norms. For example, when different ethnic groups struggle over the distribution of educational resources and rewards, this implies that each party already recognizes the value of education. It is also likely that there will be a common set of rules and norms about how these resources and rewards are to be distributed. For example, both groups probably agree that equal educational opportunity should prevail. During the course of conflict, the context will change and new situations not covered by existing rules and norms will come into being. This change in the context will in turn act as a stimulus for the establishment of new rules and norms. This can be seen in the school desegregation movement initiated by *Brown v. Board of Education.*[34] As a result of earlier conflict, new data and norms recast the "separate but equal" doctrine in a new context, which in turn has given rise to a whole new set of relationships, norms, and rules regarding integration. The process can also be seen in the enactment of new laws providing for equal educational opportunity for various minority groups. Conflict, then has the potential to revitalize existent norms and create a new framework of norms within which the contenders can interact. It can be seen as an agent of socialization for both contending parties.[35]

Not only does conflict establish a relationship between conflicting parties, but it also tends to create and facilitate relationships between potential allies. The formation of coalitions and temporary associations resulting from conflict may bring together otherwise unrelated persons and groups. If several parties face a common opponent, a unifying bond is created between them. The coalition may take one of two forms: new groups with distinct boundary lines, ideologies, loyalties and common values; or, stopping short of this, instrumental associations in the face of a common threat. These coalitions and associations then give structure and bind together the various elements of an otherwise individualistic society.

Intragroup Relationships. If conflict has the potential to stimulate interaction and eventually cooperation between different parties, it can also create strength in already existing groups. This happens in several ways.

One way in which groups may become internally stronger is through the development of a strong sense of solidarity and consensus produced when the group members perceive themselves to be threatened by a common enemy. Under such circumstances, members may drop any individual differences they may have to form a united front. A common sense of belonging will be stimulated, and common norms, beliefs, and perceptions may be renewed or reemphasized.

Conflict also performs group maintenance functions insofar as it facilitates communication and interaction among group members. Intragroup conflict contributes toward this end by "clearing the air." That is, "it eliminates the accumulations of blocked and balked hostile dispositions by allowing their free behavioral expression,"[36] by allowing for grievances and discontent to be alleviated in an ongoing manner. In contrast, the damming up of unrelieved or partially relieved tensions, instead of allowing conditions to change as a response to strife, leads to rigidity in the structure and creates the potential for a disruptive explosion.[37] The acknowledgement and constant adjustment of difficulties within the group clears the air and contributes to long-term stability of the group.

As a corollary to this point, it should also be noted that the absence of conflict cannot necessarily be taken as an index of the strength and stability of a relationship. If participants value a relationship but feel that it is tenuous and that conflict will endanger it further, they will tend to avoid conflict. Thus the absence of conflict may in fact indicate suppressed strain and an unstable relationship. By the same token, when close relationships are characterized by frequent conflicts rather than by the accumulation of hostile and ambivalent feelings, it may indicate the stability of the relationship. That is, evidence of conflict may be taken as an index of the operation of a balancing mechanism.[38]

Conflicts as an Agent of Change

John Dewey once wrote: "Conflict is the gadfly of thought. It steers us to observation and memory. It instigates to invention. It shocks us out of sheep-like passivity, and sets us at noting and contriving.... Conflict is a *sine qua non* of reflection and ingenuity."[39] Dewey recognized the stimulating and motivating value of conflict to human achievement. He believed conflict to be the force that drives humankind beyond the barriers of convention, to reorder what is "known" and to inquire into the nature of things. This function of conflict is also recognized in theories of contemporary psychology. Most psychologists see some state of disequilibrium or anxiety as a motivating force for human activity. That is, some discomfort, problem, or challenge stimulates humans to overcome inertia and go beyond the existing state of affairs. We can see this to be true in the world around us with only a moment's reflection. A shortage of oil stimulates the production of smaller and more fuel-efficient automobiles. The persistence of disease stimulates medical research. Indeed, most of our current space age technology has grown out of the arms race.

Conflict also has its effect in the social world. While discussing relationships, we noted that struggles within society may act to stimulate the establishment of new rules, norms, and institutions. Organizations may change their objectives, activities, or organizational structure to accommodate or resolve conflict. School desegregation, multicultural education, bilingual education, and affirmative action are examples of reorganization in the public sectors of society resulting from pressure exerted by various minority groups.

We have also noted that conflict may act as a stimulus for the formation of new social relationships as each party searches for allies. Similarly, a reordering of existing relationships may take place as parties to a dispute seek solutions. Both parties, for example, may change their behavior in order to limit the conflict through compromise. Finally, we should note the overall potential for the enrichment of society as interaction and communication, stimulated by conflict, bring together diverse ideas and perspectives. It is this principle on which the foundations of a democratic society are based.

SUMMARY

In this chapter, it has been suggested that cultural conflict will be a continuing feature of our society. We have seen that some of the more simple theories describing ethnic relationships in the United States are based on consensus theory, which projects the normal state of modern societies to be one of order and stability. A renewed interest in conflict theory, however, suggests that the consensus theory view of society is too limited and that a much more reasonable view is that modern societies involve both conflict and consensus as normal and functional interrelated qualities.

We have seen that cultural conflict may arise as a form of social conflict when diverse groups struggle to secure the social rewards distributed by society. Conflicts may arise over material rewards, status, and power, as well as over basic social values. We have seen that certain qualities of society will affect the frequency of these conflicts: The likelihood of contention increases as different groups come to view each other as competitive threats; and the degree to which different groups view each other as competitors (and thus the frequency of social strife) increases to the extent that competition and achievement are the norms of the society. Thus, because of its pluralistic nature and emphasis on achievement through competition, the United States is likely to provide fertile ground for cultural conflict.

We have also seen that value conflicts may arise independent of conflicts over social rewards. If cultural pluralism is to be interpreted to mean that there will be a goodly number of diverse cultural groups in society, we can expect that some of the values of life styles of these groups will be incompatible with those of other groups. As group interaction increases, then, so will value conflicts. Differences that could be tolerated in isolation will become an increasingly greater threat as closer cultural interactions develop.

Conflicts resulting from differences in cognitive styles, styles of interaction, and learning styles are also to be expected. It appears that culture influences the way we perceive, order, think about, learn about, and interact with the world. Some of these differences will be obvious to the observer, while others will remain latent. Stresses resulting from hidden differences are not likely to result in direct outward social conflict. Rather, that they exist will be manifest by feelings of frustration and failure, as well as by the inability of one or both parties to profit from the interaction. The more obvious outward differences have a higher potential for clear-cut social conflict, and more energy will be focused on them. But greater understanding will not necessarily follow from greater attention. Indeed, conflict resulting from obvious differences often arises precisely because of the various ways the different parties perceive the behavior in question.

Inner conflicts, too, will be a by-product of multiculturalism. Even enlightened individuals will be faced with situations that trigger feelings of frustration, anxiety, irritation, or other uncomfortable responses. As a result, people can expect to be faced with difficult choices regarding their interaction with culturally different populations. Individuals are also likely to experience a greater degree of role conflict in a multicultural setting. This is particularly true for minority individuals, who may be caught in the conflict between the expectations of the dominant culture and those of their own subculture. In addition, role conflict can be expected to arise between the personal aspirations of an individual and appropriate behavior as defined by that person's cultural group.

The chapter has explored a typology of conflicts. We distinguished between realistic and nonrealistic conflicts, the former arising from specific demands and being directed toward some end and the latter arising from a need to release tension or aggression and thus being not means to particular ends but ends in themselves. We further distinguished between displaced conflicts, misattributed conflicts, and false conflicts. Conflicts are probably rarely found in pure form, and it is sometimes difficult to distinguish among types. Such distinctions are useful, however, since management of different kinds of conflict will in all probability require different means.

Finally, we have recognized some of the functional qualities of social conflict. One such function is to provide a backdrop for the formation of one's identity. Both psychology and sociology acknowledge that one's identity is at least in part defined by the ideas and groups that one opposes. Conflict between different individuals and groups, then, contributes to the establishment and reaffirmation of both individual and group identity by providing an opportunity to clarify beliefs, values, and affiliations. This process binds individuals of like interests together, creating a sense of belonging.

Conflict also develops and maintains social relationships. By its very nature, conflict involves the interaction of contending parties, which leads to greater communication between the parties and eventually an accumulation of their knowledge about one another. Moreover, as conflict proceeds, a common set of rules and norms develops between the antagonists. Conflict also tends to create and facilitate relationships between previously unrelated groups who come together as allies and, in a similar manner, to strengthen the social ties within groups. Threatened from without, group members pull together, reaffirming their relationship and thereby building solidarity.

The last functional quality considered was the role of conflict in social change. Conflict often stimulates individuals to reevaluate, reorder, and rethink what has previously been taken for granted. Social norms and rules may be reconstructed as a result of conflict demands, as may the relationship between various individuals and groups. Furthermore, conflict often pushes human ingenuity, productivity, and technology to new horizons.

Of course, not all conflict is useful. To focus on the functional aspects of social conflict is not to deny that certain forms lead to the disintegration of specific social structures. Looking at the positive aspects of conflict, however, serves to correct a balance of analysis that has been tipped in the other direction. Conflict tends to be dysfunctional when there is insufficient toleration and institutionalization for it. What threatens the equilibrium of a social structure is not conflict itself but the rigidity of the structure, which permits hostilities to accumulate and become focused on one major issue.

NOTES

1. *Report of The National Advisory Commission on Civil Disorders* (New York: Dutton, 1968), p. 10.
2. William A Newman, *American Pluralism: A Study of Minority Groups and Social Theory* (New York: Harper & Row, 1973), p. 110.
3. R. A. Schermerhorn, *Comparative Ethnic Relations* (New York: Random House, 1970), p. 20.
4. For a critique of this view of social reality and a discussion of an alternative conflict model of society, see John Horton, "Order and Conflict Theories of Social Problems as Competing Ideologies," *American Journal of Sociology* 71 (1966): 701–13. Also see Schermerhorn, *Comparative Ethnic Relations*.
5. Michael W. Apple, "The Hidden Curriculum and the Nature of Conflict,"

Interchange 2, no. 4 (1971): 29–41; D. E. Apter, "Political Life and Pluralism," in *Pluralism in a Democratic Society*, ed. Melvin Tumin and Walter Plotch (New York: Praeger, 1977); Randall Collins, "Functional and Conflict Theories of Educational Stratification," in *Power and Ideology in Education*, ed. J. Karabel and A. H. Halsey (N.Y.: Oxford Univ. Press, 1977), pp. 118–36; Lewis Coser, *The Functions of Social Conflict* (New York: Free Press, 1965); Rolf Dahrendorf, *Class and Class Conflict in Industrial Society* (Stanford: Stanford University Press, 1959); Cynthia Enloe, *Ethnic Conflict and Political Development* (Boston: Little, Brown, 1973); Alvin Gouldner, *The Coming Crises in Western Sociology* (New York: Basic Books, 1970); John Horton, "Order and Conflict Theories of Social Problems as Competing Ideologies," *American Journal of Sociology* 17 (1966): 701–3; Newman, *American Pluralism*.

6. Newman, *American Pluralism*, p. 101.
7. Francis Hsu, "American Core Value and National Character," in *Psychological Anthropology*, ed Francis L. K. Hsu (Cambridge, Mass.: Schenkman, 1972), pp. 241–62.
8. Randall Collins, though he is not concerned with the hypothesis of a core American value, characterizes the United States as preoccupied with status and stratification, which results from and contributes to intergroup conflict. See his "Functional and Conflict Theories," pp. 118–36.
9. Newman, *American Pluralism*, pp. 112–15.
10. Kenneth E. Boulding, "Conflict Management as a Learning Process," in *Conflict in Society*, ed. Anthony de Reuch (London: J. and A. Churchill, 1966), pp. 236–48.
11. Newman, *American Pluralism*, p. 140.
12. Edward Hall, *Beyond Culture* (Garden City, N.Y.: Anchor, 1977).
13. Herbert Foster, *Ribbin', Jivin', and Playin' the Dozens* (Cambridge, Mass.: Ballinger, 1974).
14. F. R. Kluckholm and F. L. Strodtbeck, *Variations in Value Orientations* (Evanston, Ill.: Row, Peterson, 1951), p. 79.
15. Manuel Ramirez and Alfredo Castaneda, *Cultural Democracy, Bicognitive Development and Education* (New York: Academic Press, 1974).
16. Steven Scott, G. W. Hynd, L. Hunt, and W. Need, "Cerebral Speech Lateralization in the Native American Navajo," *Neuropsychologia* 17 (1979): 89–92.
17. Rita Dunn and Kenneth Dunn, *Teaching Students Through Their Individual Learning Styles: A Practical Approach* (Reston, Va.: Reston Publising, 1978); also see *Educational Leadership* 36, no. 4 (January 1979).
18. *Culture: A Way to Reading*, Tempe Elementary School District No. 3, ESEA Title IV-C Innovation, Instructional Guide, Tempe Elementary School, Tempe, AZ, 1979.
19. Ramirez and Castaneda, *Cultural Democracy*. G. P. Knight and S. Kagan, "Development of Prosocial and Competitive Behaviors in Anglo American and Mexican American Children," *Child Development* 48 (1977): 1385–94, found young Mexican American children to be more cooperative and less competitive in social problem solving than Anglo children.
20. Clyde Kluckholm, *Mirror for Man: The Relation of Anthropology to Modern Life* (New York: McGraw-Hill, 1949).

21. See for example, Martin Deutsch, *The Resolution of Conflict* (New Haven: Yale University Press, 1973), pp. 11–17; Kenneth E. Boulding, *Conflict and Defense: A General Theory* (New York: Harper & Row, 1962); and the first issue of the *Journal of Conflict Resolution* (1957): 1–104.
22. Coser, *Functions of Social Conflict*, p. 49.
23. Ibid., p. 54.
24. Ibid., p. 50.
25. Ibid., p. 54.
26. Deutsch, *Resolution of Conflict*, p. 12.
27. Ibid., p. 14.
28. Ibid.
29. Coser, *Functions of Social Conflict*, p. 23.
30. Ibid., p. 157.
31. Robert D. Borgman, *Social Conflict and Mental Health Services* (Springfield, Ill.: Charles C Thomas, 1978), p. 36.
32. Coser, *Functions of Social Conflict*, p. 38.
33. Ibid., p. 122–23.
34. *Brown* v. *Board of Education*, 347 U.S. 483 (1954).
35. Coser, *Functions of Social Conflict*, p. 128.
36. Ibid., p. 39.
37. Ibid., p. 45.
38. Ibid., p. 45.
39. John Dewey, *Human Nature and Conduct* (New York: Modern Library, 1930), p. 300, as quoted in Lewis Coser, "Social Conflict and Theory of Social Change," *British Journal of Sociology* 8 (1957): 198.

7

Making the Schools Work

The preceding discussion has been offered as the theoretical foundations that policy makers at all levels—including senior administrators of federal, state, and local educational agencies, program and project directors, school administrators, and classroom teachers—should consider if they are to respond to the needs of a pluralistic society. Yet much of what we have said has not been school specific; we have not offered specific recommendations to guide school policy. This approach has not been unintentional, for one premise of this study is that there are no clear-cut answers to the problems and alternatives we have investigated. Rather, policy must be established within a specific context by informed individuals who clearly understand the issues at hand. Nevertheless, it might be appropriate to point out some immediate issues that policy developers need to consider and to make some suggestions regarding the curriculum and administrative structure of the school. We turn to these shortly, but before we do, it may be useful to investigate the historical role schools have played in the Americanization of the poor and ethnic minorities.

ETHNICITY AND THE HISTORICAL FUNCTION OF THE SCHOOLS

Theoretical descriptions of the dynamic nature of ethnic groups have been developed and presented as models capable of explaining, depicting, and predicting the changing characteristics of ethnic groups in the United States. It should be apparent, however, that in the development of these models we have largely ignored the social and political dynamics that have influenced the direction in which ethnic groups have changed. In our discussion of the inadequacies of the theories of assimilation and amalgamation we suggested that the political and social ideologies of each group would influence the relationship of one group to another. For example, if the dominant group blocked structural assimilation for a minority group by refusing access to its institutions or refusing to share its power, the processes of both assimilation and amalgamation would be limited. Similarly, assimilation and amalgamation would be restricted to the extent that a minority group chose voluntary segregation or refused to give up certain cultural features. In the discussion of ethclass Gordon suggested that structural assimilation has been inhibited by prejudice, discrimination, and conflict. It may be useful at this time to explore in more detail the social and political factors that have influenced the quality of ethnic groups in the United States. Because of our interest in education, we focus our analysis on the public schools.

The Interpretation of History

All social institutions take shape in response to some perceived need. They are created for some purpose. The need or purpose does not always have to be articulated, though it often is. It would probably be accurate to say that most institutions take shape partly as a result of conscious planning and partly in response to unrecognized and less understood influences. In either case, the evolution of an institution occurs because it is supported by a constituency that perceives its function as valuable and is willing to support it ideologically, financially, and operationally. Because of the way they take shape and their need for support, social institutions necessarily have a value or normative component. That is, they are conceived and function to serve some set of values, and as a consequence their nature is value laden. It should come as no surprise that the values institutions support tend to be those of the individuals who contribute to and maintain them. Hence, in analyzing public schools we note that they have been developed and supported by the relatively affluent in society and as a consequence reflect the values and life styles of that group. Let us consider how these values might be interpreted.

It has been popular to believe that free public schools were conceived by their founders as a means to democratize the nation. The father of American public education, Horace Mann, writing in the mid-nineteenth century, was representative of the boundless faith in universal education, and in the words of Lawrence Cremin, believed that "once public schools were established, no evil could resist their solitary influence. Universal education could be the 'great equalizer' of human conditions, the 'balance wheel' of the social machinery, and the 'creator of wealth undreamed of.' Poverty would most assuredly disappear, and with it the rancorous discord between the 'haves' and the 'have-nots' that had marked all of human history. Crime would diminish; sickness would abate; and life for the common man would be longer, better, and happier."[1] As Cremin sees it, the theory supporting Mann's faith represented a mix of early American progressivism, elements of Jeffersonian republicanism, Christian moralism, and Emersonian idealism. Mann understood well the relationship among freedom, self-government, and universal education. Like Jefferson, he believed that freedom would rest secure only as free men had the knowledge to make intelligent decisions.[2]

In the past decade or so, some historians have tended to reinterpret educational history and assign a different set of intentions to the supporters of public education. Called revisionists, these historians have attempted to show that the schools have actually functioned in a conservative manner to reinforce the prevailing class structure by selectively screening out and failing "undesirables."[3] Colin Greer, in his highly critical historical analysis of the public schools, argues that the schools' mission is and always was to maintain and transmit the values considered necessary to prevent political, social, or economic upheaval. Similarly, Michael Katz suggests that class bias is inherent in the structure and functioning of school systems and that it is the children of the well-to-do, not the children of the poor, who have benefited most from public education. He further argues that schools operate as a continuous social sorting device enabling well-to-do children to retain or improve their advantage while doing little for the rest.[4]

While revisionists do not hypothesize a conscious conspiracy, carefully orchestrated, to manipulate and exploit the poor over the past century, they argue that events leading to and culminating in the development of contemporary social institutions have had precisely that impact. This is particularly true for the public schools. As an example, according to Greer, the humanitarian reaction to nineteenth-century poverty never rose above a profound disrespect for the poor. "The paupers of the city for the most part ... [were thought to be] depraved and vicious and require support because they [were] so."[5] According to the revisionists, schools for the poor were at least in part motivated out of fear of the poor.

Even the democratic rhetoric of Horace Mann, which depicted the schools as the great equalizers of the human condition, can be reinterpreted to support the view that the schools were the servants of those who built them. While Mann viewed the schools' chief function as a so-cial and economic "balance wheel" balancing conflicting interests; according to Greer, the balance was to be the imposition of controls for social stability in favor of the moneyed and powerful and was thus to protect the social order. The common school protected the rights of property, first, by teaching children of the propertyless to believe that the economic system was reasonable and just, rewarding to people according to their natural abilities and real contribution to society; and second, by teaching that if one practiced puritan virtues, he too could be successful.[6]

Interpreted from the perspective of liberal democratic ideology, the public school system took the poor and ill-prepared ethnic minorities who crowded into the cities, educated and Americanized them, and shaped them into the productive middle class that is America's strength and pride. From the perspective of ideological class struggle, the public school system selected "individuals for opportunities accord-ing to a hierarchical schema which runs closely parallel to existing so-cial patterns."[7] To recount the history of education strictly from either of these ideological points of view is to miss the true nature of the evolution of the public schools.

There is a connection between the politics of the school and the politics of the society at large, and schools generally reflect the society. But as Diane Ravitch has pointed out, demands made by society are simultaneously liberal and conservative, and the distinction between the two is not always clear. For example, when individuals like Mann sought to persuade people to support schools generally, he appealed alternatively to those who wanted a more equal society than existed and to those who wanted a more stable society. Mann argued both that education would be a great equalizer and that it would disarm the poor of their hostility toward the rich.[8]

A second reason to avoid a strict ideological interpretation of American education can be found in the nature of the political process. Within the system, compromises on conflict demands often results in conciliation and coalition building and leads to settlements in which there is neither a winner nor a loser. Compromises are reached, goals are only partially realized, and change takes place incrementally and sporadically. In this manner, whatever the issue at hand, educational reformers had to take into account the necessity of persuading others to agree. If the public schools did not satisfy voters, there were various ways by which their dissatisfaction might be expressed: by voting against the school board, by sending their children to nonpublic schools, by opposing a school board issue, or by lobbying their elected representative.[9]

A third reason to avoid a strict ideological interpretation is that there is no one-to-one correspondence between the ultimate effect of a policy and the intentions of its creators. Thus it would be a mistake to attribute certain functions to an institution as intentional simply by observing the outcomes of that institution. This is true for several reasons. Given the best of intentions, one's goals may simply be overly ambitious and beyond attainment. Even if attainable, things may go wrong: Strategies may be ill conceived; policy may be based on faulty assumptions, inadequate or inaccurate information; or other variables may simply fail to cooperate.

On the other hand, the true intentions of some actions are not those that are explicitly stated. We must agree with Greer's warning that to evaluate the public school system solely by its rhetorical spirit is dangerous and misleading.[10] We have learned that the manifest (openly stated) function of a policy or action can be distinguished from its latent, hidden function. In recognition of this, revisionists, not convinced that ethnic minorities have been integrated into society on the basis of equality and justice, have sought an alternative explanation for policy reform in American education. Because they could not find convincing evidence of the democratic inclusion of the poor and minorities into mainstream society, they have looked to the latent function of school reform as an explanation. That is, they have looked to effects as an indication of the true intentions of reformers.

What Happened

In the beginning, American educational institutions were cast in terms of the old English class system. In the colonies secondary and higher education served primarily the needs of a small directive class. "Schools concerned with the teaching of reading and writing in English—where they existed at all—were primarily terminal schools for the masses. They were designed to teach the children of the common people to read, to grasp the principles of some religious sect, and to conform to existing principles of social organization."[11]

With the advent of capitalism and industrialization, a free public educational system began to evolve. By the 1850s, Horace Mann and other supporters of the public school movement were successful: Almost every northern state had provided its citizens with common schools, governed and supported by the general tax pioneered in seventeenth-century Massachusetts. Fifteen years later, the southern states began to establish statewide systems of public education.

After the Civil War, large numbers of immigrants, primarily from Eastern and Southern Europe, along with poor, unskilled, rural, native-born Americans, began to pour into the cities to fill the labor requirements of the exploding manufacturing industries. The social conditions that resulted can only be considered as tragic for the poor; high mortality rates, suicide, alcoholism, vagrancy, pauperism, and a general sense of cultural and social disorientation brought on by unfamiliar and unresponsive social institutions were the rule. All will concede that the schools had their problems along the way, particularly those associated with the growing pains brought on by industrialization and urbanization. Hindered by skyrocketing enrollment and school buildings that were poorly heated, poorly lighted, and frequently unsanitary, the cities' schools in the 1890s responded to the need and tried to accommodate the students.

Many educational innovations took place during this time. Along with widespread public access to schools came the professionalizing of education and eventually pupil evaluations, ability grouping, and differentiated curriculum based on tests of intelligence. Progressive education and the transformation of the schools associated with it began as part and parcel of the broader program of social and political reform that developed. It grew out of the effort to cast the schools as a fundamental lever of social and political regeneration. Proponents of virtually every progressive cause from the 1890s through World War I had a program for the schools. Humanitarians of every stripe saw education at the heart of their effort toward social alleviation.[12] Essentially education was viewed as an adjunct to politics.

But if schools were adjuncts to politics, political goals were not always altruistic or humanitarian. According to Samuel Bowles, "the progressive education movement, spanning the period from the 1890s to 1920s, can be seen as a response to conflicts associated with the integration of peasant labor, both immigrant and native, into the burgeoning corporate capitalistic relations of labor."[13] Michael Katz concurs; many of the individuals concerned with altering society at the turn of the century had no higher opinion of poor city families than did their predecessors a half century before. Insofar as reform efforts had an educational purpose, for many that goal again reflected one of the large aims of municipal reform: the attempt to find new modes of social control appropriate to a dynamic and fluid urban environment. Their aim remained one of inculcating the poor with acceptable social attitudes.[14]

In addition to this view of superiority, some reformers were concerned with protecting their self-interests. They tended to hold immigrants and their spokesmen responsible for a decline in the quality of municipal life. Consequently, attempts to reform civic conduct necessarily included efforts to reduce the power of newcomers. One power to be contended with was that of local immigrant politicians. Because neighborhoods tended to attract people of common ethnic origin, local ward politics and, consequently, local schools were influenced by the ethnic vote.

The consolidation of school districts and the development of a centralized school bureaucracy was one response to these perceived threats. Based on ward politics, school committees had grown large and unwieldy. There were valid questions about graft and ineptitude raised against these large school boards and the decentralized power characteristic of schools prior to bureaucratization. But of no less concern was the uncertain power of conventional sources of authority under the existing system. Thus, one purpose of reform during the first quarter of the twentieth century was to put control of urban schools under boards that were small rather than large, unrepresentative rather than unwieldy and inefficient, and elected from notables in the city as a whole rather than by ward and the more broadly based "partisan politics" wards represented.[15] The powerful upper and middle classes thereby gained control of local ethnic schools, and large, centralized school districts came into their own.

Another set of reforms produced intelligence testing and ability grouping. Following World War I, intelligence testing was hailed as a scientific and objective way to provide appropriate opportunities to individuals based on their abilities and native potential, thereby furthering efficiency while respecting the equal opportunity of democracy. By determining the intellectual capabilities of students, schools could develop and offer a curriculum best suited for the occupational stations for which students were destined. Schools, it was argued, could become more streamlined and efficient; and students with limited ability could be spared the frustration of failure resulting from expectations beyond their means.

While there is validity to the arguments supporting standardized tests and ability grouping, these innovations also tended to support class bias. As Karier describes the testing movement, from the beginning standardized tests were seen by those who created them as modeled on the then existing social order. Influenced by social Darwinism, testers like Binet, Terman, and Thorndike recognized that social-class differences would not only influence the performance of an individual on a test; these differences were the basis of the tests. These same men usually accepted the social-class system as a given and then proceeded to argue that social-class differences added validity to their observations. The assumption supporting this position was that the rich were obviously brighter than the poor.[16] For example, Goddard, the American psychologist who translated the work of Binet, assumed a positive correlation of social class and native intelligence. He expressed the need not only for the intelligent to rule the ignorant masses but also the need to educate the masses so that they would accept intelligent leadership. Part of that acceptance would depend on the organization and use of tests in the schools. Similarly, Terman, using tests originally based on skills appropriate for varying occupational classes and eventually standardized on the basis of class, correlated IQ and occupational levels, which were now to be used to design a curriculum appropriate for a particular social class and to guide and channel the child toward that occupation for which his assumed "native brightness" fit him.

If the evolution of the common school can be described in part as an attempt by the upper and middle classes to maintain the status quo and preserve social order and stability through the socialization of immigrants and the poor, it was not entirely a process of imposition. Many of the would-be victims saw the advantage of education and of acquiring the ways of America. According to one educational historian, statistics for literacy and school attendance in the federal census of 1910 suggest that immigrant families showed as much or more zeal for education as families in which the parents were native born.[17] Apparently, not only were parents interested in seeing their children educated but, as evidenced by the commitment of ethnic associations to undertake educational ventures such as night classes in English, adults saw a value for themselves as well.

There were perhaps many reasons for immigrants to be concerned about education in their new land. One was the economic benefit to be gained by learning to read and write English; but there were also commercial and civil aspirations. Immigrants were in the process of creating new identities and communities. The use of education to enhance group status, develop leadership, and provide cultural benefits was apparent from the beginning. Thus, quite as much as any coercion from compulsory education acts or any pressure from professional Americanizers, the immigrants' own hopes for creating a better life account for the success of the public school in drawing the mass of working-class children into its embrace.[18]

We can see, then, that immigrants and poor children were encouraged into the public schools at once as a move by the elite to preserve social order and as a hope for mobility and cultural stability on the part of the poor. For some of these children the school experience proved beneficial and rewarding; for others, it was a failure. During the first three decades of the twentieth century, the younger children of immigrants were as likely to be in school as were children of native-born whites. At older ages, however, immigrants' children neither attended nor completed school in the same proportion as children of native whites. Throughout the schooling process, they were more likely to be older than other children in the same grade and were more likely to drop out when legally permitted.[19]

These are general trends and, if overstressed, may be misleading. In fact, it can probably be argued that there was no single immigrant experience in the schools. Nationality groups varied substantially on such measures as elementary school retardation, grammar school continuance, high school entrance, school continuance and completion, and the ratio of males to females in high school.[20] In addition, students from all groups made progress of the sort depicted in popular folklore, but some made more than others over comparable periods, and significant parts of all groups made minimal or no progress. Of those that did well as groups, Eastern European Jews and Slavs were among the most successful; southern Italians and Poles were among the groups that did poorly.

The successes that schools provided did not come immediately. Many first-generation adults attended night classes or schools established by ethnic organizations, but it was the second generation that used the schools as a steppingstone. Typically, school success came after the establishment of an economic foothold and ethnic communal stability through, for example, the development of successful ethnic businesses or political organizations grounded in the community and the subsequent need of a high school diploma to advance it. According to Greer, there is a hard core of reality behind the story that depicts the entry of the Eastern European Jewish immigrant into small business enterprises and then of his son into the university and the professions.[21] In a similar fashion, Greeks were prominent in foods and restaurants, the Irish in organized labor and politics, and the Scandinavians in the cultivation of farmland. During these years manpower set the tone for assimilation; the local business, the local church, and local fraternal societies, followed by the factory, the union, and the political machine, as much as the schools, were the agents of acculturation and mobility. Often economic stability for an ethnic group preceded rather than followed entry into the broad middle class by means of education.

The manner in which school reforms affected ethnic minorities of the past is of particular interest to the investigation we have undertaken in this book. Reforms for the schools are again being proposed, among them the adoption of cultural pluralism with its expression in multicultural and bilingual education. Though many reject the assimilation function schools played in the past, contemporary ethnic minorities ask to be included in the mobility function extended to previous groups. Accepting the public schools both as a historical and current means to power and affluence, advocates of pluralism argue that the schools should provide the same opportunities that allowed other groups to pull themselves up out of poverty and despair and into the middle class.

We have seen, however, that the schools were not as successful in furthering mobility as they were once thought to be. As late as 1950, more than 80 percent of New York and New Jersey workingmen of

Italian, Irish, and Slavic extraction were employed in unskilled or semi-skilled occupations.[22] And, in 1973, recognizing that power and afflu-ence still flow along group lines, a study designed to investigate the extent to which Poles, Italians, Latins, and Blacks have penetrated the centers of power and influence in large corporations found that among Chicago's largest corporations, less than 3 percent of the corporation directors were from these backgrounds, even though they accounted for more than 34 percent of the metropolitan area's population.[23]

We see, then, that the full integration even of white ethnics has not been complete. And perhaps the greatest danger in continually under-estimating the lack of social and economic mobility among this seg-ment of our population is its impact on the urban poor of today. As long as we believe that other groups have successfully used the public schools to better their position in society, there will be a tendency to hold those who are unable to do the same responsible for their failure. As with the rest of us, contemporary social reformers, social scientists, and school personnel are convinced of their goodwill toward the dis-advantaged. When efforts to help the disadvantaged fail, someone else must be at fault. And one of the most likely candidates is the social, cultural, or intellectual inferiority of the disadvantaged poor. It is im-portant, then, to recognize that schools in earlier times were only mar-ginally successful as a means of mobility. It is in the recognition that schools in the past served certain groups more than others that we must evaluate our contemporary efforts. Public schools are and have always been basically conservative institutions. It may not be possible, without major changes in their structure and function, for them to serve today's minorities, who continue to put their faith within them. We have more to say about this in the final section of this chapter, but first let us turn to a discussion of contemporary policy and curriculum issues.

POLICY ISSUES FOR SCHOOL PERSONNEL

Today we are involved in another movement to reform American education, making it more responsive to the needs and demands of the nation's minority groups. Beginning with *Brown* v. *Board of Education* in 1954, the current thrust gained momentum and power from the civil rights movement and from a conservative concern about crime and so-cial disorder on city streets. Clearly something was the matter, and the schools were called upon once again as the primary social institution to address the ills of society.

Initially, integration provided the rallying point that united Blacks, whites, liberals, radicals, and even many conservatives around two clear-cut goals: improving urban schools and ending de facto segregation. A broad base of support existed during the Kennedy and Johnson years, producing a proliferation of government programs and liberal funding. But the strains and contradictions inherent in the movement began to show themselves particularly between integration and compensatory education, integration and decentralization, and radical pedagogical reform and community participation.[24] To provide compensatory programs often meant homogeneous grouping and thus segregated classrooms within institutions. To decentralize the school bureaucracy often made impossible the cooperation necessary for integration among school districts in large metropolitan areas. And the goal of many radicals to "liberate" children was often contradictory to the belief held by community members that a stricter educational environment was necessary for social mobility.

A core issue underlying these strains centered on school control. Faced with court orders to desegregate and with incontrovertible evidence that minority students were not receiving the same benefits as white middle-class students, metropolitan school districts proposed sophisticated technological innovations within their existing bureaucracies to improve the content and procedures of schooling. Among other things, educational professionals and specialists proposed large educational parks drawing from a wide residential area and/or wide scale busing to overcome the problems of residential segregation. Compensatory education programs, such as Head Start, and enrichment programs were offered for children from preschool through postsecondary education to help minority students compensate for their "cultural deprivation."

But while the schools responded by building larger and more complex systems within their existing structures, a challenge to their control supported mostly by minority spokesmen and radical reformers developed. They proposed the decentralization of city school systems into small districts governed by local community organizations. Those supporting community control stressed the value of a close relationship between school and community, the drawbacks of the large school bureaucracy, and the relationship of community control to democratic theory. In its more extreme forms this position voiced a general distrust for professionals and central-city government and the belief that white, affluent bureaucrats could not and would not act in the best interests of the poor, particularly poor minorities.

Also, recognizing the limitations of a large, self-perpetuating bureaucracy, another challenge developed. This time the proposal was to replace the public school monopoly with competing private groups operating their own institutions. The means to activate this proposal was a voucher system whereby parents or students would cash in tax-supported vouchers at the school of their choice. Underlying the voucher proposal was the belief that free competition among schools would foster quality education and that the fight for funds would produce a variety of schools and a continuing effort to offer an education attractive to its customers.

Fundamental to the current school reform movement, then, is the control of the schools. Both community control and voucher proposals stress structural changes and are predicated on the assumptions that meaningful educational change must be preceded by political change and that a move to schools more politically representative of the communities they serve will foster positive pedagogical reform.[25] The existing public school bureaucracy argues that the above positions oversimplify the problem, that a highly specialized professional staff and the efficiency of a centralized district are required to tackle the complex task of education, and that locally and privately operated schools are likely to serve the special interests of the community rather than the best interests of the child or the larger community.

The solution to the question of who should control the schools is not an easy one. As historians of American education have shown in recent years, the large, bureaucratic schools that grew out of earlier reform, despite their rhetoric to the contrary, have not served the poor well. Given both their past and current records there is little reason to believe that the large, centralized public schools of today will or can provide the social mobility minorities continue to seek. For example, despite the heavy funding of federal programs during the past two decades, minorities have not shown significant gains.

Yet it does not necessarily follow that political reform, such as decentralization, will result in pedagogical reform or that when it does, these changes will increase educational achievement. In fact, some proposed pedagogical reforms deemphasize the skills of reading, writing, and arithmetic in favor of more humanistic statements such as freedom to "become" or freedom to "be." Also, some pedagogical "reforms" instituted by community-operated schools have been extremely conservative, even reactionary, emphasizing corporal punishment and rigidly structured classrooms reminiscent of eighteenth- and early-nineteenth-century education. Furthermore, we know that locally operated schools will reflect the special interests of their sponsors. It is not unreasonable to expect racism, sexism, and religious fundamentalism to materialize as part of the locally operated public schools. As for voucher systems, it has been argued that they will continue to serve the affluent for at least two reasons: (1) Affluent children are easier, and cheaper, to educate; and (2) the affluent are in a position to supplement the vouchers and thus contract for more expensive educational programs. Critics argue that the poor will be left in the public schools, segregated to an even greater extent than they are now, or they will tend to pool in the poorer private schools.

Some modified program of decentralization, combining both the advantages of community control and professionalism, is probably the best solution. It would seem reasonable to have some means of control to prevent the exploitation of ignorant consumers and enforce minimal safeguards for the larger community as well as students. Teachers too should retain (or perhaps develop) some professional autonomy in order to preserve sound pedagogical practices in the classroom. Yet there needs to be flexibility and diversity in and among schools of the kind large, centralized school systems seem unable to provide and which seem most likely to occur under the influence of smaller, more responsive political units. But even if such a compromise can be reached, we are still faced with the problem of integration, for integration and decentralization seem incompatible given the existing housing patterns in most metropolitan areas. Decentralized community schools must of necessity be small and local, which means that in large urban areas they most likely will be ethnically homogeneous. It would be possible to attain integration in many metropolitan areas if large educational parks or magnet schools were created, but contrary to decentralization, these would be large and formal and tightly administered and distant from the communities they serve.

Court orders withstanding, we may choose to abandon or at least revise our hopes for integrating schools. As we have seen in the various ideological models of pluralism, this has been the trend for some minorities, and as evidenced by the volatile political actions over busing, many whites (though for different reasons) would go along as well. But even if we set aside integration in favor of the more insular versions of cultural pluralism, we are still faced with the problem of improving educational achievement for minorities. Our experience with compensatory education indicate that we do not know how to improve the educational achievement of minority children through pedagogical means. Yet, as the Coleman Report demonstrated, integration can have a positive effect on the academic achievement of minorities when affluent whites compose the majority of the student body. Further, data from the Coleman Report show an improvement in racial attitudes among students in integrated schools.

We appear, then, to have a standoff between the benefits of decentralization and those of integration. It is important to note that there are, of course, other grounds that influence whether integration or decentralization is to be preferred. These include the moral and value preferences of the communities that will be affected, as well as specific situational factors. Also of significance are legal requirements and court precedent.

As we saw in Chapter 4, the First and Fourteenth amendments provide primary support for the ideal of cultural pluralism, but the Constitution has not provided a single clear and concise interpretation.

The Amish, for example, found support for their separation from mainstream society, but Blacks found support for integration into social institutions. Nevertheless, the review of cases did unearth some general principles the courts used in defining American pluralism. We can conclude that the Constitution generally protects citizens from arbitrary or unreasonable control by the government and protects the rights of parents to raise and educate their children as they see fit even when the life style is inconsistent with existing social patterns. But we also see that this right is limited to a large extent to expression through private institutional means and that even in the private sector it may be limited if a threat to the well-being of society exists.

In regard to equal educational opportunity, we can conclude from court rulings that the racial or ethnic separation of children in schools is impermissible; school systems must pursue a policy of integration. It is possible, however, to have a school with a population from predominantly one ethnic group, provided that this situation neither contributes to nor is a result of discrimination. In addition, school systems must provide instruction for non-English-speaking students in a language from which the students can benefit, and remedial English must be taught when necessary.

While useful, these general principles provide only general guidance in the design of educational policy. Courts are reluctant to rule in a broad manner; they are much more likely to apply certain principles to a specific case in a specific context. Because of this individual treatment, we should expect multicultural and bilingual education to vary from group to group and from situation to situation. Note, for example, that in a Denver desegregation suit (*Keyes* v. *School District No. 1*) some schools were allowed to remain predominantly Mexican American, but in San Francisco (*Lee* v. *Johnson*) a Chinese American school was denied a similar request. The policies of each school system, then, must be assessed in terms of general legal principles as they apply to the particular setting. In addition, state law influences local educational design. While federal law supersedes state law, it provides only the minimum standards with which districts must comply, leaving much to state discretion. State constitutions and legislation make specific legal requirements, which must be considered prior to the establishment of any program.

So even legal guidelines force the policy developer into assessing specific local circumstances and conditions. And this is how it ought to be. As we have argued before, there is no one answer that is right for all the diverse groups in their unique circumstances and with their varying hopes, fears, needs, and desires. As Michael Katz concludes: "There is no way, nor even a few ways, of rightly arranging for education. . . . [T]he particular form education should take in any one place should be worked out by the people involved."[26]

It is likely that those faced with improving the quality of education of minorities or with establishing educational policy will find little comfort in knowing that they must assess specific local conditions or that, as an ideal, cultural pluralism is not capable of establishing specific organizational or pedagogical direction. Even though we have argued throughout this book that there is a wide range of alternatives school personnel ought to address if they are to be responsive to the communities they serve, it still may be possible to develop a general policy of multicultural education applicable to a large number, perhaps a majority, of the possible groups and contexts.

Support for a broad, overarching policy statement can be found in the fact that most of the diverse groups within the United States see themselves as part of the overall society and wish to participate in it. They do not want total isolation in their schools; rather, they want the public schools to work for them. In short, most people believe that education is important and that it can function as a means to enhance upward mobility. But what is becoming increasingly clear to these same people is that, generally, the schools have not worked well unless the students are white and middle class, and whether they have worked or not, they have presented a biased white Anglo-Saxon Protestant view of the world. Thus, much of the thrust behind cultural pluralism is the demand that the schools meet halfway the communities they serve.

Perhaps a more practical reason for developing an overarching conception of multicultural education for the public schools is the recognition that the existing school structure represents a large, bureaucratic social institution, and as such, it will probably not undergo radical change in the near future. While some organizational change can be expected if cultural pluralism is to have an impact on education, such change will probably be within the public schools as we know them today. Thus it would be wise to develop and offer a conception of multicultural education that can be adopted by public school personnel currently within the system. We might search for a policy statement of multicultural education general enough to include most groups who perceive themselves to be functionally related to mainstream society, yet specific enough to guide and evaluate pedagogical and curricular considerations.

GOALS AND PRINCIPLES OF MULTICULTURAL EDUCATION[27]

Perhaps the place to begin the development of our conception of multicultural education is by stating a working definition on which our goals and principles are based.

Multicultural Education is an educational program which provides multiple learning environments that properly match the academic and social needs of students. These needs may vary widely due to differences in the race, sex, ethnicity or social-class background of the students. In addition to enhancing the development of their basic academic skills, the program should help students develop a better understanding of their own backgrounds and those of other groups that compose our society. Through this process, the program should help students learn to respect and appreciate cultural diversity; overcome ethnocentric and prejudicial attitudes; and understand the sociohistorical, economic, and psychological factors that have produced the contemporary conditions of ethnic polarization, inequality, and alienation. The program should also foster the ability to critically analyze and make intelligent decisions about real-life problems and issues through a process of democratic, dialogical inquiry. Finally, it should help students conceptualize and aspire toward a vision of a better society and acquire the necessary knowledge, understanding, and skills to enable them to move the society toward greater equality and freedom, the eradication of degrading poverty and dehumanizing dependency, and the development of meaningful identity for all people.

Embedded, sometimes implicitly, in this definition are several broad and general goals of multicultural education. For purposes of clarification it will be useful to list the major long-range goals. Some of these goals pertain to students and others to teachers. We begin with goals for students.

Goals for Students.   The full achievement of these goals would undoubtedly require a comprehensive multicultural education program that encompasses all grade levels and affects all aspects of the schools including their policies, practices, and curriculum. While such a program is not likely to exist in most schools, the goals listed below may nevertheless be viewed as ideals toward which teachers should at least help their students aspire.

1. Students should be helped to develop positive feelings, attitudes, and perceptions toward their own and other ethnic groups, and to develop a better understanding of their own ethnic background and those of other groups that compose our society.
2. Students should be helped to acquire a knowledge, understanding, and appreciation of the experiences and contributions of racial minorities, white ethnic groups, and men and women in American society.
3. Students should be helped to overcome their stereotypes of ethnic groups, transcend their ethnocentrism, and gain an understanding appreciation of the related concepts of cultural pluralism and democracy.
4. Students should be helped to understand the nature of pluralism and interethnic conflicts including the basic causes of

racism, sexism, and poverty, and to recognize the need for depolarizing such conflicts.

5. Students should be helped to develop the ability to critically analyze and make intelligent decisions about complex societal problems and issues through a process of democratic, dialogical inquiry.

6. Students should be helped to acquire knowledge of the historical and social realities of American society in order to increase their understanding of our pressing societal problems and how they may possibly be solved.

7. Students should be helped to conceptualize and aspire toward a vision of a more equitable and democratic society, and to develop the skills, knowledge, and commitment to enable them to create the necessary changes leading to such a society.

Goals for Teachers. The second set of goals pertains to the knowledge, skills, and attitudes teachers must acquire in order to effectively implement multicultural education as defined above. These goals are the following:

1. Teachers must acquire knowledge, understanding, and appreciation of the experiences and contributions of racial and ethnic minorities and women and men in American society.

2. Teachers must understand the nature of pluralism and intergroup conflict in American society and the basic causes of racism, sexism, and class inequality.

3. Teachers must develop a sound, coherent philosophical and pedagogical rationale for multicultural education and acquire knowledge of the basic principles of designing and organizing a multicultural curriculum in all subject areas.

4. Teachers must acquire knowledge and skills in identifying, evaluating, and utilizing multicultural curricular resources, including human and institutional resources in the community.

5. Teachers must learn how sociocultural factors influence learning and how to diagnose the learning styles and needs of students from different sociocultural backgrounds to maximize the academic and social development of every student.

6. Teachers must understand how their attitudes, values, and expectations can affect the motivation and performance of students, particularly those from sociocultural backgrounds different from their own, and how to transcend their sociocultural biases.

7. Teachers must acquire knowledge of various multicultural

approaches to teaching, including those that utilize dialogical and cross-cultural techniques to enhance and personalize learning and create a more democratic classroom environment.

8. Teachers must acquire the necessary knowledge and skills in human relations for effectively managing a classroom of students from diverse sociocultural backgrounds, including the mediation of interethnic conflicts.

9. Teachers must be able to help students increase their academic achievement level in all areas, including basic skills, through the use of multicultural materials and teaching approaches that are sensitive and relevant to students' sociocultural backgrounds and experiences.

The conception of multicultural education we have developed by means of providing a definition and then supplementing it with goals for both teachers and students should be specific enough to direct educators to the key relevant considerations but be general enough to apply to a variety of contexts. It is hoped that this framework will prove useful by enabling educators to more consistently translate the ideal of cultural pluralism into effective practice. Perhaps it will be beneficial to go a step farther in this direction by offering a set of principles for translating theory into practice.

Guiding Principles for Translating Theory into Practice

To facilitate the translation of our conceptual framework into classroom practice, we now suggest a number of guiding principles that should help educators implement multicultural education in practical and effective ways. The list includes those principles thought to be generally useful to most educators at all levels and in most areas of education.

Principle No. 1. Multicultural education should start "where people are." Basically, this is just a different way of stating John Dewey's well-known principle that the education of children should take into account their sociocultural backgrounds and begin with the experiences they bring with them into the classroom.[28]

In terms of multicultural education, the principle simply means that everyone should begin by confronting his or her own ethnic identity and background first. Its importance lies in the fact, shown by many studies, that the self-concept of children can strongly influence how well they do in school. In view of the negative impact that racism has had on the self-concepts of ethnic minority children, it is especially important for teachers to help these children develop positive attitudes and feelings about their ethnic identities and heritages.

Many teachers make the mistake of thinking that teaching about groups in their native lands helps develop positive self-concepts among descendants of these groups now living in the United States. Unfortunately, it often has the opposite effect. Since most Americans almost automatically assume that members of other cultures and ethnic groups are foreigners and not Americans, teaching about China, Japan, Mexico, Africa, and other countries may reinforce the feelings of ethnic American students that they are not full-fledged American citizens. Certainly teachers should teach about these other countries, but only after teaching about the ethnic American experience. It is important for students to learn that ethnic minority Americans have made significant contributions to the development of the United States and that they have as much right to be in this country and call themselves Americans as has anyone else.

The curriculum of many schools still conveys the impression that the only people who have been of consequence in the development of this country have been white, Anglo-Saxon, and Protestant. The experiences and contributions of ethnic groups are rarely mentioned in the school curriculum; when information is presented, it usually is meager, superficial, or condescending; and it often perpetuates time-worn stereotypes. These biases, omissions, and distortions can subtly denigrate the self-image of minority students and have long-lasting, detrimental psychological effects.

Interestingly enough, members of white ethnic groups also often have little knowledge of their ethnic backgrounds. For some, ethnicity may be a taboo subject that should not be explored. This being the case, it should not go uncorrected. Unless people feel good about their ethnic backgrounds, they can hardly relate positively to those of others. This axiom applies not only to students but also to teachers, particularly if they are teaching students whose ethnic backgrounds are very different from their own.

Moreover, people must see some personal relevance to their own lives in multicultural education. Unless they receive some personal gratification, they are not likely to develop a genuine interest in or commitment to the ideal; otherwise, one must assume they are becoming involved in it for purely altruistic, perhaps missionary purposes. But that can only result in a paternalistic attitude. Anyone who becomes involved in multicultural education with a "Gosh, we must help (or learn about) these poor, culturally deprived people" attitude is off on the wrong foot. This is one reason why the experiences of white ethnic groups, women, and other social minority groups must be included in multicultural education. When their experiences are included, their involvement can become much more personally rewarding.

Principle No. 2. Multicultural education should help de-center people and thereby help depolarize interethnic hostility and conflict. That is, multicultural education should not simply result in increasing ethnic consciousness but must be followed by a process of de-centering whereby members of different groups see themselves existing interdependently. Without this attainment individuals may become so preoccupied with issues of ethnic identity and ethnic self-interest that they may be misled into believing these issues are ends in themselves. Such an orientation has often led to a self-indulgent ethnocentrism that may be psychologically gratifying but does little to promote greater intergroup understanding and cooperation.

An effective way to de-center a person is to use his or her ethnic background as a cross-cultural bridge by showing the parallels between that group's experience and those of other ethnic groups. For example, many white ethnics, like racial minorities, have been victims of oppression and discrimination. However, due to a rather curious social amnesia, many people have never learned about or have repressed this unpleasant aspect of our historical past. Increasing awareness of such parallels in experience can help develop mutual understanding and empathy between different ethnic groups and contribute to the process of depolarization. The analysis of such parallels could also lead to a deeper understanding of why ethnic groups have historically been in conflict with one other, despite their many common grievances, and perhaps lead to ways by which such conflicts can be avoided. In fact, if serious and realistic efforts are to be mounted to bring about the societal changes envisioned by multicultural education advocates, broad-based coalitions of various groups having similar interests and goals will have to be formed over the long run.

Principle No. 3. The implementation of multicultural education should be approached as a long-term process that will not produce dramatic, overnight changes in the schools. Too many people become involved in multicultural education with the idea of implementing it in a big way and become quickly frustrated when little happens after an effort of only one or two years. It is probable that most teachers are not adequately prepared to immediately begin implementing multicultural education in a big way. Many teachers would do better to start off with fairly modest goals, such as supplementing their existing curriculum with small multicultural units. With small initial successes and growing confidence, teachers are more likely to develop a long-term commitment to multicultural education and actively pursue their personal growth and development in the field.

In addition to starting too big, the strategy of bringing in outside experts with prepackaged programs also has its limitations. In order for such experts to be effective, they must be willing and able to work with the staff of a school for several years to involve them in the planning of the program and to gain their trust and confidence. Only in this way will the administrators and teachers involved gain a sense of ownership in the project and develop the genuine interest and commitment necessary to sustain it.

Finally, teachers should bear in mind that racism, sexism, and elitism in school environments are usually conveyed in subtle but pervasive ways. Therefore, if they wish to reverse this process, perhaps they will find an equally subtle and pervasive approach to be the most effective over the long run. An approach that infuses multiculturalism throughout the school environment, including even such seemingly innocuous aspects as bulletin board displays, may ultimately have more of an impact than a highly visible, short-term effort.

Principle No. 4. Multicultural education should ultimately be integrative, comprehensive, and conceptual. Although teachers who are just getting started in the field may wish to begin with small, specialized units of instruction, the most effective approach over the long run is to incorporate multicultural concepts and perspectives into the total curriculum. This is most easily done in the language arts and social sciences, but it can be done in science, mathematics, and physical education with some thought and effort (we have more to say on this in connection with the guiding principle 7). In this respect, multicultural education is not a specialized area of education but a general approach to education. As Carl Grant points out, the term multicultural education is somewhat of a misnomer; what we are really talking about, he asserts, is "education that is multicultural."[29]

Of course, it would be impossible for any teacher to incorporate the experiences and perspectives of the more than three hundred ethnic groups in the United States into the curriculum. As an alternative, one might include at least those groups that are present in significant numbers in the local community, along with a few that might not be present. There is still a massive amount of factual information even on these groups. Since there is little merit in having students memorize a lot of low-level facts about groups, a conceptual approach that provides a framework for understanding the experiences and perspectives of all the groups would seem to be the most effective strategy. James Banks has developed a conceptual model of this kind for the social studies.

He suggests taking a particular historical event and then analyzing it from the perspective of different ethnic groups.[30]

History teachers might try to develop other alternative conceptual frameworks that go beyond so-called contribution history and minorities/women-as-victims history and provide a broader perspective on U.S. history as a whole.[31] For example, the building of the first transcontinental railroad could be viewed not only as a major contribution of Chinese workers but also as part of the larger pattern of capitalist development in the western states and Asia, through the exploitation of cheap labor and raw materials. As another example, consider the internment camp experience of Japanese Americans during World War II. It is not enough for history teachers to introduce this long-omitted episode into U.S. history by recounting the trials and tribulations of the victims. They should also raise basic questions as to why such a gross violation of the Constitution was allowed to occur. In order to find answers to these questions, students will have to study not only the victimized group but also some of the broader forces that were at work in the nation and the world during that period.

The need for such innovations in the curriculum may even be greater at the college level. College courses in the humanities and social sciences still generally exhibit an overwhelming bias toward Anglo conformity. The experiences and perspectives of racial minorities, working-class white ethnics, and women are rarely given serious or substantive consideration. The bias is even greater when you compare the preponderance of Western perspectives in the college curriculum against the paucity of non-Western or Third World perspectives. For example, despite the fact that Asians comprise over one-half of the world's population, courses on Asian cultures and societies are generally a minuscule proportion of the total course offerings available in most institutions of higher education.[32]

Principle No. 5. Multicultural education should produce changes not only in the content of the curriculum but also in the teaching practices and social structure of the classroom. Most classrooms are not exemplary models of democracy in action. Studies have shown, for example, that rules of behavior and conduct are usually established unilaterally by the teacher and rarely in democratic collaboration with students. They have also shown that teachers ask most of the questions, which usually require rote-recall answers of low-level facts.[33] Students are rarely engaged in true dialogue in which they are stimulated to do most of the questioning and participate in higher-level analysis and critical evaluation. These and other aspects of classroom interaction constitute part of the hidden curriculum that transmits powerful subliminal messages to students and socializes them into patterns of conforming, obedient, and passive behavior that are dysfunctional for participating in a truly democratic society.*

Teachers must be willing to change their teaching practices in ways that will make their classrooms more democratic. An approach that has great promise in this regard is the dialogical approach of Paulo Freire, who originally developed it to teach illiterate peasants in Brazil how to read.[34] Properly adapted to American schools, the approach can dramatically increase student-initiated dialogue in the classroom and greatly stimulate critical thinking. Since the approach utilizes the learners' culture and experiences as the basis for learning, it is also more likely to be sensitive to the cultural backgrounds of students. Through such an approach, students can gain a much better understanding of the deeper meaning of democracy, freedom, and equality and the power they potentially have to exert some control over their destinies. The approach also has major implications for curriculum theory and design and could lead to fundamental changes in this area.[35]

Unfortunately, many teachers become so concerned about covering a certain amount of material in a given time that they often lose opportunities for spontaneous, creative learning that may occur around issues of intense interest to students. Such occurrences are more likely to happen through process-oriented approaches to teaching, such as role-playing, simulation games, nondirective styles of leading discussions, having students lead discussions, breaking the class down into small discussion groups, or having students pursue individual or group projects and having them report back to the class on their findings. All these approaches can potentially lead to changes in the social structure of the classroom that may give students a greater sense of power over their learning, stimulate their interest and motivation, and result in more democratic relationships between teachers and students.

Principle No. 6. Multicultural education should be affective as well as cognitive, and should relate to issues that are personally relevant to students. Feelings and emotions are generally suppressed in schools because educators widely view them as inhibitors of learning. Nevertheless, studies have shown that feelings and emotions can be powerful stimulators of truly creative and meaningful learning experiences, and properly directed, they can be exploited to greatly enhance learning.[36] Feelings and emotions are generally aroused by sensitive

* The reader should remember that the conception of multicultural education being presented here is one thought to be appropriate for many *but not all* of the ethnic groups the public schools must serve. For some students an inquiry or question and answer approach to learning may not be an appropriate learning style. Prior to the adoption of any curriculum or methodology teachers should reflect upon the composition of their class.

issues that are personally meaningful to students and often produce some anxiety in them. For example, teachers generally avoid discussing such issues as racial name-calling or peer relationships and how they develop among students. Yet such issues are often potent aspects of the immediate social reality of students and can be used by teachers to give students a deeper, more personal understanding of broader social issues. By personalizing learning in this way students will gain not only cognitive knowledge but, and equally as important, they will develop greater empathy and sensitivity.

The affective dimension is especially important in learning about cultures different from one's own. Too often we study other cultures from a distance, viewing them in the abstract as something foreign and outside the realm of our experience. We may acquire a lot of factual knowledge and cognitive understanding of these cultures, but little feeling, empathy, and sensitivity toward them.

Principle No. 7. Multicultural education should help students increase their academic achievement levels in all areas, including basic skills, through the use of teaching approaches and materials that are sensitive and relevant to the students' sociocultural backgrounds and experiences. Multicultural education should not be used as an excuse for not developing the academic skills of students on the grounds that such skills are not compatible with the cultural characteristics of a particular ethnic group. To the contrary, multicultural education should enhance skill development by increasing motivation, stimulating interest, and properly matching teaching approaches to learning styles. In fact, McDermott contends that many minority and culturally different children fail to learn how to read because of the incompatibility of their culture and the culture of the classroom.[37] When cultural compatibility exists, literacy is apparently not difficult to achieve. As we saw in Chapter 6, a number of preliminary studies indicate that there are distinct cultural differences in learning styles among children from different ethnic groups.

Of course, it may be difficult to assess and match learning styles for a number of children in a classroom. Another approach for addressing this problem may be the mastery learning technique, which has been largely developed by Benjamin Bloom and his associates. This technique, in essence, consists of breaking down a course of study into a series of sequential learning tasks of about two weeks duration each. Students are tested after the completion of each task to determine what they have learned. Those who have not achieved mastery level on any task are given a second chance. In their second attempt at the task, the students are helped by the teacher to find alternative ways to get through the task. Bloom's research has shown that, done correctly, mastery learning will enable 80 percent of students to master 80 percent of the tasks. The technique has been applied to a number of inner-city schools and has apparently met with considerable success.[38]

The mastery learning technique would appear to be quite adaptable to multicultural education. The idea of giving students a second chance to master a task through alternative approaches is consistent with the idea that different students have different learning styles. The challenge is to find a sufficient variety of alternative ways of approaching each task so that a wide range of learning styles can be accommodated. The technique seems to be mainly applicable to cognitive learning tasks in such areas as reading, mathematics, and science. In these basic skills, it may prove to be a practical and effective way of achieving one goal of multicultural education, that is, to match teaching approaches to learning styles. The behavioristic nature of the technique may not lend itself well to teaching some of the more important, affective aspects of multicultural education, such as empathy and cross-cultural sensitivity.

Principle No. 8. Multicultural educators should utilize multicultural resources in their local communities and should increase the involvement of parents in the education of their children. Inviting guest speakers from ethnic organizations, visiting museums of social history, and exploring various aspects of local ethnic communities are some of the ways teachers could utilize multicultural community resources. Such activities would not only stimulate interest and enhance learning, they could also help develop community support for multicultural education programs, support that is often necessary in order to sustain such programs.

The involvement of parents in the schools can play a very important part in multicultural education. Children from culturally different families often experience serious family/school discontinuities as a result of the differences between their cultures and that of the school. By inviting the parents of the children into their classrooms as guest speakers, or simply as observers, teachers could help reduce the detrimental effects of these discontinuities. Involving parents in this way would also give teachers more understanding of and sensitivity to the social problems and needs of these children.

Of course, in many families both parents work or, in the case of single parent families, the one parent works, making it difficult for parents to visit and participate in school activities during the normal school day. This is particularly true for minority parents. In order to include these parents and to avoid the further exclusion and alienation of lower class and minority populations, teachers may need to go to parents. Indeed, teachers taking the initiative to interact with parents in this manner will have two advantages. First, teachers typically contact parents only when the child is in trouble with the school. The tenor of these interactions is often negative and defensive and may contribute to the development of greater distance between the school and the parent. By contacting parents on a positive note, teachers will give parents the opportunity to participate in school affairs in a constructive manner. Second, parents often feel threatened or insecure when confronting public institutions such as the schools. By meeting in their own homes or community settings parents are likely to feel more comfortable.

Principle No. 9. Multicultural education must deal with the social and historical realities of American society and help students gain a better understanding of the causes of oppression and inequality and ways in which these social problems might be eliminated. This principle is included because many teachers often deal with only the more superficial aspects of multicultural education by introducing students to ethnic foods, holidays, and costumes. As one critic has commented, such activities expose students to only the more exotic expressions of culture.

What, after all, would a foreign student understand about Anglo-American culture by celebrating the Fourth of July in a classroom setting? That Americans like firecrackers? That they are addicted to fried chicken and watermelon? But more to the point, if that student did understand these particular activities on a cognitive level, what has he comprehended about the values that nurture the things Americans traditionally do on the Fourth?[39]

On the other hand, many teachers avoid confronting such issues as racism, sexism, and class inequality. Yet, these are among the most important issues which multicultural education must address. Students are often more open to dealing with these issues than teachers may think. Nevertheless, introducing and effectively handling these issues in the classroom requires considerable knowledge, skill, and experience on the part of the teacher. It is particularly important for the teacher to create a climate in which students feel comfortable in actively participating in discussions of the issues and free to express unpopular opinions about them.

Principle No. 10. Multicultural educators must understand that the care, understanding, and sensitivity they show toward their students may, in the final analysis, be the most important influence on student motivation and performance. After all that has been said, this principle may still be the most important one for teachers to keep in mind; there is no such thing as a "teacher-proof" curriculum. Unless teachers are sincerely concerned about their students and seriously committed to educating them, none of the principles discussed earlier will ultimately lead to the desired results.

At the same time, it should be emphasized that good and sincere intentions on the part of a teacher are not enough. In fact, the detrimental effects of monocultural education discussed earlier may have even more insidious and damaging effects on children if they are unconsciously promoted by a well-meaning teacher who is sincerely concerned about his or her students. Therefore, if teachers wish to effectively implement multicultural education, it is essential for them to acquire the knowledge, skills, and attitudes embodied in the principles that have been set forth above.

We conclude our list of guiding principles here. Although a comprehensive listing has by no means been provided and several other principles could easily be added, we have tried to present those that might be of the most interest and relevance. It should also be noted that the appropriateness of each principle must be considered within the particular educational context to which it is applied. For example, some of the principles may be appropriate for highly multiethnic schools but not for largely homogeneous schools. Similarly, some may be appropriate for urban schools, others for rural schools, and still others for suburban schools. In any case, it is hoped that these few principles will offer some practical guidance to educators who may wish to apply the conceptual framework for multicultural education.

We now shift our application focus from a general conceptual framework to a more specific problem area facing the public schools. In Chapter 4 we saw that cultural conflict will be a normal and permanent feature of a pluralistic society. It seems reasonable for schools to anticipate the different forms of conflict likely to arise and to prepare themselves and students for it. This will be the focus of our next set of recommendations, beginning first with curriculum reform and then followed by institutional reform.

DEVELOPING A CONFLICT-SENSITIVE CURRICULUM

Current Curriculum Practices

Schools have often been the battleground on which diverse groups have fought for their special interests. In addition, schools have often been thought of as the vehicle for solving or resolving the ills of society. Both roles point to the schools as an extremely important institution in our social response to cultural conflict. Because of their importance in the development and reinforcement of values, belief, and knowledge, schools have the potential to play an important role in the development, management, and understanding of cultural conflict.

It is vital, however, to understand that as social institutions schools tend to reflect and support the norms, values, beliefs and structure of the larger, dominant society. Some of the support is intentional, consciously and systematically conceived and applied. Direct curricular objectives and many policies that control the operation of the schools have functions of this type. Other beliefs, norms, and values are supported through less obvious means. They are implicitly but effectively taught in schools. Not usually talked about in teachers' statements of goals or included as the underlying rationale of policy statements, these ideas and norms have been called the "hidden curriculum."

Attitudes and beliefs affecting conflict, as well as attitudes and beliefs about conflict itself, are transmitted to students in both ways. An overview of our existing curriculum and practices suggests that we are very ambivalent about conflict, reinforcing it in some ways but rejecting or avoiding it in other circumstances. It is important to look more carefully at what we teach about conflict both explicitly and implicitly, since these learnings will affect the nature of conflict in society in a number of ways.

Perhaps the most striking feature of conflict in the curriculum is its absence. Rarely do we find a systematic treatment of conflict as a component of human existence. As Michael Apple points out, even in the social studies, where we would most expect conflict to be considered, consensus models rule the day.[40] Apple found that much of the literature examined accepts society as basically a cooperative system and that observations in classrooms over an extended time reveal a similar outlook. In his words: "The perspective found in schools leans heavily upon how all elements of a society, from the postman and fireman in first grade to the partial institutions in civics courses in high school, are linked to each other in a functional relationship, each contributing to the ongoing *maintenance* of society."[41] As support for this conclusion, Apple cites two examples he considers typical. The first is from the Science Research Associates' economics "kit" *Our Working World*, a tool designed to teach basic concepts of economics to elementary school students. Statements such as the following pervade the primary grade course of study subtitled "Families at Work":[42]

When we follow the rules, we are rewarded; but if we break the rules, we will be punished. So you see, dear, that is why everyone does care. That is why we *learn* customs and rules, and why we *follow* them. Because if we do, we are all rewarded by a nicer and more orderly world.

The second example comes from a more sophisticated inquiry-oriented curriculum. The following is a hierarchy of generalizations that are to be internalized by the student through active participation in role playing and inquiry.[43]

1. The behavior of individuals is governed by commonly accepted rules.
2. Members of family groups are governed by rules and laws.
3. Community groups are governed through leadership and authority.
4. Man's peaceful interaction depends on social controls.
5. The pattern of government depends upon control by participation in the political system.
6. Stable political organization improves the quality of life shared by its citizens.

To compound the problems of students coming to understand conflict, when it is discussed in the social studies curriculum, a somewhat biased view is presented. The true nature of, the amount of, and possible uses of internecine strife are generally misrepresented.[44] Students learn, in not very subtle ways, that our side is good and their side is bad. "We" are peace-loving and want an end to strife, "they" are warlike and aim to dominate; "we" are civilized, "they" are barbarian; "we" support progress and development, "they" are ignorant and backward.

It is apparent that social studies tends to teach students that consensus, order, and stability are normal and proper and that conflict is deviant, dysfunctional, and disruptive. This view is reinforced by the way we approach other subject matter. The stories children read in language arts programs rarely deal with personal or social conflict. When conflicts do occur, they are usually the result of misunderstandings and are successfully resolved through cooperation and sharing. Similarly, science organizes content around fundamental regularities and almost never examines inherent intellectual and personal struggles. Thus, students fail to perceive that what we consider scientific knowledge today was often born in the midst of conflict generated by the introduction of new and usually revolutionary paradigms that often effectively divided the scholarly community, nor do they recognize the ever-present conflicts over different interpretations of data or disagreements over methodology and goals.

The school curriculum, in effect, teaches students that consensus is normal and desirable. The results of this are reflected in student attitudes toward conflict. Torney and Tesconi,[45] in their review of the literature, found that children do not value conflict and dissent as important to the growth of the democratic system. They found that elementary school students in particular tend to believe that the system fails as a whole if threatened in any part. They also noted that this belief contributed to a lack of tolerance for legitimate protest. Support for dissent or diversity of opinion was absent even in many high school students.

But if school practices and curricula tend to teach students that conflict is dysfunctional and abnormal, some aspects of the curriculum, both hidden and otherwise, reinforce behavior and attitudes that contribute to the matrix of conflict. The development of nationalistic feelings among American citizens, for example, while developing cohesiveness within the nation, tends to increase the possibility of conflict between nations. Similar results may issue from emphasizing the "free enterprise" nature of our social-economic-political system. We tell students that competition, self-reliance, and achievement are good; and we reinforce individuality, independence, and aggressiveness. To the winner belong the spoils. But to the extent that students come to perceive the system as a negative-sum game—a system with limited resources and rewards, where winners gain at the cost of the losers—we can expect the intensity and urgency of conflict situations to increase and the possibility of collaboration and cooperation between conflicting parties to decrease.

Finally, the structure and mode of operation of schools contribute to the development of tendencies toward conflict. Schools tend to stratify students. Clearly there are winners (those who do well in school) and losers (those who fail). Examinations, report cards, ability grouping, tracking, promotions, and diplomas all underscore this fact. Stratification also occurs along the lines of authority and power, and few would deny that schools are prone to autocracy at times. Those with power, the teachers and administrators, clearly are in a position to command, and those without power (the students) are compelled, at times physically, to obey.

From the foregoing we can conclude that schools do indeed teach about conflict. But they teach the wrong things. Moreover, much of what needs to be taught is not considered. We must realize that what we teach and how we teach affects social-cultural relations in society. In addition, we need to understand that students, like all of us, probably live in a social environment displaying various degrees of cultural conflict. We need a curriculum that addresses these issues in a realistic, straightforward, and productive manner.

A Conflict-Sensitive Curriculum

Learning about Conflict.   Perhaps the place to begin if we are to cope with conflict, manage it, or even maximize its functional possibilities, is with the recognition that conflict is a normal, pervasive component of a healthy pluralistic and democratic society. All of us—students, educators, and the general public—need to begin to view conflicts as systematic products of the changing structure of a society, which by their very nature tend to lead toward progress. Thus, the "order" of society is the regularity of change, and the "reality" of society is conflict and flux and not a "closed functional system."[46] In particular, students need a great deal of help to understand what a pluralistic system is, to learn to value its diversity, and to comprehend how such a system operates and persists over time.[47] Students must come to realize that criticism and the accommodation of conflicting ideas are part of democratic pluralism and that altercation or antagonism among some social elements will not necessarily destroy the whole system.

It is feasible to build this more realistic view of conflict and society into the everyday school curriculum. Michael Apple[48] suggests several curriculum considerations for science and social studies. For example, he believes that in science classes a more balanced presentation of some of the espoused values of science is essential, particularly recognition of and focus on the historical importance of the overriding skeptical outlook in science. Similarly, he argues, the history of science can be seen as a continuing dialectic of controversy and conflict between advocates of competing research programs and their theories, between accepted answers and challenges to these "truths." In this connection, the study of conceptual revolutions in science and how they have proceeded would contribute to a less overbearing perspective on consensus as the only mode of progress.

For the social studies, Apple suggests a more systematic presentation of the role of conflict in social change, and the conditions under which such conflict occurs. As an example, he suggests the comparative study of revolutions—perhaps the American, French, Russian, and Chinese revolutions. He also suggests a more realistic appraisal and presentation of the uses of conflict in the civil rights movement by Blacks, Hispanics, Native Americans, and others. Through such a focus, the realization would be inevitable that laws *had* to be broken before they were abolished by the courts. Clearly, a good deal of progress was and is made through the activities of conflict. Apple also suggests comparing different theories of social structure and the differing value assumptions of each.

This last suggestion might be particularly relevant to helping students understand conflict in a pluralistic society. It should be evident that the focus on foods, ethnic dances, dress, folktales, and "unusual" or intriguing customs and practices that frequently comprises multicultural education curricula will not suffice. Rather, students need to see that real differences exist and that these differences can be critical in intergroup relationships. There is a real need to learn that understanding, respect, and tolerance are not always possible and will not always be adequate to lubricate cultural friction.

Two current curricular methodologies seem particularly useful in helping students understand the conflicts arising from cultural differences. The first is law-related education. With the encouragement of the American Bar Association, educators and lawyers have developed a variety of excellent teaching materials and have introduced law studies into hundreds of school systems throughout the country.[49] While these materials may not deal directly with cultural conflict, they provide a framework that can easily be adapted. By focusing on court cases and legal decisions involving cultural conflict, students will gain a better understanding of the basis and content of conflicting interests, how they evolve, and how some have been legally resolved. A sampling of cases that might be used is included in the Appendix.

A second methodological approach is associated with the movement in values education. For example, Robert Stahl offers what seems to be a particularly promising and effective approach in developing values dilemmas for content-centered social studies instruction.[50] The model allows teachers to explore problems in values within the context of the social studies program. Thus, the opportunity exists to teach culture-specific content (i.e., information about one or more cultural groups) so as to encourage students to acknowledge and consider potential conflicts that may arise from cultural differences. Through this process, teachers can develop value clarification activities that have a high probability of resulting in real intellectual conflicts or dissonances in the values or morals of the students involved in the activities. Two such activities are included in Appendix B as examples.

Some individuals see inherent danger in teaching students that cultural conflict has been and continues to be a prominent feature of our social landscape. Nathan Glazer believes that the danger in such teaching is that it may lead to greater social conflict and strife between groups. In his mind, "we must judge what we teach by what we want to attain."[51] Glazer believes that the goals of the American educational system are the teaching of skills (e.g., reading, writing, calculation), socialization (learning to work alone and in groups, respecting common rules, regarding achievement as possible and rewarding), and the making of Americans (he defines America as a distinctive nation based on the primacy of no single ethnic group). He argues that we could emphasize in our teaching that a dominant ethnic group, the Anglo Americans, enslaved, suppressed, and carried out physical or cultural genocide against all other groups; that these other groups attained equality through organization, force, and violence; and that every gap in education, income, or political influence between the groups is fully ascribable to prejudice and discrimination. But Glazer believes such teachings are likely to interfere with the development of the nation we desire. Our selection and choice of what we teach in history, economics, and sociology, he argues, "must be guided not only by truth . . . but also by our conception of a desirable society, of the relationship between what we select to teach and the ability of people to achieve such a society and live together in it."[52]

Glazer's position is troubling and presents something of a dilemma. On the one hand, cultural conflict is real and has played in the past and continues to play a major role in group relationship in the United States. To downplay it, gloss over it, or ignore it in the hope that it will soon go away or never existed is to deny reality. Indeed, one of the central theses of this study is that social conflict is part of the normal order of things and that cultural conflict, as one kind of social conflict, is part of the normal order of a culturally plural society. The kind, frequency, and intensity of cultural conflict may change, but it will not disappear; nor should we desire that it do so. Rather, we should work to maximize its functional qualities. By failing to recognize the prevalence of conflict, we lose the opportunity to help prepare individuals to manage it and function effectively in its presence.

On the other hand, there are sound bases for Glazer's fears. If we teach students that conflict characterizes group relationships, that conflict is the rule and not the exception, we might predispose students to create and engage in conflict. That is, we might create a self-fulfilling prophecy. It has been well documented by a number of researchers studying the dynamics of conflict that the knowledge and perceptions an individual brings to a conflict situation significantly influence the evolution of that conflict.[53]

Individuals enter any potential conflict situation with a well-established cognitive map. It is composed of information, beliefs, attitudes, and perceptions that the person uses to make sense of the world. These have been acquired through direct experience and through sources of general information such as talking with others, reading, television, and school. Among the information and beliefs an individual holds will be views about other people and groups and how they fit into one's social world. This cognitive map—the composite of the individual's general information—tends to determine the way a conflict situation is interpreted.[54] For example, an individual who has learned that the world in general is rather hostile and malevolent is likely to interpret even benevolent moves of another in a hostile and malevolent way. And preconceptions are often self-confirming. A person who believes the world is fundamentally hostile will tend to behave in such a way as to make it so. Thus, if we teach students that American cultural groups are in competition with one another and that each group is out to exploit and dominate the others, it is likely that this will serve as the basis for group interaction. Groups will constantly be on the defensive and will tend to interpret the actions of other groups in a hostile manner. Under these conditions, we should expect stereotyping, prejudice, and discrimination to increase, each fueling the escalating spiral of conflict.

It is precisely the recognition of this dilemma that provides a way out. Glazer is rightly concerned over what we teach students about group relationships. It would be inadvisable and an unwarranted exaggeration of the facts to portray the relationships of culturally different groups as consisting solely of exploitation, domination, and struggle; but it will also not do to deny the relevance of cultural conflict to both historical and contemporary social dynamics in the United States. We need to provide an understanding that will put conflict in its proper perspective. Students need to understand that conflict is a social reality subject to certain determining factors, as are all other social phenomena.

Contemporary conflict must be understood in the light of current economic, political, social, and psychological factors and as a product of history. Historical conflict, in turn, must be understood in the light of the perceptions and values of its period as well as the economic, political, and social factors that existed during that time. Also, the functional aspects of both past and current conflict need to be emphasized. Rather than attempts by one group to destroy another, conflict can be seen as a means by which constructive social change takes place. By literally forcing conscious attention on social ills, we can define issues and explore new dimensions. Thus, cultural conflict in the United States can in large part be seen historically as constructive social change, the medium through which minority groups have been able to secure a more equitable and just position in society.

Teaching students directly about the dynamics of conflict (i.e., the variables that tend to affect all conflict situations) will also help bring conflict under control. For example, we need to teach students how the general information one brings to a situation can influence the way the situation is perceived. This puts the students in a position to evaluate the accuracy and applicability of beliefs and knowledge to any specific situation. That is, while students may know that at times interpersonal relationships can be understood in terms of cultural conflict, with this additional skill they can determine if a particular situation is one of those times or not. Thus, the study of cultural conflict enables individuals to define the nature of a particular social relationship. In making discriminating judgments, in deciding whether or not a given interaction is an instance of cultural conflict, the student is able to influence the form of the interaction. This will be a considerable improvement over the way many people are often trapped by mindless and unconscious stereotypes and prejudices.

The dynamic nature of conflict suggests other matters that would be profitably included in a conflict-sensitive curriculum. Not only is conflict influenced by our prior learning but it entails a learning component of its own. The involvement in a conflict situation tends to "teach" us about the situation, the other individuals involved, and many other factors that become part of our general store of information. All these perceptions influence both the present conflict and future conflicts. For example, if someone hits me, I "learn" that he is hostile toward me. (This may not in fact be the case; it may have been an accident, or he may have done it for my own good.) If I then respond in a hostile manner, it is likely that the other person will also develop a more hostile perception of the situation than he had before. Kenneth Boulding suggests a reason why conflict, in spite of its many generally beneficial effects, continually tends to get out of hand and become destructive: He says that the conduct of a conflict frequently results in a pathological learning process.[55] In other words, conflict tends to teach (or otherwise create) attitudes, perceptions, and beliefs that increase the probability of sustained hostility.

As a way to avoid "pathological" learning from conflict, Boulding believes people need to understand how to learn about conflict. While we may learn many things from a conflict situation, we may be learning the wrong things. What we learn may not be true, or we may be focusing our attention on irrelevant aspects. We need to become more skilled in analyzing a conflict situation to determine its true nature: how the other party perceives the situation, how the other party is likely to receive certain moves on our part, and how the other party is likely to respond to certain moves we may initiate.

One of the components of this learning is what Boulding calls "long-sightedness,"[56] the projection of long-term consequences of various actions due to the chain of events they put into motion. People need to realize that taking a short-term advantage often results in a long-term loss because of the reactions of other parties.

Another step toward the reduction of pathological learning would be the development of a propensity to inquire further about the reasons behind another person's behavior. In other words, individuals need to make sure that their perceptions are indeed an accurate description of the actual state of affairs. From time to time we need a reality check.

To summarize how the foregoing discussion relates to curriculum: People need to learn about conflict. It is important that an individual know the occurrences around which conflicts develop. One must be aware of the different kinds of conflicts that can develop in order to assess a situation accurately and determine the most functional response. It is important to understand the dynamics of conflict, as well as how general background information affects the way a situation is perceived and how engagement in conflicts affects the participants' perceptions of them. Only through understanding will individuals gain control of conflict rather than be controlled by it.

Socialization. Earlier, we mentioned the ambivalence displayed toward conflict in the schools. We noted that some teaching methods and materials may unwittingly contribute to the frequency of social conflict. For example, it was noted that we tend to reinforce competition, individuality, and aggressiveness in school, and also suggested that the authoritarian nature of school may reinforce the misuse of authority while it legitimizes dominance and the use of power.

Some students of conflict have recognized these tendencies and recommended that we take a closer look at the way we socialize our children.[57] If we want to avoid aggression and open conflict, they argue, we must achieve a culture that deliberately trains its members to avoid them. That is, children should be taught to live the kind of lives that will equip them to live the adult lives we want for them. If our goal is a society in which aggressive behavior is no longer seen as functional, children should not be allowed to play aggressively and should be rewarded for cooperation. Furthermore, we may wish to attempt to socialize people so that certain methods of waging conflict are so alien that they become "unthinkable." Thus, we can recognize the role and presence of cultural conflict in society, but can define the rules that govern it in such a way that violence is not permitted. An illustration of a step toward both these goals is Sweden's ban on the sale of violent toys (guns and the like). A law has also recently been passed in Sweden that forbids the spanking of children even by their own parents.

We might also wish to reconsider some of the organizational qualities of school that lead to a hidden curriculum reinforcing aggressiveness along with the notion that it is usual for some people to "win" and others to "lose." We must realize that in the course of socializing our children it may not be possible to educate them both to be aggressive and to empathize fully with others.

There is no clear answer to these questions of socialization. Any specific curriculum recommendations we could offer here would be premature. The issues, however, are important and must be raised in regard to the course future conflicts will take. Those affiliated with the schools will have to take some stand, but ultimately the decisions will rest with the larger society.

Personal Conflict and the Curriculum

In our earlier discussion of personal conflict (see Chapter 6), we recognized that at times individuals find themselves in situations that give rise to feelings of anxiety, frustration, irritation, and the like as a result of cultural differences. One may feel ill at ease among people speaking a language that one does not understand. While recognizing that a noisy and active classroom may be a normal environment for students, a teacher may nevertheless be irritated and distracted by the situation. This may occur even when the individual intellectually understands the cultural roots of the disconcerting behavior. These feelings do not arise from ethnocentrism, misunderstanding, or the fact that one is competing for social resources with members of the other groups; rather, they are involuntary responses stemming from earlier socialization.

The curriculum emphasis, if one is to be able to cope with and function in such situations, will be on the development of self-awareness and positive self-attitudes. Before being able to confront one's physiological, psychological, or emotional responses rationally, one must become aware of them, understand their origin, and accept them. Carl Rogers sees this kind of awareness as the basis for inner freedom.[58] When associated with one's ethnic identity, this awareness is what Michael Novak argues is needed for an individual to be "ethnically literate."[59] As long as the responses of discomfort remain at a semiconscious or unconscious level, and as long as their origins remain hidden, the individual will be under their control; but when he identifies and understands them, the individual takes control. This is not control in the sense that the feelings can be *willed* away (though this is sometimes possible) but that one can choose how to react to them and whether to escape or endure the discomfort.

Michael Novak offers several possible sources of greater self-understanding. First, he believes that at home young children need to be provided with folktalks, images, and rituals that objectify the actual emotional and intellectual rhythms governing family relations. When family relations move on levels that can be experienced only subjectively, or when the external images and rituals determine the family's dynamic interaction, he believes serious emotional distortion arises. "Anger, resentment, misunderstandings, and dreadful silences multiply, intertwine, and feed on each other, not only those that occur in the complexity of all human relationships, but also special cultural distortions that heighten them."[60]

The second source of understanding is the responsibility of the school. The school curriculum, like the home, needs to help students objectify their inner tendencies. Currently, Novak argues, schools offer no ethnic illumination to children about the various family patterns and emotional contexts from which they came. "Anger is a legitimate and frequently exhibited emotion in some traditions, but is regarded as a lapse in self-control in others. Ambition is nourished in some, but much chided in others. Children are lavishly praised in some traditions, and systematically "humbled" in others."[61] Such differences could and should be threaded through subject matter implicitly (e.g., through character development and story focus in reading materials) and explicitly (e.g., as topics of investigation in their own right).

Third, the curricula of universities should include, along with other studies, courses focusing on the waves of immigration to the United States; on the lives and life styles of the immigrants; and on the roles these people played in political, economic, and social development. We might argue, as James Banks does, that such a focus should be incorporated into the social studies of the secondary schools as well.[62]

Each of these sources will contribute to a greater cultural self-awareness and should also facilitate the development of positive self-attitudes. These in turn enable individuals to tolerate both inner and outer stress. Internally secure individuals are less threatened by alternative positions and more able to cope in stress-producing situations. Therefore, we must face the task of developing persons who understand and feel good about themselves.

HOW INSTITUTIONS CAN COPE

We have indicated some curriculum concerns to which schools need to address themselves if they are to prepare individuals to function successfully in a culturally plural society. Yet this presupposes that the schools themselves will be able to survive the continued pressures of cultural conflict. In view of the trend for schools to play an increasingly active role in the amelioration of social problems, we should expect schools to continue to be a frequent battleground in which conflicting interests are fought out. If the schools are not able to manage the conflict successfully, a real threat exists to their viability as educational institutions.

The best time to manage social conflict is before it starts, or at least in its early stages. This is because, as conflicts develop, antagonistic groups undergo various transformations and shifts in objectives that often result in polarization and increased rigidity in the positions they hold. This is similar to the pathological learning process we observed earlier. But for the conflict to be managed, it must first be acknowledged. Playing down differences, smoothing over rough spots, or placating those with legitimate complaints (i.e., denying the existence of conflict or hoping that it will go away) will in the long run aggravate a conflict situation. Educational personnel must recognize and accept the likelihood of conflict, and rather than fear it, must face it in a straightforward and honest fashion. Indeed, it would be useful for educational personnel to view conflict situations as one of the main sources of hu-

man progress and to recognize that the historical roots of the democratic form of government and of society are deeply embedded in conflict.
If the probability and legitimacy of conflict are understood in this way,
it is evident that institutions should prepare for it.

Structural Accommodations for Conflict

The literature on conflict regulation and management suggests that
certain institutional arrangements and forms of organization tend to
contribute to the peaceful management of subcultural differences.[63] De-
parting from the principles of majority rule, these arrangements
endeavor to prevent subcultures from falling into a position of "stable unrepresentation," an institutional position that perpetuates underrepre-
sentation and powerlessness. If subcultures perceive themselves as
permanent minorities, unable to significantly influence a policy process
by which decisions are made that affect their well-being, they are increasingly likely to behave in a disruptive or violent fashion. If subculture minorities are guaranteed access to policy-making processes, they
will perceive themselves to be sharers in the policy process rather than
winners or losers. In such an arrangement, unlike a winner-take-all
system, no significant group will ever be unrepresented. Likewise,
schools at all levels need to provide formal institutional mechanisms
for culturally different groups to protect themselves and their interests
against majority domination. Marc Levine suggests that such an
arrangement would entail the following:[64]

1. The principle of proportionality should be applied in political
   representation and resource allocation. This should hold true
   at the state, district, and school level. Each group must have a
   fair say in determining the goals and objectives of education,
   the distribution of educational resources (e.g., which programs will be funded), and in policy decisions that affect
   the organization and operation of the schools, which might
   include decisions on matters ranging from integration to
   discipline.
2. "All parties" government, in which minority subcultures are
   invited to share power, should be created. In majority rule,
   winner-take-all arrangements, the winning party ends up
   with the policy-making power, leaving the "losers" without
   representation. An "all parties" government guarantees that
   all groups with a vested interest will have a continuing voice
   in the decision-making process. In addition, it has been common in such arrangements for the distribution of power
   (democracies notwithstanding) to reinforce the principle that

each legitimate group is entitled to its fair share. However, since those with power are in a position to define which groups are legitimate, the greatest difficulty for a minority group has often been to achieve the status of legitimacy. Thus, in the formation of policy-making bodies, it is important that each group with a vested interest be included.

3. Concurrent majority and minority vetoes should be utilized. This is an arrangement similar to that found in the United Nations. Each group has the power to refuse any proposal that affects its well-being. Because each group with a vested interest can veto a policy decision, no central policy-making body can produce a decision that any particular group views as a threat to its interests. Rather, the issue is thrown back for further negotiation until it can be successfully resolved. One might think that this arrangement would make it very difficult to agree on policy issues, and in some cases it will. But the alternative is to simply override the interests of one of the parties, giving the appearance of resolving the conflict but in fact suppressing it, which is not the same thing. The consequences of suppression are likely to be increased hostilities, frustration, alienation, and a general movement away from functional outcomes.

4. Subcultural policy-making autonomy should be bestowed in specific administrative areas deemed strategic by the subculture. Some considerations fall solely within a particular group's legitimate domain and thus need not be subject to the approval of the collective governing group. These will not affect the well-being of the larger group but do have meaning to the particular subculture. Religious practices have traditionally fallen within this domain. For example, whether or not an individual will participate in prayer in the classroom and in flag salutes is not within the bounds for the majority to decide. However, when the practice affects the larger group, as, for example, refusal to immunize children before they enter school, it becomes the legitimate domain of the larger group. The tendency is for the dominant group to be overzealous in its claims of interest, and this must be guarded against. A case can probably be made for the position that many of the traditional concerns of schools (e.g., hair, dress, and language) properly belong in the hands of subcultures. One might even argue, as certain Chinese American and Chicano communities have, that the decision whether to integrate or not should belong to the subcultural group.

Communication and Conflict

Besides distributing power and creating the opportunity for competing groups to protect themselves, the institutional arrangements mentioned will have the added advantage of facilitating open and accurate communication. Since many conflicts arise from what parties *think* may happen—from their anxieties, prejudices, fears, and uncertainties—rather than from any phenomena that are threatening in an objective sense, open communication would appear to be very desirable. It would even seem advantageous to have a communication system whereby a third party could facilitate the communication process. In this way, a reality check for the perceptions of the potentially conflicting parties could be provided.

Third-party informational input is valuable because within a potential conflict-producing situation there are usually any number of ways in which the parties can interpret the sequence of events. The evocation of a particular situational reality by either party depends upon the social cues that prompt that response. Since the images and responses cued will influence the direction the conflict will take, management of the conflict may depend on the information a third party provides and hence on the way in which the conflicting parties ultimately interpret the situation. Thus, facilitating conflict management by improving communication may depend on information fed in from the outside (i.e., by a third party). That is to say, when conflict exists in a social and organizational matrix that allows for a generous input from outside parties, an accurate perception of reality and a constructive interpretation of the situation are more likely to be produced. Gerald Moulton has suggested some criteria to be used by either a third party or the conflicting groups in evaluating the communications process during negotiations:[65]

1. To what degree is there an attitude or climate which supports a cooperative search for a win/win agreement?
2. To what extent do all parties understand and agree on what is appropriate subject matter and process?
3. To what degree is it clear what each party involved desires to achieve through negotiative problem solving?
4. To what degree is there agreement on what the "facts" are in the situation (as contrasted with "assumptions")?
5. To what extent do the parties involved understand and agree on what the major and minor issues are in the situation?
6. To what degree are the positions and priorities of each party understood?

7. To what extent are the parties aware of the relevant needs requiring fulfillment in the situation?
8. To what extent are the negotiative strategies and tactics being used consistent with a creative win/win solution for all parties?

Constant and accurate communication can facilitate conflict management, and third parties have the potential to play a significant and constructive role toward attaining this end. But while a third party can provide information and cause the conflict to focus on constructive social and cultural perceptions, this party must be seen as being neutral by each of the other two parties if the intervention is to be accepted. Since schools are likely to be associated with the interests of the state or the dominant culture, individuals identified with a school can expect to have a difficult time mediating conflicts in which that school is involved, but they may be able to help mediate conflicts between other conflicting parties when the school is seen as having no vested interest. Mechanisms should also be established to provide for disinterested third parties to help resolve conflicts in which the school is involved.

As with political representation, so also communication and mediation in school matters entail being able to identify which parties or factions within conflicting groups communication should be addressed to. While this seems straightforward enough, often a community or group is divided within itself or lacks cohesion and consensus. One result of internal dissent, suspicion, or disorganization is that a group may not be able to find leaders who can negotiate and accurately represent the community's views. In such cases it would be fruitless for the school to try to resolve the conflict with only one faction (which often occurs), since other factions can deny the legitimacy of the representation. While divide-and-conquer tactics work well in attempts by one group to dominate or exploit another, if a democratic and pluralistic end is to be reached, it would be much more expedient for the school or some neutral third party to either help the divided group come to terms or find some way to include everyone in the conflict negotiations.

Flexibility and Conflict

Another institutional quality that may facilitate conflict management and regulation is flexibility. By maintaining a relative degree of flexibility the schools can increase their ability to manage many divergent interests. By manipulating the institution so that it can accommodate a number of alternatives and thereby minimize potential conflict, we can avoid a negative-sum arrangement. Thus, the schools should avoid limited, opposing alternatives. Rather, by developing a multiplicity of curricula, teaching strategies, and organizational structures; by accommodating different language and cultural preferences; and perhaps by decentralizing—the schools may be able to accommodate a diversity of individuals and views. A workable pluralistic solution will be to provide ways for differences to exist separately or structures that incorporate but accommodate the legitimacy of a variety of differences.

Preparing School Personnel

The above suggests some ways schools, as social institutions, can prepare themselves structurally and organizationally to manage cultural conflict in a functional way and the manner in which the curriculum can contribute toward this end. But content does not flow spontaneously through the structure of an institution. It must be selected and processed by individuals who assume positions within the institution. Ultimately, the character of the institution depends on how individuals do their jobs and interrelate. Within the schools, individuals who affect how the institution functions are administrators, teachers, and staff. These individuals must work together in support of the avowed content objectives and purposes if the schools are to function effectively. To manage cultural conflict effectively, school personnel will need a broad understanding of cultural conflict, as well as appropriate skills and attitudes. These skills, attitudes, and knowledge are much the same as those outlined for students earlier.

School personnel must first recognize the ubiquitous nature of conflict and the probability that cultural conflict will continue and be particularly manifest in schools. Second, they need to understand the bases of cultural conflict, issues that will precipitate it, and the different kinds of conflict that may develop. Third, they need to recognize the functional aspects of conflict and see that even if at times disagreement is disruptive and unpleasant, it is an important means of social change. Fourth, school personnel must understand the dynamic process of conflict. In this regard, they need to see how an individual's general store of information influences not only personal perceptions but the direction a conflict situation will take. They need to see how "pathological" learnings can arise during conflict and how to extract accurate information from a conflict situation. Fifth, school personnel must have dispositions and a set of attitudes suited to conflict management, and these must include recognizing the need for a reality check from time to time to verify the objectivity and accuracy of the information they are receiving. The use of "long-sightedness" in conflict situations is another invaluable technique. Sixth, teachers need to guard against unintentionally creating or reinforcing conflict by carefully reviewing what and how they teach and their personal style of interacting with people. And seventh, school personnel must become more sensitive to their personal feelings and reactions and the role culture plays in both the formation and the evocation of these feelings and reactions. Such a sensitivity involves more than identifying a reaction and its source—it also includes being able and willing to choose among alternative behaviors in response.

THE PUBLIC SCHOOLS AS A SOCIAL INSTITUTION: A WORD OF WARNING AND HOPE FOR THE FUTURE

The Need for Change

A casual reading of the preceding pages might produce the impression that conflict among different cultural, racial, and ethnic groups in the United States is acceptable and no great cause for concern. Such an impression is far from the thesis of this study. We have argued that, the ideal of cultural pluralism notwithstanding, conflict is a normal part of society, and have emphasized its functional aspects and discussed ways to prepare people for it. Yet our experience tells us that cultural conflict is a very real problem. Property has been destroyed; the operation of social institutions has been disrupted; large sums of material and human resources have been diverted from other needy concerns to control and combat it; and most important, cultural conflict has resulted in injury—emotional, psychological, physical, and sometimes fatal—to human beings. Indeed, if cultural conflict were not clearly a social problem, this book would never have been written.

The arguments in the preceding pages should not be seen as condoning cultural conflict; one can neither condone nor disapprove of something that is largely beyond choice or control. And conflict is largely beyond volition or strict regulation. It is a part of all of us, in both our personal and social lives. But this is not to say that the *ways in which conflict is manifested*—the expression it takes—cannot be influenced by conscious choice and national regulation. Conflicts are significantly influenced by situational and personal factors, and such elements are largely within the realm of human decision. Thus, while cultural conflict may always be with us in some form or another, violence and destruction need not be, nor should we resign ourselves to continued human casualties. The omnipresence of conflict has been illustrated, as have its functional elements and dynamics, in order that we may manage it and direct it, rather than let it control us. Thus, in regard to cultural conflict, one purpose of this book has been to dispel the naive notion that understanding, respect, and toleration will lead to love and harmony among different groups. With increased knowledge of the more complex variables influencing the development and expression of conflict, we will be better able to manipulate these factors and hence maximize functional outcomes and minimize violence and destruction.

Much research and writing about conflict has been conducted during the last two decades, but the phenomenon is complex and the answers are not easy. Furthermore, there is a traditional lag between theoretical development and practical application. Perhaps here, if at all, our efforts will be most useful. We have, for the most part, discussed cultural conflict in relation to the public schools and made recommendations regarding curriculum and organization.

Other recommendations for change have also been offered. We have addressed the issues of cultural conflict as a requirement in the pursuit of the ideal of cultural pluralism. In this same pursuit we offered guidelines for providing an approach to education that is multicultural. Therein we suggested goals for the school that would help transform certain aspects of society to be more consistent with the ideal. But there is a risk that must be avoided: the danger of again imposing upon the schools the primary responsibility to ameliorate society's ills. A corollary is that there is a growing potential for a discontinuity developing between the schools and other social institutions.

The Problem of Change

We are asking that schools change and thereby help bring about changes in the greater society. The engineering of social change, however, is complex and requires the cooperation of a number of different components. In order to understand the subtitles of these requirements we need to look more closely at the components that might be changed within a social institution.[66]

The first step in analyzing the potential areas of change within a social institution is to recognize that all social institutions are a system of interrelated parts. That is, at least conceptually, there are different interrelated components, each serving a different function in the operation of the institution. Simply speaking, these components consist of formal organizational structure of the institution, the informal network comprised of the individuals who people (operate) the institution, and the product or content that the institution processes. Let us look at each of these more carefully.

First, we should recognize that the structure or organization of an institution can be separated from its content. The structure, as the term implies, pertains to the form or arrangements of the parts; it is the interrelation of parts as dominated by the general character of the whole. The structure can be best understood as made up of two elements: the formal structure and the informal structure of the social system. The

formal structure consists of the formal positions, the status relationships among them, and the interaction of the people who occupy
them. This may be thought of as a hierarchy of positions into which
people are assigned different roles. For example, the formal structure
of the judicial system, in simple terms, is composed of the various
courts; the respective roles and positions associated with the functioning of the courts (judges, attorneys, jurors, plaintiffs, etc.); the rules
that govern the mechanics of court operations (the Constitution, statutes, the principle of precedent, etc.); and the respective positions and
functions of each in relation to one another. This structure remains relatively intact regardless of who peoples the positions or what actual
laws are being enforced.

The public schools, for their part, have a different formal structure
from the judicial system and every other social institution. School structure is generally composed of different levels of schools (e.g.,
elementary, and secondary, and higher education), with each subdi-
vided further into grades based on chronological age. The roles within
the structure include students, teachers, administrators, and staff, with
each possessing a particular power and status relationship with regard
to the others. And there is a set of rules (federal, state, and local law)
that governs the operation of the institution.

It can be seen, then, that the formal structure makes the public
schools different from social institutions such as law enforcement, government, judiciary, and business. That is, different rules, positions,
and purposes make up each institution and distinguish one from the
other. Thus, the schools are organized in a different way, to do a different job, with (for the most part) different people, than the police
department. Similarly, while they may tend to deal with the same individuals, the police department and the judiciary are organized in different ways and have different formal positions (e.g., patrolmen and
detectives rather than judges and attorneys) and different purposes from
one another.

The informal structures of a social system parallel that of the formal
organizational structure. Such structures encompass interactions not
prescribed by the positions held by the individuals involved but by the
dynamics of the group or individual personalities involved. Informal
structures evolve out of personal interaction rather than out of the formal structural positions of the institution. For example, though each
session of the U.S. Supreme Court is sanctioned by the same prescribed set of rules—the U.S. Constitution—each Court takes on a
character of its own in regard to its function and relationship to other
courts, laws, precedents, and the like. (Compare the Warren Court to
the Berger Court.) This informal structure is evident at all levels of the
system and influences how the formal structure in fact functions; it can

either support or subvert the intended purpose of the formal structure and content. Consider a building designed for structural flexibility and creativity, a structure with movable walls for maximum interaction, cooperation, and the easy flow of individuals involved in it. This may be likened to the formal structure. But now place in the building individuals who reinforce authority, status, competition, and individual self-reliance. The intended function of the formal structure can be effectively neutralized. Similarly, consider a police department organized so as to identify and respond to the needs of minority groups in a community. Furthermore, assume that fair and equitable laws exist for the police department to enforce. If the police officers themselves act in a responsive and just manner, the whole system will function smoothly; but if the officers exhibit authoritarian, partisan, and racist attitudes, the formal intentions of the system will fail. When we look at the informal structure of the schools, we shall investigate the values, attitudes, and styles of interaction of teachers, administrators and support staff.

The content of a social system, as with the structure, is of two kinds. The first may be aptly described as structural content. Structural content, whether formal or informal, refers to the assumptions, values, and beliefs that are inherently part of the structure. This concept is based on the recognition that no structure is value free. Rather, the design of any given structure, whether intentionally or unintentionally, has an agenda imposed on all functions of that structure. Our judicial system, for example, is the system it is because of an ideological commitment to certain notions of justice, fair play, and equality. Furthermore, by its nature it reinforces certain authoritarian and authoritative roles and a sense of tradition and order. The schools, in the same manner, reinforce certain values, perceptions, and behaviors. These are the "hidden curriculum." Some of the more evident features of this curriculum are: (1) Differential power and status arrangements are legitimate (e.g., teachers have power over students, and administrators have power over teachers); (2) time is linear and one-directional (e.g., grades progress through K-12); (3) each activity has its own time and place (e.g., math, reading, and social studies each have their own time slot); (4) each person is rewarded on the basis of accomplishments and some receive greater rewards than others (e.g., grades are based on individual achievements and some students receive *As* while others fail).*

Our examples illustrate the content found within the formal structure. It should be noted that informal structural content varies from that of its formal counterpart in at least one important respect. Because

* There are, of course, many more hidden values existing in the formal structure of public schools. Unfortunately, we cannot enumerate them here.

the formal structural content tends to emanate from the extant administrative structure, it tends to be more fixed and enduring, and its contents tend to be more stable. Informal structural content, on the other hand, extends from the values held by the people in the institution, tends to be more fluid, and varies with regard to the dynamics of the groups and individuals involved. It is derived primarily from the assumptions, values, and beliefs of individuals who people the formal structures.

The second kind of content found within a social institution may be described as the subject content or subject matter. This refers to the values, beliefs, and information directly and intentionally funneled through the structural system. The relationship of the content to the formal structure is like that of a product to a factory. The physical plant of a factory (i.e., the buildings) is the structure that manufactures some product. The product, however, remains in a very important way separate from the physical plant. Often, any number of different products could be made in the same factory. Thus certain subject contents are selected by someone or some group from a vast number of alternatives to be "plugged in" to the mechanical or administrative apparatus. In the judicial system these would be the actual laws and statutes. Seemingly, the judicial system can function to digest legal actions on any number of otherwise contradictory positions. For example, given one set of laws, it may function to protect civil liberties; given a different set of laws, it may function to reinforce state repression. In this sense, the judicial system does not make law or establish policy but is the structure through which these are enforced. The same can be said of the schools. Their structural existence is relatively independent of their content, and thus any number of different curricula could make up the content of the school.

Let us stop for a moment to review the system we are constructing. To this point we have sought to clarify several components of social institutions. First, there is a formal structure that entails a set of assumptions and values (the structural content). This may be likened to a building. The particular design and construction of the building are based on and reinforce certain perceived functions and the values and assumptions that support them. Hence we find considerable differences between a high-rise office building and the structure that houses an industrial manufacturing plant. This point can also be illustrated by comparing the structural changes in public schools accompanying the rise of the contemporary infatuation with "open education" to older, more traditional, and "closed" designs.

Second, there is an informal structure paralleling this formal structure that at once functions within the formal structure and affects the actual functioning of the formal structure. Again, for illustrative purposes, consider a building, as a structure, designed with movable walls for maximum interaction and cooperation and easy flow of those individuals involved. Now consider the effects on this formal structure of an informal structure (e.g., the role established by those who work within the building) organized to reinforce authority, status, and individual self-reliance. The intended function of the formal structure could be effectively neutralized.

Third, there is the actual content (subject content) that is fed through the institutional structures. In schools this is the curriculum; in media it is the programming; and in industry it is the product.

The relationship of these three components to one another is one of mutual dependence. Content cannot be processed without some structure to disseminate it. Likewise, a structure can serve no function without something to process. Both components are dependent on the groups and individuals that set the entire process in motion, and give rise to the informal structures. We may now explore the relevance of these interrelated components to social change.

By drawing attention to the fact that formal and informal structural components, their corresponding structural content, and the subject content all belong to the same structural system, the potential difficulties in instituting changes within any given social structure are made more obvious. Consider, for a moment, a school wishing to modify its curriculum (i.e., subject content). If the curriculum changes are incompatible with some of the values of the school system (the structural content), the proposed changes will have little chance for success; that is, to a large extent the formal structure of the school will determine the nature of the content that can be disseminated. For example, if within the formal structure success and rewards are distributed unequally on the basis of the ethics of competition and achievement, curriculum goals of cooperation or success of all students will be impossible. Even if the proposed curriculum is compatible with the formal structures and its structural content, the effort may still be frustrated by the informal structure and its corresponding structural content. To bear this out, one need only speculate for a moment as to the probability of eliminating ethnic bias from schools by modifying curriculum while maintaining a prejudiced staff. Applying this reasoning to the problem of cultural conflict above, in our recommendations we suggested structural and organizational changes in the school (formal structure), changes in the curriculum (content), and areas in which personnel should be trained or retrained (informal structure). Thus, to bring about changes in the schools, or in any social institution, there are three main areas on which we need to focus. We might add that we have also identified three main areas that need to be explored for possible changes that ought to take place.

There is yet another consideration in the process of change that is equally as significant as the system described above. This is the relationship of schools to other social institutions found in society. The public schools, as social structures, are components of a larger social system. They do not exist in an autonomous state but are part of a dynamic complex of social institutions that make up society. The family, churches, schools, government, judiciary, and private business are all examples of units in this larger structure. While it is common to talk about each institution as existing separately, only a casual look is needed to see that each influences and in turn is influenced by the others. Certainly, the way children are brought up and what they are taught in the home influences the way they behave at school. Similarly, what they are taught and how they are treated in school has a great deal to do with their behavior at home and their later behavior as adults. Business affects government and government affects business; and both affect the school budget, programs, and curriculum. The religious community, too, has a very broad influence.

Generally, all these social institutions tend to reinforce one another. The values and knowledge taught at home are those reinforced in school (at least for the dominant culture). Compatible patterns of authority exist in the home, school, workplace, government, and church; and attention is paid to time and scheduling in all these places, to mention but a few of the regularities. On occasion, however, some aspect of one of these components of the social system falls out of step with one or more of the other components, and reverberations are felt throughout the entire social system. For example, if the home and school fail to develop in young people a sense of pride in workmanship and achievement, businesses, particularly those involved in manufacturing, will suffer a drop in production. Similarly, if business—and government—fail to provide jobs for those graduating from school, young people are likely to have less incentive for attending school. They may tend to drop out earlier and put a greater strain on the economy, and these students will also be more difficult to motivate and control while they remain in school.

One of the dangers of focusing efforts to develop a society based on the ideals of cultural pluralism and to manage cultural conflict in the schools is that by altering the existing state of affairs in schools regarding these two concerns without simultaneously addressing the issues in other components of the social system, discontinuity and conflict may develop. For example, school systems that confront conflict in a progressive manner may be viewed as a threat to other, more conservative institutions. Thus, should a school set a precedent for the principles of proportionality in political representations, all-parties government, and concurrent majority and minority vetoes, it would not be surprising for the school to be heavily criticized by other agencies that wished to avoid such a relationship with minority groups. Similarly, individuals—school personnel, students, and members of the community—accustomed to confronting members of other ethnic groups and conflicts in a straightforward manner may alienate those who prefer to talk around or avoid troublesome issues. Conversely, schools wishing to confront and manage cultural conflict in a progressive manner and be responsive to community needs may be frustrated when their intentions are mistrusted. As long as conflicting groups continue to learn from other interactions that the world is generally hostile, it is not likely that they will view the schools any differently. Thus, a focus on the schools as a primary means of social change, to the exclusion of other social institutions, may alienate both the schools and the groups they influence.

A second but related problem is to focus too narrowly on the schools as agents of change. If change is to have any broad and lasting effects, it must be accepted and reinforced beyond the school gates, a lesson frequently overlooked by various educational reform movements. Reforms not supported by the larger social system will simply wither and die, whether they focus on progressive education, multicultural education, or cultural conflict. If those graduating with the new skills or attitudes are penalized for their new ways, or if they fail to find reinforcement, they will adopt more rewarding behavior. If programs are not compatible with the felt needs of other segments of society, funds will eventually dry up and administrative personnel with more "down-to-earth" ideas will replace those who have "failed." Michael Katz underlines this point when he states that "[d]espite substantial financing and a captive audience, the schools have not been able to obtain the goals set for them. . . . They have been unable to do so because those goals have been impossible [for the school] to fulfill. They require fundamental social reform, not the sort of tinkering that educational change has represented. If, by some miracle, the radical reformers were to capture the schools, and only the schools, for the next century, they would have no more success than educational reformers of the past."[67]

While it is true that social change is complex, it is *not* impossible and is not dependent on radical or revolutionary means.[68] Indeed, there has been dramatic and significant change in the direction we require in the past quarter century or so. For example, we have seen the integration of traditionally all white schools, civil rights extended to a large minority segment of our society, the questioning of traditional sex roles and stereotypes, the movement of women and minorities into higher levels of education and professions heretofore off limits, and the development of a generally greater tolerance for alternative life styles.

More particularly, changes are also evident in school programs and policy. We have begun to pursue sex and race equality; curriculum material that portrayed women in passive and docile roles and that either ignored minorities' contributions to society or represented them in demeaning ways is being questioned and rewritten; concepts like multicultural and bilingual education, which were not even in the vocabularies of many educators and politicians a few years ago, are now widely discussed and in some cases even considered legitimate.

Critics might argue that these alleged changes are more apparent than real or that they are far short of what is needed to achieve social justice. The latter claim is undoubtedly true. There is still much to be done; we have a long way to go in pursuit of our ideals. But from this observation it does not follow that we have not made headway. In fact, significant changes have taken place; if they had not, this book and others like it would never have been written or published. At times when we feel overwhelmed with the task before us and the obstacles in our path, there is the inclination to throw up our hands in frustration and despair. But to give in to these reactions is to forfeit the control and influence we have and to allow other forces to shape the nature of society.

In our review of past educational reforms we adopted the position that schools have not been particularly effective in initiating social change. Indeed, there is much evidence to suggest that they function more to reinforce the status quo and maintain social order. But schools need not assume total responsibility for positive change. It is significant to note that the changes mentioned above are not restricted to educational settings. They are reflected in nearly all aspects of life. Television programs, movies, and advertisements that would have gone unquestioned a decade or two ago now are considered offensive and inappropriate. Faces representing a variety of ethnic and racial backgrounds are evidence in visual media, in executive offices and graduate schools. Even the barriers that historically functioned to exclude some minorities and women from the trades have been cracked. While the forces behind these changes may not be clear, it is relatively clear that public schools have not been their primary causes. Nevertheless, the schools have contributed and currently stand in a position to contribute further. Schools, by educating and preparing individuals for the ideal society in which the highest human ideals are achievable, contribute toward the creation of that society.

SUMMARY

We began this chapter with a brief consideration of how the public schools have historically dealt with ethnic populations. It is popularly held that the schools played a major role in helping immigrants who came to America seeking a new life between 1860 and 1924 make a successful transition into the middle class. A more careful study of history, however, suggests that the schools were only marginal in providing mobility for these populations and that in some cases school reforms can be seen as an attempt to reinforce the existing class structure and maintain social stability.

Next, we explored some of the considerations to which educational policy developers might address themselves in regard to instituting the ideal of cultural pluralism and in addressing cultural conflict. One central issue to be faced is that of school control and its implications for selecting between integration and decentralization. Evidence suggests that it is difficult for large, centralized school systems to be responsive to the needs of the various communities they serve. Decentralization, on the other hand, seems incompatible with integration, which in turn can have a positive effect on school achievement of minorities and on racial attitudes. In addition, the ideal of cultural pluralism is compatible with either integration or decentralization. We recommend that some compromise between community and professional control be reached.

To provide further guidance to educators wishing to implement the ideal of cultural pluralism, we considered some policies that might be appropriate for a majority of the diverse groups the schools currently service. We first established a set of goals for students and teachers as outcomes of a multicultural education program. To support the attainment of these goals, we offered a set of procedures to guide the development and implementation of multicultural education.

In regard to cultural conflict, we saw that currently schools portray conflict in a very negative light, contributing to student perceptions that conflict is generally undesirable and dysfunctional, and that some school practices may actually tend to reinforce the frequency of conflict. On the basis of these observations, several recommendations were made for the development of a curriculum sensitive to cultural conflict.

One recommendation was that a more realistic and functional view of conflict be inserted into the curriculum, in part by showing the role conflict continues to play in both the sciences and social studies. Another was that students should learn about conflict. They should understand the bases of conflict, what issues will provoke conflict, and the different kinds of conflicts that exist. They should also understand the dynamics of conflict: how their perceptions influence the direction a conflict will take and how conflict functions as a teaching mechanism. However, we also observed that if we are to develop a curriculum that addresses conflict directly, the curriculum and school practice should be reviewed. This is necessary in order to assess the extent to which the school itself contributes to aggressiveness and conflict-prone atti-

244 CULTURAL PLURALISM IN EDUCATION

tudes and behaviors. Finally, we made recommendations regarding the development of a curriculum that would lead to greater cultural self-understanding and awareness and help an individual cope with the personal conflicts likely to arise in a culturally plural society.

Regarding institutional considerations, we recommended several ways to develop an institutional structure able to accommodate and manage cultural conflict. The approach focused on how to avoid stable unrepresentation and maximize open and effective communication. The advantages of flexibility were presented as well. Further, the chapter discussed the need for school personnel who are knowledgeable and trained to cope with conflict. Even if the organizational structure of the schools is designed to manage conflict and a conflict-sensitive curriculum is in place, without supportive personnel in the vital positions in the school, the total effort will fail.

We concluded the chapter and book with a word of warning. As social institutions there are several components of the schools in which change may take place. Each of these must be considered if significant change is to occur. Further, schools in themselves are not capable of broad social change. They exist in a dynamic relationship to other social institutions that must cooperate if educational reforms are to be effective. Indeed, even educational change itself is dependent upon the support of influences beyond its control.

NOTES

1. Lawrence A. Cremin, *The Transformation of the School: Progressivism in American Education 1877–1957* (New York: Vintage, 1964), pp. 8–9.
2. Ibid., p. 9.
3. See, for example, Colin Greer, *The Great School Legend: A Revisionist Interpretation of American Public Education* (New York: Basic Books, 1972); Michael Katz, *Class, Bureaucracy and the Schools* (New York: Praeger, 1971); Michael Katz, ed., *Education in American History* (New York: Praeger, 1973); Clarence J. Karier, *Shaping the American Education State* (New York: Free Press, 1975).
4. Katz, *Class, Bureaucracy and Schools*, pp. 108–10.
5. Greer, *Great School Legend*, pp. 62–63.
6. Ibid., p. 75.
7. Ibid., p. 152.
8. Diane Ravitch, *The Revisionists Revisited* (New York: Basic Books, 1978), p. 16.
9. Ibid., pp. 16–17.
10. Greer, *Great School Legend*, p. 152.
11. Newton Edwards and H. G. Richey, *The Schools in the American Social Order* (Boston: Houghton Mifflin, 1963), p. 22.
12. Cremin, *Transformation of the School*, p. 85.
13. Samuel Bowles, "The Integration of Higher Education into the Wage-Labor System," in Katz, *Education in American History*, p. 141.

14. Katz, *Class, Bureaucracy and Schools*, p. 116.

15. Greer, *Great School Legend*, p. 81.

16. Karier, *Shaping the American Education State*, pp. 161–62.

17. Timothy Smith, "Immigrant Social Aspirations and American Education, 1880–1930," in Katz, *Education in American History*, pp. 236–50.

18. Ibid., p. 250.

19. Michael Olneck and Marvin Lazerson, "The School Achievement of Immigrant Children: 1900–1930," *History of Education Quarterly* 14, no. 4 (Winter 1974): 454.

20. Ibid., p. 458.

21. Greer, *Great School Legend*, p. 287.

22. Ibid., p. 86.

23. Russell Barta, "Minority Report: The Representation of Poles, Italians, Latins and Blacks in the Executive Suites of Chicago's Largest Corporations," Institute of Urban Life, Chicago, Illinois, cited in Michael Novak, "Cultural Pluralism for Individuals," in *Pluralism in a Democratic Society*, ed. M. Tumin and W. Plotch (New York: Praeger, 1977), p. 51.

24. Katz, *Class, Bureaucracy and Schools*, p. 126.

25. Ibid., p. 129.

26. Ibid., p. 146.

27. This section has been adapted from Bob Suzuki, *An Asian-American Perspective on Multicultural Education: Implications for Practice and Research*, ERIC ED 205 633, November 1980. Reprinted with the author's permission.

28. John Dewey, *Experience and Education* (New York: Collier, 1963).

29. Carl Grant, ed., *Shifting and Winnowing: An Exploration of the Relationship Between Multi-cultural Education and CBTE* (Madison, Wisc.: Teacher Corp Associates, 1975).

30. James Banks, "Ethnic Studies as a Process of Curriculum Reform," *Social Education*, February 1976, pp. 76–80. Geneva Gay and James Banks, "Teaching the American Revolution: A Multiethnic Approach," *Social Education*, November-December 1975, pp. 461–65.

31. For example, see Tsukasa Matsueda, "Developing and Implementing a Multicultural U.S. History Course: A Case Study in a Suburban High School" (Ed.D. dissertation, University of Massachusetts, Amherst, 1980).

32. Asia Society, *Asia in American Textbooks* (New York: The Society, 1976); Harold R. Issacs, *Scratches on Our Minds: American Images of China and India* (New York: John Day, 1958).

33. E. C. Susskind, "Questioning and Curiosity in the Elementary School Classroom" (Ph.D. dissertation, Yale University, 1969); Adam Scrupski, "The Social System of the School," in *Social Forces and Schooling*, ed. N. K. Shemahara and A. Scrupski (New York: McKay, 1975).

34. Paulo Freire, *Pedagogy of the Oppressed* (New York: Herder and Herder, 1970); idem, *Education for Critical Consciousness* (Cambridge, Mass.: Center for the Study of Development and Social Change, 1974).

35. Helen Roberts, "Design for Developing Multicultural Curriculum" (Ed.D. dissertation, University of Massachusetts, Amherst, 1975).

36. Richard Jones, *Fantasy and Feeling in Education* (New York: New York University Press, 1968).

37. R. P. McDermott, "The Cultural Context of Learning to Read," in *Papers in*

Applied Linguistics, ed. Stanley F. Wanat, Linguistics and Reading Services 1 (Arlington, Va.: Center for Applied Linguistics, 1977).

38. Benjamin S. Bloom, *Human Characteristics and School Learning* (New York: McGraw-Hill, 1976).

39. Ernece Kelly, "Language Arts in a Multicultural Society," in Dolores Cross et al., *Teaching in a Multicultural Society* (New York: Free Press, 1977).

40. Michael W. Apple, "The Hidden Curriculum and the Nature of Conflict," *Interchange* 2, no. 4 (1976): 29–41.

41. Ibid., p. 33.

42. Ibid., p. 34.

43. Ibid., p. 35.

44. Ibid., p. 38.

45. Judith Torney and Charles Tesconi, Jr., "Political Socialization Research and Respect for Ethnic Diversity," in Tumin and Plotch, *Pluralism in a Democratic Society,* pp. 95–132.

46. Rolf Dahrendorf, *Class and Class Conflict in Industrial Society* (Stanford: Stanford University Press, 1959), p. 27.

47. Torney and Tesconi, "Political Socialization Research."

48. Apple, "Hidden Curriculum," p. 37.

49. For a directory of projects and a bibliography of law-related materials, write the Special Committee on Youth Education for Citizenship, American Bar Association, 115 S.E. 60th Street, Chicago, Ill 60637.

50. Robert Stahl, "Developing Value Dilemmas for Content-Centered Social Studies Instruction: Theoretical Construct and Practical Application," *Theory and Research in Social Education* 7, no. 2 (Summer 1979): 50–76.

51. Robert Stahl, "Achieving Values and Content Objectives Simultaneously Within Subject Matter-Oriented Social Studies Classrooms," *Social Education,* November–December 1981, pp. 580–85; Blanche Sherman Hunt, "The Effects of Values Activities on Content Retention and Attitudes of Students in Junior High Studies Classes" (Ph.D. dissertation, Arizona State University, 1981).

52. Nathan Glazer, "Cultural Pluralism: The Social Aspect," in Tumin and Plotch, *Pluralism in a Democratic Society,* p. 17–18.

53. See Kenneth Boulding, "Conflict Management as a Learning Process," in *Conflict in Society,* ed. Anthony de Reuck (London: Churchill, 1966), pp. 236–48; Morton Deutsch, *The Resolution of Conflict* (New Haven: Yale University Press, 1973).

54. Boulding, "Conflict Management," pp. 242–43.

55. Ibid., p. 246.

56. Ibid., pp. 243–44.

57. S. L. Washburn, "Conflict in Private Society," in Reuck, *Conflict in Society,* pp. 3–15.

58. Carl Rogers, *Freedom to Learn* (Columbus, Ohio: Charles E. Merrill, 1969).

59. Novak, "Cultural Pluralism for Individuals," pp. 41–44.

60. Ibid., p. 42.

61. Ibid., p. 43.

62. James Banks, "Cultural Pluralism: Implications for Curriculum Reform," in Tumin and Plotch, *Pluralism in a Democratic Society*, pp. 226–48, esp. pp. 242–46.
63. Marc V. Levine, "Institution Design and the Separatist Impulse: Quebec and the Antebellum American South," *American Academy of Political and Social Annals* 433 (September 1977): 60–72.
64. Ibid.
65. Gerald Moulton, "Some Criteria for Evaluating Negotiations" (mimeographed materials, Arizona State University, Tempe, Arizona, 1980).
66. Nicholas Appleton, D. Jordan, and M. Daniel-Jordan, "Cultural Pluralism and the Social Structure: A Systems View," *Bilingual Education Paper Series* 1, no. 11 (June 1978). National Dissemination and Assessment Center, California State University, Los Angeles, Calif.
67. Katz, *Class, Bureaucracy and Schools*, p. 142.
68. Jean Francois Revel, *Without Marx or Jesus: The New American Revolution Has Begun.* (Garden City, N.Y.: Doubleday, 1971).

Suggestions for Classroom Use

This book is intended to serve a variety of interests, and the background and purposes of the reader will influence the way it is used. Policy makers, for example, may wish to use the book as a resource to familiarize themselves with the issues and alternatives to be faced in developing educational policy for a pluralistic society; others may use the work as a springboard for more systematic inquiry and research. It is anticipated the book will also be used in college and university courses designed to present the theoretical foundations of multicultural education to students who are, or soon will be, working within the public schools. It is in these courses that the suggestions and exercises offered in these appendixes will perhaps be most useful.

1. Prior to instruction, help students identify their current attitudes toward cultural diversity by completing the following inventory:

If you strongly agree, circle SA
If you agree, circle A
A If you disagree, circle D
If you strongly disagree, circle SD

   a. The United States would be a stronger   SA   A   D   SD
   country if we all thought of ourselves as
   Americans first and reserved any identity
   for private matters.
   b. In making laws and providing for the   SA   A   D   SD
   general welfare of society, government

should recognize and make allowances for
different cultural and ethnic groups.

c. Bilingual education should be offered as a   SA   A   D   SD
positive recognition of the cultural diversity
of America and should be available to all
students who wish to participate.

d. Government must be careful to assure that   SA   A   D   SD
its actions in no way support or encourage
the maintenance of cultural or ethnic groups
that deviate significantly from the
mainstream of society.

e. Under some conditions, it might be desirable   SA   A   D   SD
to allow culturally or ethnically different
groups to establish and operate their own
tax-supported schools.

f. Bilingual education, if it is used at all,   SA   A   D   SD
should be seen as a temporary means to
help non-English-speaking students make a
rapid transition to English.

g. The public schools should be integrated as   SA   A   D   SD
near as possible and strive for the
development of a unified society.

h. To allow for a variety of different and   SA   A   D   SD
sometimes contradictory values, beliefs, and
life styles in the United States makes life
richer and more interesting for all.

i. A cultural and ethnic heritage is a part of us   SA   A   D   SD
all, and the public schools should help us
recognize and appreciate our differences as
well as our similarities.

j. While it is perfectly all right to join political   SA   A   D   SD
and social special-interest groups and to
lobby on their behalf, these groups should
not be formed on the basis of ethnic criteria.

k. For matters of importance such as voting   SA   A   D   SD
and education, we should do everything
necessary to accommodate those citizens
who have limited English-speaking ability.

l. Ethnic consciousness is an abstacle to   SA   A   D   SD
individual social progress in a technological
and competitive society.

*m.*The history of all the pertinent cultural   SA   A   D   SD
groups should be taught as an integral part
of the history of the state and the nation.

n. Schools should strive to provide nonwhites   SA   A   D   SD
with equal educational opportunity even if
their education is more expensive than for
whites.

o. Minority-group parents have an obligation   SA   A   D   SD
to prepare their children to function
effectively in the United States by guiding
them to learn the language, values, and
practices of American society.

p. The schools should be structured to   SA   A   D   SD
maintain an English-speaking environment
and to discourage the use of other
languages.

q. Children of aliens without passports have a   SA   A   D   SD
right to an education that is at least
equivalent to that of citizen children.

r. Ethnic-minority parents who do not provide   SA   A   D   SD
their children with an academically
competitive orientation are responsible for
their children's academic failure.

s. It is enriching to incorporate the values and   SA   A   D   SD
views of many other cultures into one's own
life.

t. We should look forward to the day when all   SA   A   D   SD
people speak without any accents that
identify them ethnically or regionally.

u. If all people were the same color, the world   SA   A   D   SD
would be a better place to live.

v. Nonwhite children should learn about their   SA   A   D   SD
physical unity with their racial past.

w. Along with social justice all ethnic groups   SA   A   D   SD
should have political equality.

x. Within the public schools, the emphasis   SA   A   D   SD
should be on the common characteristics we
share as humans with the differences among
cultural and ethnic groups minimized.

SCORING KEY:

Strongly agree	+2	Nonpluralism preference = NP
Agree	+1	Cultural pluralism preference = CP
Disagree	−1	
Strongly disagree	−2	

Non-pluralism preference   *Cultural pluralism preference*

a. _____   b. _____
d. _____   c. _____
f. _____   e. _____
g. _____   h. _____
j. _____   i. _____
l. _____   k. _____
o. _____   m. _____
p. _____   n. _____

$r.$ ____　　　　　　　　　$q.$ ____
$t.$ ____　　　　　　　　　$s.$ ____
$u.$ ____　　　　　　　　　$v.$ ____
$x.$ ____　　　　　　　　　$w.$ ____

SCORE: *NP* _____　　　　　　*CP* _____

2. Individually interview or invite to class individuals from different ethnic and cultural groups, individuals who represent different ethnic organizations (e.g., Black Student Union, La Raza, Greek-American community organization), or school administrators. Prepare questions to determine:
   a. What they think their own people (Anglos, Blacks, American Indians, etc.) are like? What specific characteristics of their people make them different from other groups?
   b. What values do their group hold most dearly?
   c. What do they think people of some other specific group, to which they do not belong, are like?
   d. Name a group that they think may be prejudiced against them.
   e. Do they think they are prejudiced against any group? Explain.
   f. What do they think is the best way to cope with prejudice?
   g. What does cultural pluralism mean to them?
   h. Do they support multicultural and/or bilingual education? If so, what are the goals of each and who is it for?
   i. Do they favor integration?
   j. Should ethnically "pure" schools be permitted if voluntarily chosen?
   k. What role should ethnic communities play in the control of the school?
   l. What role should government play in the recognition and preservation of different ethnic and cultural groups?
3. Brain teasers for the legal beagle: Have students complete the following questionaire. Compare the answers in the left-hand column with the court cases discussed in Chapter 4. Compare what students think is legal with what they think should be legal.

It is legal　　　　　　　　　　　　　　　　　　　　　　　*Should be legal*

Yes ____ No ____　a. A state legislature believing that　Yes ____ No ____
　　　　　　　　　　all citizens must first and
　　　　　　　　　　foremost be committed to
　　　　　　　　　　American ways and values
　　　　　　　　　　prohibits instruction in or the
　　　　　　　　　　teaching of a language other
　　　　　　　　　　than English in either public or
　　　　　　　　　　private schools during the years
　　　　　　　　　　of elementary school.

Yes ____ No ____　b. In violation of a state's　　　　　Yes ____ No ____
　　　　　　　　　　compulsory education law a
　　　　　　　　　　student may refuse to attend
　　　　　　　　　　high school when the refusal is

based on strong religious beliefs.

Yes ____ No ____   c. When one's actions are based on strong religious beliefs, one is not subject to state law even if the state can show it has a compelling interest at stake.   Yes ____ No ____

Yes ____ No ____   d. A state may override the authority of parents to raise a child the way they see fit even when the parent's actions are based on religious beliefs if the state can show a compelling interest to protect the child or society.   Yes ____ No ____

Yes ____ No ____   e. A state may require all school-age children to attend public rather than private schools as the main source of their education.   Yes ____ No ____

Yes ____ No ____   f. A school district may require all students to salute the flag as a regular part of opening exercises each day even if a student claims that the salute violates his religious beliefs.   Yes ____ No ____

Yes ____ No ____   g. Generally, a school district may establish or maintain racially separate but equal schools.   Yes ____ No ____

Yes ____ No ____   h. A school district may be required by the courts to bus children to another part of the district to effect desegregation.   Yes ____ No ____

Yes ____ No ____   i. Generally, an ethnic minority (racial group) may choose to maintain primarily one-race schools in its neighborhood in order to preserve its language and cultural heritage.   Yes ____ No ____

Yes ____ No ____   j. A school district faced with a sudden influx of Vietnamese refugees may place the children in regular classrooms without the aid of special English-language instruction or bilingual education.   Yes ____ No ____

Yes ____ No ____   k. A school district with three non-English-speaking children   Yes ____ No ____

decides not to provide special
English-language instruction or
bilingual education.

Yes ___ No ___ *l.* Following a court desegregation   Yes ___ No ___
order, the wishes of a remotely
located Mexican American
neighborhood within a large
city to retain predominantly
one-race schools supplemented
by bilingual education is
honored.

Yes ___ No ___ *m.* A private school, receiving no   Yes ___ No ___
federal or state funds, refuses to
integrate.

Yes ___ No ___ *n.* Navajo Indians on their   Yes ___ No ___
reservation in Arizona elect to
establish their own schools and
refuse to abide by Arizona
educational guidelines.

Yes ___ No ___ *o.* Mexican American children in a   Yes ___ No ___
school tailored to the needs of
middle-class English-speaking
families demand that the
educational program become
bilingual/bicultural.

    a. Meyer v. *Nebraska* (1923)
    b. Wisconsin v. *Yoder* (1972)
    c. Reynolds v. *United States* (1878)
    d. Prince v. *Commonwealth of Massachusetts* (1943)
    e. Pierce v. *Society of Sisters* (1924)
    f. Barnette v. *West Virginia* (1943)
    g. Brown v. *Board of Education* (1954)
    h. Swann v. *Charlotte-Mecklenburg Board of Education* (1970)
    i. Johnson v. *San Franciso Unified School District* (1971)
    j. United States v. *Texas* (1971)
    k. Lau v. *Nichols* (1974)
    l. Keyes v. *Denver School District I* (1973)
    m. Griffin v. *County School Board of Prince Edward County* (1964)
    n. Williams v. *Lee* (1957)
    o. Serna v. *Portales* (1974)

4. Determine the students' ideological preferences for a model of cultural pluralism by responding to the following statements. Ask students to explain why they take the position they do on each of the items. Compare each statement to the alternative ideologies discussed in Chapter 3.

	Agree	Disagree
a. Social workers who practice in an area populated by a particular cultural group should be native speakers of the group's language and should belong to the same cultural group as the clients.	A	D
b. Nonwhite parents should teach their children to resist domination by white society's values and by the English language.	A	D
c. Ideally the school should teach each non-English-speaking child the subjects in his native language while it introduces him to English as a second language.	A	D
d. The schools should allow each cultural community to decide which language is to be used to teach the children of that cultural group.	A	D
e. The children of interracial marriages are encouraging evidence of the future of equality and harmony among racial groups in the United States.	A	D
f. The mixing of white students with black students outside their own neighborhoods leads to a healthy exposure of these students to different values and life styles.	A	D
g. Learning about the cultures of other people is as important as learning about one's own heritage and should be taught to all children.	A	D
h. English-speaking white children should also benefit from bilingual education.	A	D
i. It is important that members of an ethnic group develop a strong sense of identification exclusively with their ethnic group.	A	D
j. An ethnic group should share its cultural uniqueness with other ethnic groups, including the dominant society.	A	D
k. Cultural groups need to be introduced into the mainstream of society in order for them to improve their life styles.	A	D
l. Nonwhite groups must develop a political power base before they can communicate as equals with the dominant white society.	A	D
m. Cultural differences and uniqueness should receive far more attention than cultural commonalities among the various ethnic groups.	A	D
n. A school district's responsibility to the education of cultural groups is best met by implementing a program that teaches standard English to non-English and limited-English speakers.	A	D

o. Members of a cultural group should use their native language among themselves even if it means socially excluding English speakers from conversation.	A	D
p. Powerless ethnic groups have a better chance of cultural survival if they share their culture than if they isolate themselves from the rest of society.	A	D
q. A member of a cultural group should work for the survival and advancement of his or her cultural group even at the expense of all other groups.	A	D
r. It is more important for people to maintain and share their cultural identities than to progress economically.	A	D

5. Have students administer the above questionnaires to groups of teachers, administrators, and lay people. Analyze the results for trends and compare differences.

6. Instruct your students to read the conflict situations presented in Appendix B and see if they can identify the basis of the conflict and the contributing variables. Brainstorm alternative ways of handling the conflict, projecting the probable consequences of each method.

7. Have students search their newspapers for items related to cultural pluralism and cultural conflict. See if they can identify the nature and kind of the conflict. Have them suggest ways that they might manage the situation if they were involved.

8. Have students review the examples of conflicts given in Appendix B and those found in the newspaper. Is there anything that suggests that if the situation had been handled differently initially, it would have evolved in a different manner? Suggest different organizational structures that might have controlled the conflict in earlier stages if they had been in effect.

9. Ask students to review the conflict examples in Appendix B and those found in the newspaper, and identify the functional qualities of the conflicts. For example, what positive outcomes resulted from each conflict?

10. Using volunteers from the class, role-play selected conflict situations. In each of these examples, there are important ideas and strong feelings represented on both sides of the issue. Through role playing, the alternative positions become explicit, and their logic as well as their emotional appeal can be more clearly examined. This exercise may also help students to see how their perceptions influence the nature of the conflict and to understand the perceptions of others.

11. Lead the class through one or more of the simulations included in Appendix B.

B

Teaching Resources

EXAMPLES OF CULTURAL CONFLICT

Court Cases

The following examples of cultural conflict are actual situations that found resolution through legal proceedings.

1. Students in Southside High School in Muncie, Indiana, voted to adopt symbols associated with the Old South. Accordingly, the school flag resembled the flag of the Confederacy, the athletic teams were called the "Rebels," the glee club was named the "Southern Aires," and the homecoming queen was called the "Southern Belle." Black students, who constituted 13 percent of the enrollment of Southside, felt that these symbols were offensive and inflammatory and that they discouraged Black participation in extracurricular activities.[1]

   As a school administrator, what would be your policy on this matter? Why?

2. In Tahoka, Texas, a group known as "Concerned Mexican American Parents" became dissatisfied with certain educational policies and practices in their school system. They attempted to have these matters corrected through letters, meetings, and legal action. To support the view that these grievances were justified and that corrective action would be taken, a number of students wore brown armbands to school one day. The next day, the Board of Education passed a regulation prohibiting any unusual dress or wearing apparel that is "disruptive, distracting, or provocative so as to incite students of other ethnic groups."[2]

256

In your view, did the Board of Education handle the matter properly? What might they have done differently?

3. The president of predominantly Black North Carolina Central University withdrew financial support from the official student newspaper because of its announced segregationist editorial policy. The first issue of the newspaper under this new policy made clear its opposition to the admission of more white students. For example, one article stated: "There is a rapidly growing white population on our campus. . . . We want to know why they are here? How many are here? Why more and more come every year (by the hundreds)? . . . Black students on this campus have never made it clear to those people that we are indeed separate from them, in so many ways, and wish to remain so."[3]

   What are the issues underlying this conflict? How might this conflict situation be approached from an administrative point of view?

4. A Mexican American counselor in Tempe, Arizona, became concerned that children of Mexican American and Yaqui Indian backgrounds in the school in which she worked were being placed in classes for the mentally retarded because they were tested in English rather than in their native tongues. To no avail she attempted to correct this problem internally through contacts with the principal of the school and special services division of the school district. Becoming frustrated by the lack of action on the part of the school, the counselor advised parents of the children to sue the school district. Relations between the counselor and school authorities became more strained, with the result that she was denied access to the files of children placed in special education classes and was told not to retest children without first obtaining a written parental consent form. When she refused, she was transferred to another school. Upon this action she filed suit against the school district claiming she was punished for exercising her free speech right.[4]

   In your view was this dispute handled properly? What might be the reasoning behind each of the parties' actions?

Cultural Differences

The following situations suggest how conflict potentially may arise from differences in values, perceptions, and life styles among different cultural groups.

1. One of the target areas of a director of an Alaskan Teacher Corps Project included a remote village that had relatively little contact with Caucasians and virtually no modern conveniences. When the director arrived at the village, the inhabitants obtained their water by hauling large blocks of ice from the river at the bottom of the hill on which the village was situated. The villagers would place the ice in garbage cans inside their homes and allow it to melt. But things had recently improved. With considerable difficulty, the village people were able to secure federal money to build a pipeline, pump station, and storage tank that drew water from the river and deposited it in the village. The system seemed to work well, and everyone seemed satisfied.

   One day, however, the director arrived to find that villagers had stopped using the new water system and gone back to hauling ice. When he asked one of them what had happened, he was told that the water had bugs in it and they were not going to drink it.

Now, as it happened, a new young Caucasian science teacher had recently been hired to teach in the village. For one lesson, he had obtained a sample of water from the storage tank and put it under a microscope to show his students the micro-organisms, or "bugs." The lesson, of course, had been overwhelmingly successful. Since no one in the village much relished the idea of drinking water with bugs in it, they would no longer drink water from the storage tank.

The director pulled the teacher aside, pointed out the situation, and asked what he could do. "No problem," the teacher said. He placed a drop of chlorine in a water sample and showed that the micro-organisms could easily be killed. But drinking water full of dead bugs was not much better than drinking water with live bugs, and the villagers still would not drink the water. The teacher next suggested taking a sample of water from the melting ice the villagers were using for drinking water and showing them that, like all water it, too, had micro-organisms.

The director, fearing the villagers would be left with no acceptable water supply, talked him out of it. The water transport and storage system still sits idle.[5]

2. "Of some seventy settlements in the Canadian Arctic, this [Umingmaktok] was one of the few with no resident whites and almost no services. No airstrip, not an inch of road, no telephone, school, TV, electricity, or sewer systems. . . . In a mere 60 years [the native Inuit inhabitants] have jumped from Stone Age self-sufficiency to contemporary consumer society."

Some of the observed characteristics of the Inuit include the following:

a. "'. . . they showed the greatest delicacy in asking questions. They were interested, but they knew that if I wanted them to know something, I would tell them. Asking many questions of strangers was not their custom . . . [Vilhjalmur Stefansson, quoted in article cited below].'"

b. "For the Inuit, survival has meant flexibility. Long-range planning is impractical, since only fools pretend to know what marvelous happening or calamity will occur tomorrow."

c. Time schedules were unknown. "[Inuits] would flock to [the tent of a visiting anthropologist] at three o'clock in the morning, saying as they entered, 'Somebody is coming to visit.'"

d. "Once [Inuit children] started walking, they came and went with amazing freedom. If a 5-year-old chose to visit [a visitor's] camp for several hours, he wouldn't ask or say where he was going. The children learn not by do's and don'ts but by imitating those who appeal to them most."

e. "Corporal punishment does not exist. Except for pointed ridicule [children are never scolded], even for vicious tantrums. Children are [thought to be] born with no sense, and only years of experience can teach them maturity, goodness, and manners. To be mad at them would be unreasonable."[6]

What conflicts might arise should public education be attempted here?

3. The Sanapaws are Menominee Indians. ". . . like their ancestors, [they] are leisurely people. The land knows no eight-hour day or five-day week. Har-

vest and hunting become social times. Life is lived day by day, and each moment cherished for its own.

Some would consider them superstitious about being too successful. "'You know, my brother Le Roy, he died a year ago,' Jerry [Sanapaw] recalled. 'His bad luck came, I know, because he was better than the rest. He was an Indian dancer, winning awards, ribbons, recognition all over. When you're a Menominee you can't stand out, you can't be better off than your brothers.'"

"Indian teachers . . . are being recruited and Indian culture is being emphasized in the primary grades, but the effort is dissipated further along. High-school students are bused to a neighboring county that has no Indian teachers and no Indians on its school board. Racial tensions have flared, and federal investigations have found discrimination. Under such conditions, more than 75 percent of the Menominees fail to graduate from high school and fewer than 4 percent see the inside of a college classroom."[7]

What conflicts exist here?

VALUES DILEMMAS[8]

"Images"[9]

Mr. and Mrs. Colon wanted a larger home, a yard, peace and quiet, and a better school system for their children. So they moved to the suburbs. They got what they wanted.

But the Colons are Puerto Ricans. In spite of their established place within the American middle class, as Puerto Ricans they will never consider themselves average suburbanites. They live in what appears to be two worlds. As Americans, they participate in Little League and have a backyard swimming pool. As Hispanics, they serve beans and rice on their dinner table and frequently speak Spanish at home.

The middle-class Puerto Ricans in this particular suburb include many families with yearly earnings of $25,000 to $30,000. There are many small business owners, professionals, and a smaller number of managers of non-Puerto Rican-owned businesses. Many of these people are second- and third-generation Americans; few are recent immigrants.

Mr. Colon served in the army, graduated from college, and works in the local school system. For nine years he served on the school board, being the first Puerto Rican in the state elected to such a post. His two daughters are college graduates; one is becoming a doctor.

Yet, in spite of all these accomplishments, the Colons and their Hispanic neighbors find themselves perceived as stereotyped Puerto Ricans—"needy, underprivileged, and lazy."

The Puerto Ricans who have made it to the middle class must still deal with the realities of Hispanics who have not made it. These realities include poverty, crime, and political impotence. Welfare is a mixed blessing for the successful. To whites (Anglos, as they are called), all Latins living in New York are Puerto Ricans, regardless of their origin. Thus, the struggling non-Puerto Rican newcomers are considered a "Puerto Rican problem," and all Hispanic crime is "Puerto Rican crime." All the poverty, crime, and need for welfare among

these Hispanics hurt the Puerto Ricans by increasing the stereotypes and negative images, and it also affected them as taxpayers.[10]

 a. According to the article, what are some symbols of the American mid-
    dle class?
 b. Would Mr. Colon be considered a successful Puerto Rican? A success-
    ful American?
 c. At what time should an immigrant from Puerto Rico call himself or
    herself an American?
 d. What population group in America has never been stereotyped?
 e. What does the word "stereotype" mean?
 f. Would you enjoy being a Puerto Rican?
 g. How is it bad to be a member of a stereotyped minority group?
 h. In what ways would it be good to be a Hispanic? A Puerto Rican?
 i. What should be done to erase the negative images created by stereo-
    typing?

The Power of Medicine Men[11]

You are assigned by your health care agency to supervise a clinic and plan the
health care for an Indian tribe on a reservation. If you are successful, then
promotion will come very rapidly for you. Should you not succeed in this
assignment, it may be years before you are promoted.

Upon your arrival at your new position, you find that the health care
workers at the clinic are about evenly divided in ethnic representation between
Caucasians and tribal members. You also find that each group represents some
opposing beliefs about medicines and health care. The tribal members advocate
the use of a certain herb which the non-Indian members state "causes diarrhea
and anemia in infants and children." The tribal members argue that the use of
the herb is tied to past traditions and is a cure for infant illnesses.

Shortly afterward, you find that the infant death rate is 50 percent higher
than in the area surrounding the reservation. The leading cause of infant death
on the reservation is severe diarrhea and anemia.

Upon further investigation you discover that the Caucasian staff members
warn their patients not to use the herb. However, the Indian staff members
secretly tell their patients and their families to use the herb. You also learn that
the tribal medicine man opposes certain practices at your clinic. One of the
practices he dislikes is the giving of vitamins with iron to infants. He also advocates use of the herb in question. Because of his influence, few tribal members
are likely to go against the wishes of the medicine man.

Recent staff meetings held to discuss the opposing views have ended in
more alienation and polarization of the staff. You cannot afford to let this division continue. Being new to the situation, you may be able to resolve the differences. Your immediate goals are to reduce the infant death rate and at the
same time preserve the dignity of all your health care staff. Reaching these
goals would be the mark of success you want.

You are very aware of the fact that consistent trial-and-error methods to resolve the conflict would lessen your effectiveness with your staff—and all the
Indians. They respect authority and confidence. However, they are frequently

very suspicious of too much white man's authority and confidence. Therefore, you decide that you will list your alternatives and decide which three you believe have the greatest chances of bringing success. You also decide to identify the two alternatives you will use only as a final and last resort to "save the children." Following this procedure will help reduce the impression that you are desperate and unsure of how to handle this problem.

For the alternatives below, place the number "1" by the three alternatives you would use first to solve your dilemma. Place the number "3" by the two options you expect to use only as a last resort to solve your problem.

_____ *a.* You will call a meeting of the entire staff for the purpose of discussing causes of infant deaths on the reservation.

_____ *b.* You will issue an order that Indian staff members must support the prescriptions given by the Caucasian doctors or else be fired for insubordination.

_____ *c.* You will call a meeting of the entire staff to get them to voice their concerns and beliefs.

_____ *d.* You will call a meeting of the tribal staff and the medicine man to discuss cultural beliefs and tradition as they relate to adequate health care.

_____ *e.* You will call in a nutritionist to present a program to the Indians on dietary needs of infants stressing the side effect of the herb.

_____ *f.* You will visit the medicine man, tell him your dilemma, and ask his advice. This may make you seem like a weak and uncertain leader to many of the Indians.

_____ *g.* You will threaten to withhold the giving out of all medicine the Indians do like and do use until they agree to give up using the herb in question.

_____ *h.* You can state that you have no right to try to change the Indian tribal ways. You will let the Indians use the herb until enough of their infants die to make them want to quit using it.

_____ *i.* You can decide to use frequently enforced Bureau of Indian Affairs rules and regulations to force obedience to the clinic policies on distributing medicine and medical advice. This means Indian staff members found allowing or encouraging the use of the herb would be automatically released.

SIMULATION GAMES

The following are activities that simulate group conflict arising from a difference in roles, perceptions, beliefs, values, or some combination of these. The activities may be used to heighten student awareness of these differences, the conflicts that may arise from them, and the manner with which conflicts are handled.

Selected Games

1. The City[12]

   Directions: Any size group is divided up into 10 equal, smaller groups. Each small group is assigned a "ward" to represent.

a. The ward picks a representative to the school board.

b. They charge him with various ideas and beliefs he must expound if he is to truly represent their ward.

c. They know that their representative will report back to his "constituency" from time to time, during the course of the game.

The school board meets to face this problem: *The federal government has ordered the school system to integrate its schools. While exact percentages need not be attained, as a general formula the court order requires that each school in the district must reflect the racial makeup of the city as a whole.* (See Census Data on p. 265.)

A strong student is asked to play the nonpartisan board president who conducts the meeting. Another student is asked to play the board's attorney, and his function is to reflect the legal aspects of the discussion when they are called for.

The teacher's job is to see that the role playing is done honestly and to generally keep things moving and on target.

About every fifteen minutes, or when it seems appropriate, the board temporarily adjourns and returns to its constituencies. The board president can state the passage of time. For example, a ten-minute period spent with the constituencies may represent a passage of one week between board meetings.

Sometimes, a meeting between two wards may be called during the board's break. Various patterns will emerge. The point is, do not have the entire game played in the board meeting room. It needs to keep going back and forth from ward meetings to board meetings. It is possible that a board member will be fired and another sent in his place. Keep it flexible, but keep it *real.*

Various other rules may need to be negotiated as the game progresses.

The game may run on for several days.

All attempts must be made to make the game as realistic as possible.

WARD 1: Predominantly upper-middle-class professionals (doctors, lawyers, business executives); a rather well-to-do suburban setting for the most part; middle-of-the-roaders politically; a number of middle-class Blacks live in the southeastern section of the ward; sometimes elements of the community are called the "country club set."

WARD 2: A section of the city that sprung up during the post-World War II boom; most residents are white, Anglo-Saxon, middle-class white-collar workers; most own or are buying their homes; a very close knit neighborhood; great community pride.

WARD 3: An older section of the city; partly residential and partly the "downtown" area; many residents are of Slavic descent and second- and third-generation Americans; hard-working, lower-middle-class blue-collar workers for the most part; most own or are buying homes, although some rent apartments above stores; a number of lower-middle-class Blacks live in the southern section of the ward; some claim that the southern section will soon be all Black.

WARD 4: The city's ghetto; predominately poor Blacks but a few poor whites; many on welfare; most rent apartments or houses; a small but growing

The City

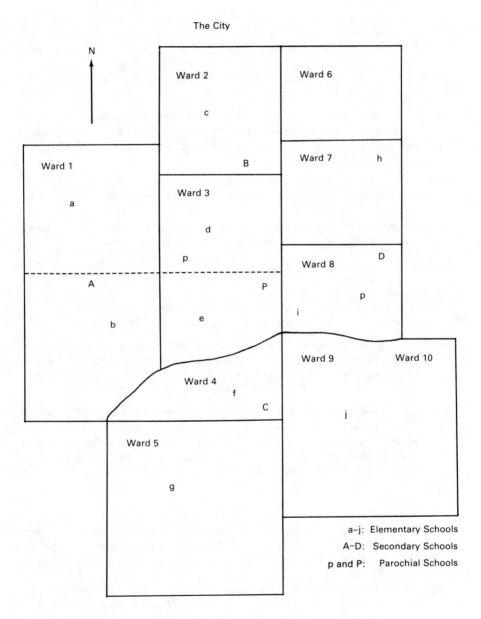

N

Ward 2

c

Ward 6

Ward 1

a

B

Ward 7   h

Ward 3

d

p

A

P

b

e

i

Ward 8   D

p

Ward 9   Ward 10

Ward 4
f

C

j

Ward 5

g

a–j: Elementary Schools
A–D: Secondary Schools
p and P: Parochial Schools

number of militants and Black Nationalists; urban renewal is in earliest stages; community feels it has few friends in city hall; politically active; a Democratic ward in a largely Republican city; minor riot in 1968.

WARD 5: The city's "southside"; a mixture of young marrieds living in newly built apartments, middle-aged homeowners, and senior citizens who are long-time residents of the area; predominantly middle-class white-collar workers and small businessmen; a number of Blacks live in the northern section of the ward; mixture of conservatives, middle-of-the-roaders, and liberals; said to be a "nice place to raise kids."

WARD 6: A section of the city that resulted largely from people "escaping" from the downtown and industrial areas as they could afford to move; many older people and a great number of these are near retirement; feel tax burdened; politically conservative.

WARD 7: An old section of the city; once a very plush residential area of the city with many large, costly homes; now on the way "downhill" as many older residents struggle to hang on; many old homes converted to fashionable town houses and apartments; residents feel greatly burdened by property taxes; politically middle-of-the-road.

WARD 8: The industrial part of the city and known as the "Italian neighborhood"; most are homeowners; lower-middle and middle-class blue-collar workers with moderate incomes for the most part; small neighborhood businesses; tendency to be "clannish"; conservative politically; section has been called a "racist" segment of the community by civil rightists.

WARD 9: A residential section of the city; upward striving middle-class professionals and businessmen; tendency toward a "keeping up with the Joneses" attitude; own or buying homes; number of Blacks in the northwestern section of the ward; very liberal politically.

WARD 10: A new section of the city; almost a city within a city; the result of sprawling middle-income housing developments, a huge shopping center, and an industrial park; a majority of the residents are either prounion, skilled workers at nearby factories, or artisans (plumbers, house painters, carpenters); politically conservative.

2. Multicultural Freeway Planning Game[13]
   a. Assign participants to one of the following groups: City Manager's Staff, Taxpayers' Association, Residents' Association, Merchants' Association, Chicano Barrio Association, Black Community Association, City Engineer's Staff.
   b. Working alone, participants develop alternative routes for the freeway so that it cost the fewest points for the groups of which they are members. The route must run from any one of the top hexagons to any of the bottom hexagons (see Freeway Planning Map on p. 267).
   c. All members of the same interest group meet together to discuss the best (least expensive) routes from their point of view.

d. Participants are formed in groups made up of one member from each interest group. Each group will be composed of one member of the City Manager's Staff, Taxpayers' Association, Residents' Association, Merchants' Association, Chicano Barrio Association, Black Community Association, and City Engineer's Staff. They attempt to reach compromises or alternative routes that are staisfactory to all.

Census Data

Ward	Population	Elementary School Children	Secondary School Children	Parochial School Children	Total School Children
1	20,000	1,700	1,300	0	3,000
2	10,000	1,080	720	0	1,800
3	30,000	3,000	2,000	1,000	6,000
4	40,000	2,700	1,800	0	4,500
5	15,000	840	560	0	1,400
6	8,000	600	400	0	1,000
7	10,000	650	450	0	1,100
8	20,000	1,400	800	1,000	3,200
9	15,000	1,500	800	0	2,300
10	5,000	600	400	0	1,000

Elementary Schools	Ward	White Children	Black Children	Total Children
a	1 (northern)	800	0	800
b	2 (southern)	860	40	900
c	2	1,080	0	1,080
d	3 (northern)	1,500	0	1,500
e	3 (southern)	1,370	130	1,500
f	4	400	2,300	2,700
g	5	730	110	840
h	6 and 7	1,250	0	1,250
i	8	1,360	40	1,400
j	9 and 10	1,910	190	2,100
Total		11,260	2,810	14,070

Secondary Schools	Ward	White Children	Black Children	Total Children
A	1	1,270	30	1,300
B	2 and 3	2,640	80	2,720
C	4, 5, and 9	1,660	1,500	3,160
D	6, 7, 8, and 10	2,000	50	2,050
Total		7,570	1,660	9,230

e. Participants meet again with their interest groups to choose a representative to the city council, select a spokesperson for the city council meeting, reconsider alternative routes, and plan strategies for the meeting. During this period, participants may also carry out negotiations with other groups concerning possible routes or strategies for the city council meeting.

f. A meeting is held of the city council, composed of one representative from each interest group. One spokesperson (other than the city council representative) from each interest group presents the group's position and answers questions. Following presentations and discussion, the city council votes on the alternative routes. As a variation, one or more "outsiders" (persons not previously involved in the game) may be asked to serve on the city council and to vote on the basis of the presentations of the different groups.

g. Game directors hold a debriefing session on the game, its relationship to "real life" situations, and possible modifications of the game for use at various grade levels.

SCORING:

Penalty points are received as follows:

a. 5 penalty points for each hexagon used.

b. Variable penalty points for going through hexagons with symbols. Each group is penalized differently according to the chart. *Note*: Penalty points are received for each symbol, so that a hexagon with 2 hills costs the City Engineer 19 penalty points—5 for the hexagon and 7 for each hill. See the figure on p. 268.

3. Albatross: An Activity in Differing Values[14]

Goals:

a. To increase participants' awareness of phenomena that occur between groups with different values systems.

b. To involve participants in a simulated society in which they encounter persons very different from themselves.

Group Size: Unlimited.

Time Required: Approximately one hour.

Materials:

a. A copy of the Albatross Role-Description Sheet for each player.

b. Newsprint and a felt-tipped marker.

Physical Setting: Two rooms, each large enough to accommodate all participants comfortably.

Process:

a. The facilitator chooses two persons, one female and one male, to act in a role play involving a simulated culture. Each role player is given a copy of the Albatross Role-Description Sheet to prepare for the role play. The facilitator emphasizes that the role-playing activity is to be nonverbal, that the role players are to express themselves in actions, not words. The role players go into another room.

b. He then asks for six to eight volunteers to be "guests" in the role play.

c. The facilitator discusses the role play with the participants, who are designated as observers. He indicates that the situation will be as follows:

LEGEND:

||| BUSINESS AREA

🔔 CHICANO COMMUNITY

▲▲ HILLS

MAP 🔺🔺 RESIDENTIAL AREA

BLACK COMMUNITY

FREEWAY PLANNING GAME

	▲	❘	▲	🔔	⬗
City Manager's Staff	5	3	1	1	1
Taxpayer's Association	1	3	5	1	1
Residents' Association	7	1	1	2	2
Merchants' Association	1	7	7	1	1
Chicano Barrio Association	2	1	1	7	2
Black Community Association	2	1	1	2	7
City Engineer's Staff	1	1	7	1	1

"You are about to be involved in an activity concerning cultural norms and values. When you walk into the next room, you will be entering a new culture—the culture of Albatross. You are a guest in this new culture. Because this is a nonverbal activity, please do not talk after entering the Albatrossian culture." The facilitator answers any questions they may have (ten minutes).

d. The observers are directed to the other room, and the role play begins.

e. After the nonverbal role play has ended, the observers, as a group, take ten minutes to list various cultural traits that they think were demonstrated during the role play. The facilitator lists these traits on newsprint. Then the role players explain, in Albatrossian terms, each trait the group listed correctly.

f. Finally, the facilitator leads the total group in a discussion about the mis-understandings that occur between groups with different value systems. Depending on the interests of the participants, the discussion may include Black-white, male-female, Arab-Israeli, or teacher-student value systems. Individual ethnocentrism and feelings of trust, empathy, disgust, hostility, and fear can also be discussed.

ALBATROSS ROLE-DESCRIPTION SHEET:

You live in a subculture called Albatross. The Albatrossian culture is viewed as counter-American because each custom is either physically or intellectually opposed to traditional middle-class American customs or ways of thinking. The following are two examples of Albatrossian customs as explained in Albatrossian terms:

a. When greeting a guest, the Albatrossian removes that person's right shoe and briefly massages the foot. Even though the right foot, in the Albatrossian view, is not considered more important than the left foot, people in Albatross tend to use the right foot more. In other words, the Albatrossians do not believe (as opposed to the dominant American view) that there must be a reason for every important custom.

b. Being second in the Albatrossian culture is more important than being first because Albatrossians view the natural world as full of dangers and fears. Hence, to be served second or to be greeted second is to be protected from potential dangers (poisoned food, an unknown enemy). Thus, males are always greeted and served first; females are served last.

This is a nonverbal activity. You are to illustrate Albatrossian customs in all your actions, including greeting your guests.

Simulation Game Bibliography[15]

1. Alternation. Simulates the problems that arise when the in-power majority in a nation makes it official policy to repress an out-of-power but substantial minority. The simulation involves bargaining skills, negotiation, and group cooperation. Participants are divided into two groups, which represent the two major ethnic/racial groups in a nation. Participants are encouraged to consider alternatives to the use of force to settle internal disputes.
   Grade: 9-Adult   *Time*: 2-4 hours   *Participants*: 15+
   Source: Center for Teaching International Relations, University of Denver, Denver, Co. 80210.
2. Bafa Bafa. Simulates the problems of cross-cultural interactions, stereotyping, and ethnocentrism. Participants are divided into two cultural groups, each of which have prescribed sets of rules that constitute norms for the particular society. Each culture sends visitors to the other culture to bring back reports about their behavior patterns. Based on the information gathered by successive visitors, each group develops and refines hypotheses about the other culture.
   Grade: 6-Adult   *Time*: 3-6 hours   *Participants*: 24-40
   Source: Simile II, 218 Twelfth Street, P.O. Box 910, Del Mar, CA 92014.
3. Center City. A game about life among the poor in a typical large city of the

United States. Participants assume the roles of junior high age residents of an urban poverty area who are attempting to live their lives and gain as much love, security, knowledge, self-confidence, spiritual growth, fun and fulfillment as possible. Participants encounter barriers as they spend time in certain areas of life, such as home, school, community, church, extracurricular activities, and in the streets.

Grade: 7-Adult   *Time*: 3-5 hours   *Participants*: 12-27

Source: John Knox Press, 341 Ponce de Leon Avenue, N.E., Atlanta, GA 30308.

4. The Cities Game. Participants assume four power roles—Business, Government, Slum Dwellers, and Agitators. The object of the game is to acquire as much money and power as possible. This is achieved by collecting "Rewards" from the Game Treasury or by negotiating under-the-table payments from other participants.

Grade: 7-Adult   *Time*: 2-4 hours   *Participants*: 4-16

Source: Ziff/Davis, Consumer Services Division, 505 Broadway, New York, NY 10012.

5. Cultural Contact. A simulation intended to demonstrate how misunderstandings and conflicts may occur when two very different cultures meet, and to develop an understanding of the concept of "cultural relativism." Conflict develops as a trading expedition comes to an isolated island inhabited by a nonindustrial tribe in order to obtain wood from trees in forests which the islanders hold sacred and untouchable.

Grade: 7-12   *Time*: 2-5 hours   *Participants*: 20-30

Source: Games Central, 55 Wheeler Street, Cambridge, MA 02138.

6. Desegregate Now. Participants are assigned roles with racial, ideological, economic, and class undertones. Their task is to desegregate the three high schools in a hypothetical school district; one is composed of primarily upper-to-middle-class white students, one is all blue-collar, and one is all Black. A desegregation formula acceptable to the participants as well as to the school board and federal district court must be devised.

Grade: 11-Adult   *Time*: 2-4 hours   *Participants*: 12+

Source: Golembiewski, J., Malcolm Moore, and Jack Robin, *Dilemmas of Political Participation* (Englewood Cliffs, N.J.: Prentice-Hall, 1973).

7. El Barrio. This simulation embodies the forces that affect a Latin immigrant to a big city in North America. He must acquire a physical skill, build a social network, learn how to use a vehicle, and decide whether to collaborate with the system or fight it. Participants may aim to become leaders in the Latin community, join the system and graduate to the suburbs, or move up and out still contesting.

Grade: 9-Adult   *Time*: 2-3 hours   *Participants*: 7-15

Source: Berkeley Gaming Project, Institute of Urban and Regional Development, 316 W. Hall, University of California, Berkeley, CA 94720.

8. Equality. A simulation intended to familiarize participants with the testing of Black Americans, allow them to feel some of the pressure that minorities feel, and explore the way people of differing ethnic backgrounds learn to live together.

Grade: 6-9   *Time*: 20-30 hours   *Participants*: 20-40

Source: Interact, P.O. Box 262, Lakeside, CA 92040.

9. Ghetto. Simulates the pains and pressures, the choices and frustrations, the bad and sometimes good luck that is in the ghetto. Each participant is given a different personal profile describing his or her education, family, and economic situation and the number of hour points available with which to play each round. In each round, the players allocate their hours among several alternatives—work, school, hustling, passing time, welfare, and neighborhood improvement. Hours invested in these activities yield a different number of satisfaction points. The aim of each participant is to maximize satisfaction points.
Grade: 7-Adult   *Time*: 5-7 hours   *Participants*: 8-10
Source: The Bobbs-Merrill Company, Inc., 4300 W. 62nd Street, Indianapolis, IN 46268.

10. Government Preparation for Minority Groups. A simulation designed to develop an awareness of some of the problems, frustrations, and aspirations of various minority groups. In this simulation of Senate subcommittee hearings, participants investigate whether or not the government owes reparations to certain minority groups.
Grade: 7-Adult   *Time*: 3-5 hours   *Participants*: 15+
Source: Edu-Game, P.O. Box 1144, Sun Valley, CA 91352.

11. Hang Up. A role-playing activity designed to develop an increased awareness by participants of their own and others' racial attitudes and prejudices. Participants start out "hung up" and move around the board encountering a number of stress activities that may exacerbate their "hang ups." The object is to get around the board and free themselves from such difficulties by acting them out in pantomine or charading the emotions felt in stress situations.
Grade: 6-Adult   *Time*: 2-4 hours   *Participants*: 2-6
Source: Synectics Education Systems, 2 Brattle Street, Cambridge, MA 02138.

12. Indian Reservation—Life Today on the Northern Plains. A simulation designed to develop an awareness and an understanding of the problems found by Indians living in the Northern Plains reservations. Participants become members of one of four families, ranging from full-blooded to quarter-blooded Indian, living on an Indian reservation of the Northern Plains. Each family experiences the problems encountered by Indians as they seek education, employment, and deal with tribal politics, all within a structure created and administrated by the Bureau of Indian Affairs.
Grade: 7-Adult   *Time*: 3-6 hours   *Participants*: 12+
Source: Institute of Higher Education Research and Services, The University of Alabama, P.O. Box 6293, University, AL 35486.

13. Race Against the Highway. A simulation designed to develop awareness of the social implications of building an interstate highway through cities. Participants play the parts of angry members of an ethnic group and militant Blacks. The issue revolves around conflicting options for highway overpasses that will affect the cost of construction, the social life of the two disparate communities, and health and fire protection for both neighborhoods.

Grade: 9-Adults   *Time*: 3-4 hours   *Participants*: 13
Source: Engineering Simulations Consultants, 1502 Scenic Drive, Rolla, MO 65401.

14. Solving Multi-Ethnic Problems. This activity simulates situations in either an elementary school or a secondary school, each of which has a high white enrollment, but serves a substantial number of minority group children, most of whom are Black. Participants assume the role of the teacher, who must solve problem situations presented through short, open-ended film sequences.

    Grade: 12-Adult   *Time*: 10+ hours   *Participants*: 10+
    Source: Anti-Defamation League of B'nai B'rith, 315 Lexington Avenue, New York, NY 10016.

15. Spectrum. A simulation of ethnic groups interacting during a student government election. As citizens with either WASP, Jewish, Black, Chicano, city white, Native American, or Oriental background, participants find themselves embroiled in a heated school election. The various participants are either apathetic or members of a radical or moderate political party; party members take stands or school issues, develop party platforms, and use persuasion to influence the apathetic voters.

    Grade: 7-Adult   *Time*: 3-6 hours   *Participants*: 20-40
    Source: Interact, P.O. Box 262, Lakeside, CA 92040.

16. Sunshine. A simulation designed to motivate participants to become concerned about contemporary racial problems and be willing to examine factual information before developing activities. Racial problems in a typical American city simulated. The room is divided to simulate Sunshine, a mythical city of six neighborhoods with varying degrees of segregation and integration in housing and schooling. While studying the history of Black Americans from Africa to the present, participants also research ways of solving current racial problems.

    Grade: 9-Adult   *Time*: 25-35 hours   *Participants*: 20-36
    Source: Interact, P.O. Box 262, Lakeside, CA 92040.

NOTES

1. *Banks* v. *Muncie Community Schools*, 433 F. 2nd 292 (7th Cir. 1970). Cited in D. Schimmel and L. Fischer, *The Civil Rights of Students* (New York: Harper & Row, 1975), pp. 31–32.
2. *Aguirre* v. *Tahoka Independent School District*, 311 F. Supp. 644 (N.D. Tex. 1970). Cited in Schimmel and Fischer, *Civil Rights of Students*, pp. 35–36.
3. *Joyner* v. *Whiting*, 477 F. 2d 456 (4th Cir. 1973). Cited in Schimmel and Fischer, *Civil Rights of Students*, pp. 71–72.
4. *Bernascani* v. *Tempe Elementary School District #3*, 548 F. 2d 857 (9th Cir. 1977).
5. Told to the author by the director of the project at a Teacher Corps multicultural education conference.
6. Extracted from Yva Momatuik and John Eastcott, "Still Eskimo—Still Free: The Inuit of Uningmaktok," *National Geographic* 152, no. 5 (November 1977): 624–47.

7. Extracted from Patricia Raymer and Steve Raymer, "Wisconsin's Menominees, Indians on a Seesaw," *National Geographic* 146, no. 2 (August 1974): 624–47.
8. For a complete description of the use of these values dilemmas in cross-cultural instruction, see Robert Stahl and Nicholas Appleton, "Achieving Cross Cultural Understanding Through a Cognitive-Based Approach to Values Education" (unpublished manuscript). For a description of the model for using values dilemmas in values education, see Robert Stahl, "Developing Values Dilemmas for Content-Centered Social Studies Instruction: Theoretical Construct and Practical Application," *Theory and Research in Social Education* 7, no. 2 (Summer 1979): N.C.S.S.
9. An example of the Standard Format of the Values Dilemma (the questions at the end illustrate the kinds of questions the teacher might use to help the follow-up discussion).
10. Adapted from Marilyn Goldstein, "Middle-Class Puerto Ricans Juggle Yankee Ideals, Native Culture," Newsday Press, as seen in the *Arizona Republic*, 19 August 1979, pp. SL 10–11.
11. An example of the Classification Format of the Values Dilemma for cross-cultural settings; (reprinted with permission of Dr. Jeannine Dahl, School of Nursing, Arizona State University. In class, students would be asked to consider the various consequences of these alternatives prior to making their final choices.
12. A simulation game developed by Professor Wil Weber and his colleagues at Syracuse University, School of Education. Reprinted with permission.
13. Multicultural revision of Michael Chester's Freeway Planning Game. The original rules can be found in *Simulation Gaming News*, May 1972. Write, P.O. Box 3039, University Station, Moscow, ID 83843.
14. The name of the author of this activity and its original were not available.
15. The description of these simulations have been adapted from *Handbook of Simulation Gaming in Social Education*, Part 2, Directory (University, Ala.: Ron Stadsklev Institute of Higher Education Research and Services, University of Alabama, 1975). Reprinted with permission.

Index

275